BEYOND COMPLIANCE

BEYOND COMPLIANCE

Reclaiming Agency in Special Education

Catherine Kramarczuk Voulgarides

Harvard Education Press
Cambridge, Massachusetts

Paperback ISBN 979-8-89557-060-9

Cataloging-in-Publication Data available from the Library of Congress.

Published by Harvard Education Press,
an imprint of the Harvard Education Publishing Group

Harvard Education Press
8 Story Street
Cambridge, MA 02138

Cover Design: Endpaper Studio

The typefaces in this book are ITC Legacy Serif Std and Knockout.

I dedicate this book to those who have held me up, inspired me, and told me to keep going—through my spirit, history, and in the present day.
Thank you to Baba, Dido #1, Bopsha, Jajo, Duno, Dido #2, Marusha, my brothers and sisters, my friends, and my foundation Anthony, Cielle, Energetic, and Flappy.

CONTENTS

FOREWORD

by Dr. Tania May
Assistant Superintendent of Special Education Office of Superintendent of Public Instruction Washington State

There are rare books that manage to both unsettle and stabilize. Books that give voice to what we feel but have not yet found language to describe. Books that call us back to our values while propelling us toward transformational change. This is one of those books.

I first encountered Dr. Catherine Voulgarides' research when launching a statewide initiative on inclusionary practices across Washington state. Her work was integral in my dissertation research on disproportionality; specifically, the intersection of race and ethnicity and segregated settings for students with disabilities. I have since had the incredible honor to get to know her and collaborate across joint efforts over the past several years. I have come to respect her deeply, not just as a scholar, but as an educator, a systems thinker, a compassionate observer, and a fierce advocate for equity. In this volume, she brings the full force of those identities to bear.

At the center of this book is a deceptively simple question: *Does compliance with the IDEA matter in the pursuit of educational equity?* But Dr. Voulgarides does not treat this as a rhetorical inquiry. She investigates it as a practitioner would—on the ground, in classrooms and districts and state offices, through IEP meetings, compliance checklists, and systems designed more for documentation than for justice. What she uncovers is both unsettling and liberating: the systems we have built to protect students with disabilities often serve to constrain them—and us. But when we pause, when we ask deeper questions, when we engage in dialogue rooted in love, humility, and praxis, we find new paths forward.

An Uneasy Truth

Dr. Voulgarides starts from a brave place. She acknowledges the good intentions embedded in IDEA, and the very real protections it offers. But she refuses to stop there. She illuminates a hard truth that many educators live daily but rarely speak aloud: that compliance with IDEA, while necessary, is not sufficient—and, in some cases, is actively harmful to the very students we serve.

She names what so many educators and leaders feel—that the procedural maze of IDEA can separate us from our students and communities. When compliance becomes a performative act, it risks becoming disconnected from meaning and student outcomes. Research and experience have shown us that, even when we follow every rule, inequities persist—especially for students of color with disabilities, for multilingual learners, and for families navigating systems from the margins. This, too, is an injustice.

Through this work, she exposes the *paradox of compliance*: that a law rooted in civil rights can, through its own procedural and individualized structure, reproduce inequity. But she goes farther, offering a sophisticated framework for understanding how this paradox is sustained—through what she calls the *logic of compliance*: a cultural web of good intentions, status quo practices, and current contexts that reward technical adherence over adaptive change.

From Technical to Transformative

What makes this book exceptional is its clarity in navigating both technical and adaptive change. Dr. Voulgarides does not reject the legal and procedural foundations of IDEA. In fact, she meticulously explains them. But she insists—rightly—that our work cannot rest there. That we must pair technical compliance with adaptive leadership. We must ask not only, "Are we doing it right?" but "Are we doing *what's* right?"

This is a book grounded in schools, in real people, in stories and voices across education. Dr. Voulgarides elevates the narratives of educators and leaders grappling with the tensions of IDEA implementation, not to indict them, but to humanize their struggles and offer a new way forward.

One of the most striking features of the book is the use of composite vignettes based on over a decade of qualitative research. These stories are not hypothetical. They are layered, rich, and authentic. They reveal the human dimensions of policy—how belief systems, relationships, histories, and social structures shape what is possible for students. In each story, readers will find echoes of their own schools, their own lived experiences, their own inner conflicts.

Chapter Four: Status Quo which examines *fragmented harm* is a strong example. The vignettes in this chapter are sobering and familiar: small, seemingly innocuous decisions, when layered across systemic barriers, produce persistent harm for students, particularly students of color with disabilities. Educators who believe in inclusion nonetheless refer students to more restrictive environments. Districts "address disproportionality" by adjusting numbers rather than practices. Teams develop legally-sound IEPs that are not fully implemented. Yet this chapter is not fatalistic. It is an honest diagnosis of how the status quo survives. And it offers a way out. As Dr. Voulgarides writes, "the same routines that preserve inequity can, when interrogated collectively, become levers for change." Only once we are brave enough to question the routines we've normalized, can we begin to dismantle them.

An Invitation to Praxis

In positioning compliance as the potential for both oppression and liberation, Dr. Voulgarides offers more than critique; she offers praxis. And she does so with deep respect for educators. This is not a book that shames practitioners. It is a book that sees them clearly—overwhelmed, well-intentioned, deeply committed—and asks them to remember why they chose this work. It is a book that believes in our capacity to change. Not just our practices, but our very systems.

Dr. Voulgarides acknowledges that IDEA is difficult to navigate. That legal literacy is uneven. That racial and economic inequities compound the challenges of implementation. But she also shows us that compliance is not destiny. That through critical reflection, adaptive leadership, and authentic dialogue, we can reclaim compliance as an act of justice. That we can move from box-checking to soul-searching. From isolation to community. From deficit to transformation.

Her work is not about tearing down IDEA. It is about rehumanizing it. It is about remembering that compliance, when rooted in care and criticality, can be an act of solidarity. Our students deserve more than procedural safeguards, they deserve a system that sees them, believes in them, and adapts for them.

I chose to write this foreword because this book matters. It matters to practitioners and leaders. And most of all, it matters to students with disabilities and their families, who are often silenced by the very systems intended to serve them.

As someone who has worked in special education for over twenty-five years, including a decade in state-level policy, monitoring, and implementation, I have witnessed firsthand the tensions between the letter and the spirit of the law. I have been in rooms where educators fear the consequences of non-compliance more than they fear the consequences of inequity. I have heard families celebrate a well-written IEP only to see its goals unrealized. I have watched as districts navigate data dashboards while missing the stories behind the data. And I have felt the deep hunger among educators and families for something more—for tools that honor both the legal mandate and the human promise of education.

This book provides a framework for making sense of our efforts. And it suggests an alternate path—grounded in research, informed by practice, and driven by hope.

Finally, this book is deeply personal. Dr. Voulgarides shares her own story—of family, migration, disability, and resilience. Her words are shaped not only by scholarship but by memory, love, and a profound sense of responsibility to those who came before and those yet to come. It is a powerful reminder that educational justice is not only a professional obligation. It is an ancestral one.

She tells the story of her Uncle Duno, whose insatiable curiosity and unconventional brilliance were not always understood by the systems around him. She tells us of her family's journey through war, displacement, and survival—and of the ways education became their way out. And she reminds us, again and again, that behind every policy is a child. A family. A possibility.

I am grateful for this book. I am grateful for Dr. Voulgarides' courage, clarity, and unwavering belief in the possibility of transformation. And I am hopeful that this book will become not only a tool for professional learning, but a spark for systems change.

To the reader—this book will challenge you. It will ask you to think differently about longstanding concepts. It will invite you into dialogue, into discomfort, and into community. And it will stay with you.

So, let us take up this call to action—not simply to comply, but to transform. Onward.

Introduction

Millions of children in the United States (US) have benefited from the passage of the Individuals with Disabilities Education Act (IDEA), which guarantees the right to a free appropriate public education (FAPE) in the least restrictive environment (LRE) for eligible US students with disabilities.[1] Enacted as a civil-rights-inspired and social-justice-oriented law, the IDEA is implemented in schools through a proceduralized, individualized, and technical framework.[2] While the act has undergone numerous reauthorizations and revisions, its primary goal—to provide equal educational access and opportunities for students with disabilities—has remained steadfast.

The *proceduralized nature* of IDEA refers to the safeguards that uphold the rights of students with disabilities and their families, ensuring that caregivers and parents are meaningfully involved in educational decisions about their child, that they have access to educational records about their child (e.g., individualized education programs, IEPs), and that they are provided with due process mechanisms to resolve disagreements with schools. These procedural mechanisms are individualized and designed to guarantee that students with disabilities receive a FAPE, which is a cornerstone of the IDEA.[3] The *individualized nature* of the IDEA refers to the way in which these procedural protections protect the rights of individual students more so than a broader collective goal of disability justice.[4] The individualized nature of the IDEA is heralded as a monumental and significant feature of the act, yet research shows that families with certain characteristics (e.g., wealth, English language proficiency, and access to advocates and lawyers) are able to secure more and higher quality educational resources via the IDEA, generating significant inequities over time.[5] These factors are compounded by the *technical nature* of the IDEA, which is a result of the dense legal environment surrounding the IDEA and the difficulty of the readability of its procedural protections which also influences the professional jargon used to determine special education eligibility and service delivery decisions.[6]

The disability rights movement is deeply connected to the broader civil rights movement of the 1960s, when disability advocacy moved away from particular disabilities (e.g., blind) to a collective disability identity (e.g., the disabled).[7] The successes of the civil rights movement and its rights-based framework provided both the conceptual foundation and political momentum for advancing protections for individuals with disabilities.[8] This shift toward recognizing and safeguarding the rights of marginalized groups directly influenced legislative action, leading to the passage of the Education for All Handicapped Children Act (EAHCA) in 1975 (later renamed the Individuals with Disabilities Education Act), just over a decade after the Civil Rights Act of 1964.[9]

The IDEA is an expansive piece of legislation that has significantly impacted students aged three though twenty-one who qualify as having a disability under the IDEA and of which the disability has an impact on educational outcomes. Among its many features are the parameters by which student disability within a school setting is defined, the services that a student with a disability has access to, and the teachers who will be assigned to their education.[10] The core statutes and procedural mechanisms that are a hallmark of the IDEA—for example, FAPE and LRE—are important mechanisms for protecting student rights, but they have also inadvertently legitimized what has become a dual system of education, dividing general and special education programs by resource allocation and administrative mechanisms.[11] Research has shown, for example, how the LRE provision can perpetuate segregation and inequality by masking exclusionary practices as inclusive ones within school settings when the IDEA is complied with and inclusive placements are codified in a student's IEP along the LRE continuum.[12] Given this, the distinction between special and general education, while theoretically justifiable and designed to provide services and supports to historically marginalized students, has been widely critiqued for its equity impacts on students despite its noble intentions; this is especially an issue with race and disability intersections, inclusionary practices, and long-term outcomes for students with disabilities.[13]

For example, racial disparities are particularly pronounced for students labeled with specific learning disabilities (SLDs), intellectual disability (ID), emotional disturbance (ED), speech or language impairment (SLI), other health impairment (OHI), and autism.[14] Nationally representative data underscore the racialized nature of these disparities. In a report prepared for the National Center for Education Statistics (NCES), de Brey and colleagues found that during the 2015–2016 academic year, Pacific Islander (43 percent), Hispanic (42 percent), American Indian/Alaska Native (40 percent), and Black students (37 percent) were more likely to receive services for specific learning disabilities than their white and Asian peers, whose rates ranged from 21 percent to 31 percent.[15] In contrast, Asian students were more likely to receive services for speech or language impairments (26 percent) and autism (21 percent) than students from other racial or ethnic groups. Black students had among the highest rates of being identified with an intellectual disability (9 percent), compared to 5 to 7 percent among other groups.

As the descriptive data indicate and as research consistently shows, historically underserved and minoritized learners with disabilities experience inequitable treatment within special education and school discipline systems. These students are more likely to be placed in restrictive learning environments, receive lower-quality services in those settings, and face exclusionary discipline at higher rates.[16] The disparities vary across racial groups, disability classifications, and geographic contexts.[17] On the other hand, other research shows that some students who require academic and behavioral support may not receive timely interventions, leading to missed educational opportunities.[18] Additionally, research shows that historically underserved and minoritized learners with disabilities are underrepresented in gifted and talented programs, often being systematically overlooked.[19] These patterns highlight that special education inequities are complex and a critical and enduring equity issue. There are noted long-term negative outcomes associated with disability status and race that extend beyond the educational system.[20]

This book is grounded in the harsh reality of this dual system of education that produces differential outcomes across intersectional identities and whose outcomes are not always consistent with the IDEA protections intended to guarantee equal educational opportunity. Given this information, this book is written for educators working within, engaging with, and interfacing with this system—for leaders, teachers, educators—who want to see it improve to support all students they work with. With this intent, this book recognizes that although the IDEA generates educational opportunity and access, it can also serve as a main driver of the split between general and special education spaces that can further perpetuate long-standing educational inequities. Indeed, despite extensive IDEA legal protections, significant inequities persist in educational outcomes that disproportionately affect historically marginalized and racialized students in special education.[21] Youth of color labeled with disabilities continue to face systemic barriers that undermine their educational outcomes, even amid decades of disability rights advocacy.[22]

These inequities are perpetuated across the diffuse layers of educational ecosystems and are driven by interconnected systems of educators' beliefs, educational policies, and educational practices.[23] This implies that dominant narratives about ability and disability are encoded in the IDEA and then are enacted across contexts.[24] Educational federalism plays a key role in this dynamic, illustrating how SEAs interpret, adapt, and operationalize federal policy, such as the IDEA, in response to their own political, cultural, and administrative contexts, which in turn shapes how local districts comply with the IDEA and how educators, related service providers, families, and students experience IDEA policy enactment and rights protections.[25] Consequently, implementation varies widely across and within states and districts, resulting in uneven access to resources and services.[26] Therefore, within districts and schools, IDEA policy enactments become responsive to community needs and local belief systems, yet it still carries with it the implicit assumptions about ability and disability as embedded in the legislation. These ideas about who qualifies for services—and under what conditions—are continuously reinterpreted through daily practices and IDEA procedural and compliance mechanisms, particularly as they intersect with other dimensions of identity, such as race and language status. Moreover, at the individual and family level, students and caregivers experience the IDEA through interactions with district and school personnel, conditions which are often shaped by unequal access to resources and power.[27] In these localized contexts, disparities emerge that reinforce existing power structures. This book elaborates on these examples and more, providing insights into how policy enactments unfold, how beliefs, policies, and practices are intertwined, and how inequities in special education outcomes persist.[28] I elaborate on these dynamics through the stories told in this book to show how this unfolding of policy to practice moves beyond technical compliance and incorporates adaptive realities of policy to practice implementation dynamics, which ultimately have real-world impacts on adults, students, families, and school communities.

This book is also firmly rooted in the reality that the IDEA is a complex piece of legislation that is difficult to navigate and understand for both practitioners and caregivers.[29] Educator IDEA legal literacy remains an aspiration, and achieving full and substantive compliance with improved results has proven difficult to achieve across states, districts, and schools in the United States.[30] IDEA administration and implementation at the local level is often compliance driven, emphasizing procedural and legal compliance over transformative possibilities, and symbolic acts of compliance with the IDEA can supersede human connection and meaningful instruction on the ground.[31] These realties limit the capacity of the IDEA to systemically address broadscale inequities on the ground.

This book is also grounded in an intersectional frame that recognizes how systems of oppression are interconnected and impact people within and across varied contexts given the persistent disparities across disability and other identities.[32] This book acknowledges that identities, like race, gender, disability, and socioeconomic status are tightly intertwined and shaped by broader power structures, contributing to both privilege and marginalization. Intersectionality, in this case, highlights how students with disabilities do not experience their disability in isolation from other identities (e.g., race, gender, sexual orientation, and socioeconomic status).[33] These overlapping identities, depending on where an individual is located (e.g., a particular school district or school within a district), create unique challenges, opportunities, and forms of oppression and privilege that cannot be fully understood by focusing on disability alone. This has significant implications for IDEA compliance, whose acts, which are inescapably situated by social, organizational, contextual, and historical dimensions, must be considered for their impacts on students at their intersections.[34]

This book is firmly rooted in educational practice. It focuses on us—the professional educators working within and across educational systems—and the decisions we make around educational service delivery. Throughout the chapters, I provide readers with critical tools and concepts to examine IDEA compliance and its equity impacts on individuals and systems. I situate acts of IDEA compliance within the technical components of education, which include the procedural and individualized mechanisms of the IDEA, and the adaptive conditions of schooling which include the contextual realties that shape policy interpretation and implementation dynamics at the intersection of policies, practices, and beliefs. I distinguish between the technical and adaptive realties of practice to provide a concrete frame for understanding how harmful practices related to IDEA compliance can be disrupted through an adapted Freirean critical cycle process, which is a process that requires reflection, dialogue, and a critical reading of our environments as it relates to compliance to identify new pathways for transformation that promote, rather than hinder, educational equity.[35]

It is important to explicitly note that I am applying Paulo Freire's work to people who are considered privileged in terms of their professional role, as this book is written for educational leaders and educators who interact with and within special education systems. I recognize that this is a departure from Freire's work, which centers on transforming the conditions of the oppressed. However, the applicability of Freire's critical ideas can be extended more broadly.[36] For example, in this book I seek to destabilize common approaches to IDEA compliance in ways that align with Freire's critique of the traditional "banking" model of education, which treats learners as passive recipients of knowledge. Freire's work, instead, calls for critical pedagogy that encourages learners to investigate, question, and understand their lived realities.[37] This approach, rooted in the need for creating a deeper understanding of intersecting social inequalities in one's environment coupled with critical thinking and problem-solving skills, is universally beneficial.

By developing a critical consciousness about how power operates across structural, disciplinary, cultural, and interpersonal domains, readers can gain a more precise and nuanced lens for analyzing and addressing social inequities in education as they relate to IDEA compliance.[38] This encounter equips them not only to recognize how inequities are produced and sustained within their own systems but also to engage in more informed, intentional, and transformative practices that challenge the status quo and advance equity for all students that go beyond compliance. The framing insists that legal literacy alone, such as knowledge of the procedural mechanisms and statute of the IDEA, is insufficient for transforming practices toward equity. Learners must engage in humanizing and critical reflection that fosters transformation.[39] When multiple ways of thinking and being are embraced and concepts related to critical pedagogy are applied, acts of compliance can become more liberating rather than constricting. At the heart of this pedagogical stance is Freire's concept of *conscientização*, or critical consciousness, which is cultivated through a cyclical process of reflection and action aimed at understanding and changing oppressive systems.[40] I position the compliance paradigm surrounding IDEA administration and implementation in this book as an oppressive and often dehumanizing system for both adults and students.[41]

To reiterate, although educators responsible for implementing and complying with the IDEA do not fit conventional definitions of oppression, Freire's theoretical constructs remain relevant.

Understanding how educational policies are implemented—and how they can unintentionally reinforce inequities—is essential for any leader or educator committed to equity. This book introduces practical tools grounded in the work of Paulo Freire to help educators reflect critically on their roles, challenge rigid compliance practices, and rethink how special education policies like the IDEA are enacted. Freire's ideas offer a powerful framework for professional growth by encouraging educators to examine how power and policy shape daily practices and to use that understanding to create more equitable learning environments. Therefore, throughout the book, I provide quotes from Freire's *Pedagogy of the Oppressed* so that the spirit of the work is honored and to encourage readers to engage in reflection about critical educational frameworks. I also provide a framework for change at the end of the book that is rooted in Freire's work to foster critical inquiry and change related to IDEA implementation and interpretation dynamics.

In essence, this book positions the IDEA as a foundational policy that both structures educational opportunities and reinforces systemic inequities. It takes an expansive and inquiry-driven approach, drawing from a multitude of theoretical and conceptual frames spanning sociological theory, critical disability perspectives, and educational law.[42] It also draws from both my past and present work to expand understandings of the role of IDEA compliance as an equity lever.

Therefore, the arguments made throughout the book are responsive to the limits of the IDEA to substantively transform educational systems. In turn, a core feature of this book is to make visible how the IDEA's impact on educational inequities depends on how educators interpret, comply with, and apply it. The everyday decisions made at the intersection of policy and practice ultimately determine whether students receive necessary supports or encounter systemic barriers. So it is here, with a focus on the role of compliance with the IDEA, that the book unfolds.

Why Compliance?

I use two frames to justify a focus on IDEA compliance: the paradox of compliance and the logic of compliance.[43]

The paradox of compliance is situated at the intersection of civil-rights-inspired protections in the IDEA; proceduralized, individualized, and technical provisions of the IDEA; and policy implementation and interpretation dynamics at the local level.[44] It manifests when educators and leaders comply with IDEA mandates in ways that meet the letter of the law, but these actions do not always lead to equitable outcomes. While this disjuncture between policy intent and application has been widely researched, starting with Karl Weick's work on loose coupling, this topic is not sufficiently explored in the special education space as it relates to equity outcomes.[45] There is a clear need and benefit in making clear how the disjuncture between documented compliance and action taken allows for inequities to persist.

The paradox of compliance is situated within the split educational system—between general and special education. At this divide lies a paradox of recognition where IDEA protections serve as an important legal resource for securing educational entitlements. But these protections also symbolize second-class citizenship, exposing students to exclusion and stigma based on their disability status.[46] The paradox of compliance also recognizes the duality of disability, which considers intersectional and historical realties related to who a student is, where they go to school, and what resources are around them that collectively influence whether disability policy and law serve as protective or marginalizing forces.[47] Thus, the paradox of compliance reveals that while acts of compliance can provide access to essential entitlements, they can also cause harm.

The paradox of compliance is a broad concept that can be empirically unpacked because legal and legislative mandates do more than dictate what needs to be done. Mandates are influenced by policy interpretation and implementation dynamics as the IDEA moves from the federal to the local level through educational federalism.[48] *Educational federalism* refers to how legislative, legal, and policy intent unravels across contexts, from the federal, to state, to local level. This results in significant variability in how IDEA is implemented and experienced across different contexts. As policy travels through the educational ecosystem, logics of compliance emerge when people utilize the IDEA.[49] Logics of compliance allow for the paradox of compliance to persist.

The logic of compliance is shaped by three forces: current cultural and social contexts, the status quo and organizational inertia of schooling systems, and the collective good intentions of people, policy, and practice. It is essential that we understand how these forces work together, because once they are named and identified, they can be used to transform educational practice, shift systems, and disrupt the paradox of compliance.

What Is Compliance?

I situate the paradox and logic of compliance within a twofold definition. *Compliance* is broadly understood to result from the interplay between technical mandates and adaptive realties.[50] By defining compliance in this manner, I provide practitioners with the tools necessary to identify how IDEA compliance can either advance or thwart equity outcomes in ways that are responsive to legislative and legal mandates and the realities of educational practice.

In the context of this book, *technical compliance* can be understood as formal adherence to the proscriptions of law, legislation, and policy, which in the case of the IDEA was designed, in theory, to protect the rights of individuals with disabilities in schools and other historically marginalized groups. Technical compliance with the IDEA is the protection of individual student rights via legally binding documents, procedures, and mandates. This could include IEPs, functional behavioral assessments, manifestation determinations, hearing notes, and so forth. Technical compliance implies that there are specific, direct, and actionable solutions to address a problem.[51] Technical compliance is thus inclusive of the procedural and individualized features of the IDEA.

Adaptive compliance is the space where the technical components of the IDEA interact with the contextual aspects of educational practice. Adaptive compliance is responsive to the social, historical, and political conditions that shape how policy and law are used to protect historically marginalized groups. This includes consideration of how a racially and economically segregated school system creates different structures of educational opportunity and access, hiring practices, experiences of school-based staff and leadership, educator knowledge of special education policies and procedures, beliefs about ability and disability, and so forth. These adaptive challenges require that educators and the educational system evolve to meet an intended outcome, rather than remain static via technical mandates alone.[52] Therefore, in this book, the adaptative elements of compliance represent the interplay of legal mandates and human interaction across varied contexts over time and their capacity to shift systems towards more equitable outcomes.

In the appendix, I leverage these two definitions of compliance as they relate to the content of nearly every chapter in the book. Through a series of questions, I ask readers to reflect on how paradoxes and logics of compliance relate to their own technical and adaptive understandings of compliance. These questions are meant as provocations for the transformative process that I describe at the end of the book. The critical questions are designed to move readers along a pathway for transformation using an adapted critical cycle process through praxis, thereby leveraging the interplay of theory, research, and educational practice whereby theory is leveraged to make clear the limiting situations that shape how we comply in schools, research is used to illustrate how these limit situations manifest in educational practice, and educational practice is applied as the medium through which transformation can occur.[53] These interconnections are made visible through the experiences and reflections of educators shared in the pages of the book.

Structure of the Book

The book's content is drawn from my decade-long qualitative empirical work on IDEA compliance—with a focus on the IDEA's accountability mechanisms related to racial and ability inequities, referred to as the state performance plan (SPP) indicators—which I use here to create composite vignettes that illuminate core concepts discussed throughout. I present these in subsections called "Stories and Voices from the Field," which are included in every chapter to provide practice-based context to the dimensions of the paradox and the logic of compliance. These stories draw from two large-scale qualitative research projects I conducted over the past ten years in school districts that were cited for racial disproportionality in special education outcomes via SPP indicators.

The projects took place in a variety of settings (e.g., urban and suburban locales) using a variety of methods: fieldwork observations, document reviews, semistructured interviews, and follow-up interviews over time. The projects were focused on understanding how racial inequities in special education relate to the policy interpretation and implementation dynamics surrounding IDEA compliance and accountability metrics. They also focused on the ways in which educators and leaders interpret and comply with the IDEA within their local contexts. The data collection focused on educator experiences and included participants working across special and general education spaces from the district to school level.

To create the "Stories and Voices from the Field" sections, I thematically reanalyzed this large corpus of data to highlight common themes, patterns, and insights related to the paradox and logic of compliance. I then created composite vignettes and stories that sometimes blended experiences and voices across time and space to illuminate core themes and concepts that reverberate throughout the data.[54] While doing so, I reflected on key patterns and insights derived from the data, prioritizing empirical and theoretical depth and ethical responsibility to participants and their lived realties.[55] In some cases, I created composite vignettes from interviews with similarly situated individuals and created a singular account that reflected shared themes and patterns across cases. I did this to create a unified and compelling narrative that highlights the central themes consistently present throughout my research. In other instances, I created a story that emerged from multiple interviews with a single individual over time. This allowed me to tell a reflective story that linked an individual's perspective and experiences as it related to one topic over time. These approaches preserved confidentiality and anonymity while still conveying the depth and complexity of participants' lived experiences. This ensured empirical rigor and depth while also making the findings accessible to diverse audiences, including policymakers and educators.[56]

In the final "Stories and Voices from the Field," two practitioners with whom I have worked with for many years tell their own story in their own voice. They speak from their own vantage point and provide an honest account of how the topics discussed in this book relate to their work around educational equity and systemic transformation. They have coauthor status for the concluding chapter.

The book is presented in three parts. Part 1, which comprises chapters 1 and 2, introduces the paradox of compliance, highlighting the tension between the IDEA's technical mandates and the equity-driven practices needed to support students. It shows how the paradox of compliance arises as IDEA core provisions, IDEA accountability measures, and practitioner actions and belief systems interact. I show how these intersections can inadvertently undermine the IDEA's civil rights inspired legacy—especially at the intersection of race and disability—and distance educator's understandings and connections to the purpose of education from how they provide special education services.

Chapter 1, "Technical and Adaptive Realities of the IDEA," begins by detailing the act's key provisions, focusing on its role in guaranteeing equal educational opportunity for students with disabilities through a civil-rights-inspired framework. I also highlight the need to use an intersectional disability rights lens when considering the history of the act. I leverage the "Stories and Voices from the Field" section to illustrate that although educators' personal connections to special education is often informed by their biographies and educational experiences, these connections can be neutralized and diluted when educators engage with the IDEA and the special education systems operating in their local contexts.

Chapter 2, "Organizational Enactment of the IDEA," examines how the civil rights aspirations of the IDEA have been narrowed into procedural accountability measures that, when leveraged in districts and schools, emphasize form over substance. I describe how the state performance plan accountability indicators in the IDEA are designed to track educational outcomes for students with disabilities. However, the focus on accountability and compliance has led to superficial engagement with the IDEA's core provisions, leaving systemic inequities unaddressed. For example, educators can find ways to comply with IDEA mandates—such as creating a legally sound IEP as it relates to FAPE—but this does not mean that the IEP is implemented in ways that assure what is on paper is substantially and meaningfully enacted in practice to support student learning. Through the chapter's "Stories and Voices from the Field," I highlight the challenges educators face in balancing the procedural demands of the IDEA with their efforts to provide equitable and effective services for students with disabilities.

Part 2 (chapters 3, 4, and 5) delves into the technical and adaptive mechanisms that contribute to the paradox of compliance through logics of compliance and explores the three interconnected forces that bear on the logic of compliance. The first force (chapter 3) focuses on how current contexts, which are shaped by complex sociocultural, historical, and political realities, influence special education service delivery and impact how the IDEA is implemented at the local level. The second force (chapter 4) addresses the maintenance of the status quo, illustrating how ingrained daily practices in schools and districts perpetuate existing inequities. The implementation of the IDEA can often uphold the very systems it aims to reform. Chapter 5 examines the third force, the good intentions of those who seek to support students with disabilities through the IDEA yet often fail to achieve equitable outcomes due to the inadequacy of good intentions alone to address systemic barriers. Understanding these three forces—current contexts, status quo, and good intentions—and how they interact is key to identifying transformative pathways that go beyond mere compliance, as outlined in part 3.

Chapter 3, "Current Contexts," emphasizes how sociocultural, historical, and political factors shape the implementation of the IDEA. Specifically, I outline how historically situated systemic inequities influence present-day teaching and learning conditions that in turn impact IDEA implementation dynamics. In the chapter's "Stories and Voices from the Field," I show how the intersection of IDEA compliance, organizational contexts, and local sociocultural, historical, and political contexts create systems of inequity and opportunity at the local level.

Chapter 4, "Status Quo," examines how institutional inertia allows IDEA compliance dynamics to persist, regardless of their effectiveness in promoting equitable outcomes. I show how seemingly benign acts of compliance perpetuate inequitable systems and remain unchecked for their impact on historically marginalized students. The chapter's "Stories and Voices from the Field" section shows how normalized and taken-for-granted educational practices often fail to address the systemic barriers that the act was meant to dismantle, thus reinforcing preexisting inequities.

Chapter 5, "Good Intentions," the concluding chapter of part 2, examines how practitioners' good intentions cannot by themselves assure educational equity. The notion of good intentions is situated within people, policies, and practices. Through the composite vignette in the chapter's "Stories and Voices from the Field," I show that while good intentions can serve as a bridging force between technical compliance and adaptive realities, they can also mask how harmful ideologies (e.g., ableism) and other systemic barriers persist if they are not directly named. Good intentions are not a solution for addressing systemic inequities.

Part 3, which includes chapters 6 and 7, provides strategies for moving beyond the paradox and logic of compliance and toward equity, utilizing an adapted culture circle and critical cycle process.[57] In chapter 6, "Praxis and Transformation," I summarize parts 1 and 2 of the book and provide guidance on how to apply the insights gained from these sections to create a locally and contextually responsive pathway for transformation rooted in an adapted Freirean critical cycle process. The process includes identifying and collaboratively naming shared experiences related to the paradox and logic of compliance, then using these shared experiences to engage in a critical dialogue—a dialogic conversation—that challenges assumptions and actions that hinder equitable service delivery. I provide a roadmap for engaging in this process and in response to the themes that arise from parts 1 and 2 of the book to challenge the paradox and logic of compliance through both an adaptive and technical lens. The dialogic process also leads to educators cocreating contextually situated plans to improve practice and student outcomes, turning reflections into concrete action steps (praxis). Thus, I introduce a transformative framework that uses ongoing, reflective dialogue among educators and school community members to uncover and address systemic inequities. Step-by-step guidance for working with colleagues through this dialogic and critical process—which involves moving from identifying local challenges to cocreating tailored solutions and putting them into practice—can be found in the appendix, "Applying the Critical Cycle Process."

Chapter 7, "Developing More Just Systems," contains a story of transformation rooted in an adapted critical cycle process focused on compliance.[58] For this chapter, I invited two colleagues, both of whom are district-level leaders, to reflect on their individual journeys of professional and personal transformation. We engaged in a loosely structured, adapted critical cycle process over a prolonged period of time. I brought research-based themes and observations about their district to our discussions. We collectively made sense of them and recorded these conversations, and they began to map out pathways for transformation based on "aha!" moments that surfaced throughout the conversations. The "aha!" moments exposed limit situations, where they then identified new ways to shift and transform their practice. These discussions gradually focused on strengthening how the district designs and implements its multitiered systems of support (MTSS). Therefore, in the chapter, I briefly frame how we engaged in the dialogic process, and then I briefly define MTSS. My interlocutors/coauthors then tell their own story. In their own words, they describe how they came to their critical insights—their "aha!" moments—through dialogue and reflection. They articulate how they identified oppressive issues in their local context and how this helped them grow professionally and personally when developing a critical sociocultural and historical understanding of their environment to foster meaningful change. Their story provides a powerful example of how the dialogic process, responsive to technical and adaptive realities, can begin to shift practice. I also provide a brief statement in the chapter that offers context for thinking about how this work can expand beyond adults working in school systems.

Last, in the appendix, "Applying the Critical Cycle Process," I provide a roadmap for integrating key insights from the book into the adapted critical cycle process. I present a series of critical questions and themes that relate to each chapter of the book, which can be used to challenge the paradox and logic of compliance through both an adaptive and technical lens. The appendix serves as a how-to guide to facilitate a transformation process rooted in compliance with the IDEA. The questions are designed to deepen understanding, encourage reflection, and guide educators toward actionable strategies for systemic change rooted in the adapted Freirean culture circle and critical cycle process. These questions are not merely reflective prompts. They are essential tools for educators to internalize key concepts presented in the book that can then be translated into meaningful action. Given that this book ultimately serves as a call to action, these questions are meant to serve as catalysts for change.

Centering Praxis

This book was designed to pull both theory and practice together through the lens of the technical and the adaptive mechanisms of policy implementation. Within this is a focus on humanizing and rehumanizing acts of IDEA compliance. Therefore, the first step in this book is to generate consciousness about the limiting aspects of compliance and then to critically unpack those limits to transform oppressive systems. It is here, embedded in the rejection of accepting what is and critically reading our environments (a Freirean logic), that a transformative process can take shape.

Freire noted that building critical consciousness (his *conscientização*) requires disrupting the status quo to achieve liberation from oppressive structures.[59] Moreover, a goal in increasing *conscientização* is to assure that the movement from oppression in one dimension does not lead to further oppression in another, which is a key marker of the dehumanization of social and political relations among people.

Therefore, the way that the paradox and logic of compliance are made visible in this book is to assure that oppressive and dehumanizing conditions for both adults and students can be named and then used to change what exists. Here, praxis is a critical feature of the work.[60] *Praxis* is the interplay of theory and practice, reflection and action, and critical transformation entrenched in political, social, and historical realties. The themes and insights gained from parts 1 and 2 of the book are meant to expose points of vulnerability as an adult and in our professional practices. They are meant to be shared with colleagues to transform what persists yet is not working and move toward actions that serve everyone better. I provide readers with questions that are meant to expose the nature and manifestation of the paradox and logic of compliance in their individual context and to connect individualized experiences to broader themes and goals.

In this sense, the adapted critical cycle process described at the end of this book is based on the idea that transformation takes place when the oppressive conditions surrounding an individual or a people is unpacked in dialogue. Through this dialogue, people, processes, and policies are rehumanized and special education service delivery is newly contextualized. In the appendix, I provide readers with the opportunity to examine how the themes emanating from the convergences and divergences between technical and adaptive realities are an opportunity to engage in praxis.

Juxtaposing the technical aspects of practice with the adaptive influences of culture, beliefs, and relationships, educators can pinpoint where their actions align and where they fall short in achieving an intended outcome. These alignments and misalignments, uncovered through dialogue, become catalysts for praxis, which we ignite in dialogue. We bridge theoretical insight with practical application. We reflect and act. We engage and transform our lived realties in ways that are responsive to our current political, social, and historical contexts. This allows for transformation and movement toward equity to be more creative, generative, and contextually situated.

To be clear, the adapted critical cycle process that is described in this book is not a pedagogy or a tool. It is solely presented as a way to encourage critical thought and dialogue around deeply entrenched practices where critical pedagogy and critical methods typically do not look—at acts of policy compliance. As a writer, and in writing this book, I am clear that, as Giroux and Robbins noted, the Western appropriation of Freire's work strips its critical nature from its revolutionary intent, reducing it to a set of pedagogical techniques rather than recognizing its foundation in concrete political struggles.[61] My use of an adapted culture circle and critical cycle process here is not to overlook the anticolonial and postcolonial dimensions of Freire's theory and practice but to leverage dialogue and the dialogic process as a way to push adults to notice, name, and begin to break free from the oppressive and limiting conditions they create when complying with the IDEA. It is for this reason that I am intentional in saying that I propose an adapted critical cycle process.

Closing

At the heart of this book is a call to reconnect the personal and professional and to rehumanize how we, as educators, engage with law, legislation, and policy as tools for expanding educational opportunity and protecting student rights. All too often, the administrative requirements associated with the IDEA and the enacting of these requirements in education practice become overwhelming and disconnected from the lived experiences of the students whom they are meant to protect. This book offers a powerful alternative to this reality. Grounded in deep reflection and collective dialogue, it invites educators to reengage with the spirit of the IDEA, to critically examine how they interpret and implement policy, and to transform compliance into a stronger equity lever.

The ideas and transformative process described in this book are not only reflective; they can also be deeply empowering, leading to a renewed sense of professional purpose and agency. The ideas encourage readers to move beyond compliance, to challenge outdated routines, and to cocreate new, equity-driven practices with their colleagues. In doing so, educators can begin to reclaim time and energy and redirect it toward meaningful instruction and relationship building with students, families, and each other in ways that lead to more thoughtful and impactful practice. Perhaps the most transformative aspect of the book, however, is its emphasis on using theoretically grounded and critically informed dialogue to surface how structural inequities and ideological barriers function while still allowing us to remain agents of change in the service of the students we serve.

* * *

A Note on Positionality

I am acutely aware that my identity and experiences have shaped my understanding of educational systems and inequities. My positioning also shapes how I critically examine the IDEA through the lenses of power, privilege, and justice.[62] As a former teacher and professor and through my family history, I have witnessed education's power to transform lives and challenge oppressive systems. In my own life, both formal and informal educational opportunities have been essential to imagining and creating opportunities that extend beyond the limits of our circumstances. This hope and belief in change guides my work. In this spirit, I offer this note on positionality in response to the core themes required to engage in authentic dialogic transformation as outlined by Freire and that are central to this book: love, humility, faith, trust, hope, and critical thinking.[63]

I include this note on positionality to connect the personal to the professional and to make visible how the theoretical and intellectual foundations that shape my work influence what is written in this book.[64] In explicitly naming who I am in relation to this work, I remain in a dialogic process with myself and the fields of knowledge that I name in this book in attempts to continuously ensure that my work is rooted in an accountability to myself, to my students, to scholarship, and to the people for whom this book is written. This note on positionality is part of a continuous assessment process that makes visible how my work engages with systems that sustain and disrupt systemic inequities, with the broad goal of transforming what is to imagine better futures for what can be.

I root this book within a dominant theme in my family story: resilience and the power of education to transform lives. I was always made aware of my family history through storytelling. These stories live in me and through me. Growing up, I was surrounded by stories and symbols of resilience and the importance of education. My dad would tell my siblings and me about his experiences and my family's escaping war, bombings, hunger, and disease in the period during the Russian invasion of Ukraine and the process of coming to the United States as displaced refugees. These were always coupled with forays into his favorite Ukrainian characters from books that helped him move out of the terror of war and find agency in frightening circumstances. They also always ended in triumph, contained a lesson in faith and love, and required us to always expand our minds.

My grandmother, Baba, was a central force in my upbringing. She never met her father, a colonel in the Ukrainian Resistance Army who fought fiercely to repel the Bolshevik advance in Ukraine. Her father's lineage traces back to the Cossacks, a proud people who fought for Ukraine. This legacy and the fight to stand up for who you are and what you believe in shaped her identity. Despite this powerful connection to history and resilience, Baba's childhood was also marked by hardship. Her mother remarried when she was young, and Baba endured severe abuse from her stepfather. It was these early struggles that led her to marry my grandfather, Dido, at the age of eighteen. Baba only completed seven grades of formal schooling.

Dido received the equivalent of only a first-grade education. In Ukraine, his family was focused on learning a trade. Despite his never finishing first grade, my grandfather had an extraordinary talent for mathematics and a keen spatial ability. He was what some might call a savant, displaying remarkable talents that he applied to machinery and his physical environment. I remember him working silently and with precise focus to transform physical spaces and fix machines, and I remember him thinking—always thinking, always tinkering. And I remember him always limping because of the bomb shrapnel left in his body.

Things were different on my mother's side. Her parents, my grandfather and grandmother Jajo and Bopsha, had formal and more advanced education obtained in Ukraine. Jajo was a doctor practicing in Ukraine when World War II forced him and Bopsha to immigrate to the United States. He was sponsored as a rural doctor and placed in a small town of barely eight hundred people.

Growing up, I remember Jajo being the "good doctor" whom people from across a vast geographic expanse came to see for their medical care. With the bakery and the drugstore, the brick rectangle of the rural clinic that sat on Main Street with about ten other structures, was the heartbeat of the town.

Bopsha was always by Jajo's side. She was an avid reader who spoke multiple languages, read heaps of books, entertained friends and neighbors who would come over for coffee and sweets, and wrote a never-ending stream of letters to friends abroad while listening simultaneously to music and the weather channel, with its constant threats of a tornado or snowstorm that could disrupt prairie life. This is where my mother and her two brothers grew up.

My uncle, my mom's brother, whom we called Duno in Ukrainian, had a disability. Neither I nor anyone in my family knew what his specific disability was. Duno, like my mother, went to a rural school for his entire life. Their formal education was contained to one school building that held all students in K–12 from the local area and where a graduating class of four students was not surprising. This was before the passage of the IDEA.

Duno was different from others, both physically and mentally, but I never thought of him as different. He was my uncle who liked to read, talked a lot and often, and had an insatiable curiosity, reflected in the thousands of books and records he collected over his lifetime that were stored in the basement of the house in that rural town. He also had a sense of adventure that was unmatched.

When he would visit the big city, he would memorize entire bus lines and then go off and travel all over the city, exploring museums on his own, trying new restaurants and cuisines, browsing bookstores, seeing movies, and soaking up everything the city had to offer. I remember his leaving early in the morning, wearing what always looked like oversized galoshes, swaying side to side with an exaggerated gait as he walked to the bus stop, ready to embark on a new adventure.

Duno was simply himself—brilliant, curious, and endlessly kind—and as a family, we watched him do what he wanted to do without constraints. Sometimes, though, I was afraid that someone would hurt him or say something bad to him because of who he was, but he never told us stories about that. He would just share his adventures.

While the history of my mother's and father's sides of the family differ in some respects in relation to education, they collectively hold common threads related to the love of learning, discovery, resilience, and exploration. They also converge on something that was told to me over and over again as a child in different ways: people can take away material things, but they cannot take away what is in your mind. Education is of paramount importance.

I share all this because my education is and always has been my culture, my family, our traditions, and my formal schooling. The connection between personal identity, history, and education is critical to me and to my career. Separating who I am from what I do or experience creates a void that weakens the transformative power of education and, frankly, undercuts my purpose in this work. It is this connection that drives my personal and professional endeavors and that inspired me to write this book. We—as professionals, as adults—must create the systems, opportunities, and supports for our students to thrive and be who they are while also honoring their stories, experiences, and culture. I have seen too often how accountability measures, compliance, and the demands placed on educators and leaders can dehumanize the educational process and separate who we are from what we do.

I find it necessary to unpack how those in power, those who make critical decisions about students' lives (us, the adults), shape structures of opportunity to learn. I was a teacher, and I faced many of the dilemmas outlined in the pages of this book. It was my students who led me to formalize the question that has shaped my entire body of work to date as they challenged me to reckon with my own actions and assumptions. They gave me the vision to ask a question that continues to drive my work: Does compliance with the IDEA matter in the pursuit of educational equity? I ask this question for them and for the memory of Duno.

I know that education can serve as a pathway through and away from the scars of war, refugee status, and newly arrived immigrant assimilation. It can create pathways for transformation across generations. It can shift and alter life trajectories. But I also know that this is more likely to happen when who you are as a person is honored and humanized in educational spaces. Therefore, I position myself in this work in a way that can help adults find ways to expand beyond the boundaries of our limited situations and move toward the transformative pathways we need for all students to succeed.

By bringing together theory and practice and by examining the technical and adaptive dimensions of policy implementation as it relates to IDEA compliance, I seek to humanize and rehumanize educational practices, processes, procedures, and policies that have reinforced limited and oppressive structures for adults, families, and students. I have attempted to make visible how the paradox and logic of compliance function so that educators can better name and identify oppressive structures in order to dismantle them and rebuild in new ways. I hope that in doing so, constructive and transformative dialogue emerge.

PART I

The Paradox of Compliance

I consider the fundamental theme of our epoch to be that of domination—which implies its opposite, the theme of liberation, as the objective to be achieved . . . to achieve humanization, which presupposes the elimination of dehumanizing oppression, it is absolutely necessary to surmount limit-situations in which people are reduced to things.

—PAULO FREIRE

CHAPTER I

Technical and Adaptive Realities of the IDEA

The development of special education is often portrayed as a straightforward and positive path of rights attainment.[1] It is also frequently framed as a race-neutral narrative of progress focusing on the legislative victories that have secured rights and protections for all individuals with disabilities.[2] While technical provisions within the Individuals with Disabilities Education Act (IDEA) are essential for ensuring that the rights of students with disabilities are upheld in schools, they exist within a broad and complex historical, ideological, institutional, and political context.[3]

The core ethos behind the IDEA was shaped by the civil rights political and legal shifts that occurred in the 1960s and 1970s.[4] Although there is a long history of disability rights advocacy prior to this time, it was not until the 1970s that rights were secured for disabled students in schools.[5]

Disability rights advocates, particularly parents and caregivers, mobilized to challenge the systemic exclusion of and discrimination against individuals with disabilities in schools.[6] These advocates drew on the legal strategies established by the landmark1954 Supreme Court decision in *Brown v. Board of Education*, which struck down racial segregation in public schools, to argue that excluding and segregating students with disabilities from educational services similarly violated the Equal Protection and Due Process Clauses of the Fourteenth Amendment.[7] Disability rights advocates framed this fight, along with other disability related issues, as a direct response to the systemic exclusion, seclusion, and marginalization of people with disabilities throughout US society.[8]

By grounding the fight for educational inclusion within the framework of constitutional rights, disability advocates effectively challenged discriminatory practices that excluded disabled students, laying the groundwork for a more inclusive and equitable educational system. These advocacy efforts led to two pivotal court cases that became the foundation for contemporary educational disability legislation: *Pennsylvania Association for Retarded Children v. Commonwealth of Pennsylvania* (1972) and *Mills v. Board of Education of the District of Columbia* (1972).[9] Both cases secured legal recognition of the educational rights of disabled children, centered caregiver and parent involvement in educational decisions, and directly contributed to the passage of the Education for All Handicapped Children Act (EAHCA) in 1975. Later, this act was renamed the Individuals with Disabilities Education Act (IDEA) in 1990.[10]

While the EAHCA and the IDEA were shaped by principles of equality drawing from the civil rights movement, they are not civil rights laws. Unlike the Civil Rights Act of 1964, which addresses discrimination based on race, color, religion, sex, or national origin, the IDEA focuses on ensuring educational access for disabled children in schools. In its prioritization of individual educational needs, its impact on broad educational equity has been limited.[11]

Currently, the IDEA operates alongside key civil rights laws to protect individuals with disabilities. Section 504 of the Rehabilitation Act of 1973, the first federal disability rights law, prohibits discrimination based on physical or mental conditions in programs receiving federal funds.[12] The Americans with Disabilities Act (ADA) of 1990 expanded these protections to the private sector, mandating the elimination of discrimination against individuals with disabilities. Unlike Section 504, the ADA covers entities that do not receive federal funding. Each of these laws serves a distinct purpose related to access and equity, with the IDEA focused specifically on educational rights and ensuring access and equity for disabled students.

Since 1990, the IDEA has been reauthorized multiple times. Yet through each reauthorization, it has consistently upheld the central mission established by the EAHCA: to ensure that students with disabilities have equal access to educational opportunities comparable to their nondisabled peers.[13] The most recent reauthorization of IDEA (2004) has several essential guiding principles, found primarily in Part B of the legislation, for safeguarding the individual rights of students with disabilities in school, which therefore must be followed by state education agencies (SEAs) and local education agencies (LEAs). These essential principles include free appropriate public education (FAPE), individualized education programming (IEP), least restrictive environment (LRE), appropriate evaluation, parent and caregiver participation, and procedural safeguards.[14]

FAPE ensures that all children with disabilities are provided special education and related services at no cost to families. These services must comply with state standards and must be customized to meet the specific needs of each child through an IEP. The IEP is a written plan created by a team that includes educators, parents, related service providers, and, when appropriate, the student. It details the student's current academic, behavioral, and social goals, the services and supports they will receive, and the accommodations or modifications needed to ensure progress in the LRE. The LRE directs that students with disabilities must be educated with their nondisabled peers whenever possible. A student's removal from general education settings must only occur when the severity or nature of their disability hinders adequate educational progress, even with the provision of supplementary aids or services. Appropriate evaluation refers to the fact that students must be evaluated comprehensively and without bias to determine their eligibility for special education and related services. Evaluations must use diverse, nondiscriminatory, and accessible assessment tools and methods. Parent and caregiver participation acknowledges that parents and caregivers are critical to the special education process and directs that they must be involved in IEP meetings, informed of their rights, and given the opportunity to contribute to their child's IEP development and educational decisions. Procedural safeguards protect the rights of children with disabilities and their families to ensure parental and caregiver involvement, provide avenues for dispute resolution, and mandate due process hearings to address disagreements regarding a child's education.

The Adaptive Realties behind the IDEA

Although the passage of the EAHCA and later the IDEA radically shifted the education landscape and how people with disabilities were included in society, the IDEA remains a flawed piece of legislation that has not systemically improved outcomes for all students.[15] Students with disabilities, particularly those at the intersection of race and disability, continue to face barriers to high quality and appropriate educational opportunities and services.[16] Research indicates that there is variability in long-term postsecondary outcomes at the intersection of race and disability.[17] For instance, Yoder and colleagues found that students with disabilities and those identifying as Black, Hispanic, or Native American faced significantly lower odds of graduation compared to their peers.[18] With regard to the labor market, Fuentes et al. found that workplace discrimination related to the intersection of race and disability contributes to significant disparities in labor market outcomes, workplace well-being, and career advancement.[19]

The adaptive realities underlying these disparities are historically situated and ideologically complex. Pettinicchio described the cyclical nature of disability rights progress, where advancements like the IDEA, the ADA, and Section 504 are often followed by setbacks.[20] This advancement and retrenchment of rights reflects societal ambivalence to disability inclusion and further illustrates how persistent structural barriers, disability discrimination, and ableism persist.[21] US disability policy has historically framed individuals with disabilities as dependent and in need of rehabilitation, reinforcing ableist views in policies that disabled people must be "fixed" to fully participate in society.[22]

Ableism perpetuates inequality by framing disability primarily as a medical problem to be cured rather than recognizing how social and structural factors impact disability experiences and how disability rights are framed.[23] Furthermore, ableism devalues individuals with disabilities and often disregards the broader systemic factors that contribute to continued marginalization.[24] When disability is framed solely as something to be fixed or remediated within an individual, the societal structures that create barriers and discrimination are obscured.[25] Instead, the onus is placed on individuals with disabilities to conform to a standard that is not responsive to their needs, which reinforces a culture of ableism.

Scholars have noted that discrimination against individuals with disabilities (*ableism*) occurs across three interconnected layers: personal, interpersonal, and structural.[26] Personal and interpersonal ableism involves individual biases, both conscious and unconscious, that devalue people with disabilities. It can be enacted interpersonally and lead to internalized ableism and stigma impacting self-esteem and a sense of self, aspirations, and individual and group perceptions about competence.[27] Structural ableism is embedded in systems that prioritize nondisabled needs, which is evident in inaccessible spaces, inadequate accommodations in education, and discriminatory employment practices.[28] These layers collectively reinforce exclusion and inequality, with disability discrimination being the sole focus.

Ableism is not a monolithic form of oppression, even though it is often centered as the axis of oppression within a disability rights narrative.[29] Intersectional ableism within a rights-based framework acknowledges that students with disabilities face interconnected forms of oppression linked to their identities, including race, gender, sexual orientation, and socioeconomic status among others.[30] These overlapping inequities show that disability rights and protections must be understood within the broader context of intersecting identities and move beyond a predominantly white-centered disability rights narrative.[31]

Throughout US history, intersectional disability discrimination has been evident. At Ellis Island, medical exams targeted individuals with physical or mental disabilities, labeling them “undesirable” under the 1882 Immigration Act, which restricted entry for those deemed likely to become a public charge.[32] Immigrants with visible disabilities, or those classified as “feebleminded,” were often subjected to invasive exams and denied entry. This exclusion reinforced a narrow, able-bodied, white, Western European, and heteronormative ideal of American identity and citizenship that marginalized those who did not conform to these standards.[33] Schalk highlighted how marginalized groups, including immigrants, Black people, and women, have historically faced ableist and racialized constructions of disability, limiting their access to opportunities and protections, including education.[34]

For example, Willowbrook, a state-supported institution for children with intellectual disabilities located in Staten Island, New York, that operated from 1947 until 1987, had deplorable conditions first noted in a documentary featuring Geraldo Rivera.[35] In the film, a doctor working in the institution is quoted as saying that Willowbrook is “hell. . . . At first you don’t get the full magnitude of it. It takes you day after day to fathom this hell. No programming going on, the most token schooling happening, no support or continuity for schooling. The minute the kid reaches beyond school age, they go deeper into the institution. No school, no future, no exit. They've got to die to get out."[36]

Rivera expressed shock at the conditions but later admitted that he did not address the racial and ethnic composition of the individuals in the institution:

> I never mentioned race. . . . I was afraid that New Yorkers were bored with the Civil Rights movement, and that if I made it a social civil rights issue, the middle-class whites—the people whose votes control the political machinery for fundamental change would say, 'Oh, it's just those poor people again. They don't pay for anything and still they're never satisfied.' But the truth, Dr. Wilkins told me, is that about 80 percent of the children of Willowbrook come from poor families. In this town, poor is translated to black or Puerto Rican.[37]

Rivera clearly thought it better to refrain from mentioning race for fear of alienating politically influential middle-class white audiences in advocating for change for disabled people.

Examples like this, of these historically situated, ideologically complex, intersectional, and adaptive realities underlie the technical components of disability rights that shape how we understand the purpose of disability law and the IDEA. Therefore, to fully understand and effectively implement the act (IDEA), it must always be interpreted within a broader sociopolitical context, one that acknowledges how multiple overlapping systems of oppression and opportunity impact students with disabilities. We must understand that behind the technical aspects of the IDEA lies a history marked by advances in disability rights, periods of retrenchment, and ongoing discrimination. These factors both implicitly and explicitly influence how the IDEA is understood and implemented in educational practice and, ultimately, how effective it can be in improving outcomes for students with disabilities. This reality is felt and experienced by educators on the ground.

Educators, particularly those in special education, articulate the purpose and motivation behind their work in ways that are responsive to the complex and layered legacy of the development of disability rights through the IDEA. The historical significance of the legacy behind the development of educational rights through the IDEA—with all its tensions and contradictions—is felt by educators when they comply with the IDEA and provide educational services and supports to students with disabilities. These tensions between the technical and the adaptive are important because they do not necessarily deter transformation or the pursuit of educational equity. Rather, they serve as an anchor of sorts for educators to make sense of their practice in ways that are linked to the purpose of the IDEA and to their desire to support students.

This manifests in conversations with educators, where it is rare for them to directly reference the IDEA as the core of their mission. Instead, they often speak passionately about their broader commitment to disability advocacy and their personal connections to the field of education and special education. For many, their mission is shaped by their unique identities, lived experiences, and personal journeys that led them to special education. These educators tend to view disability as an intersectional issue, acknowledging how it intersects with factors such as race, gender, and socioeconomic status. As a result, their approach to special education is deeply informed by their personal understandings of disability and advocacy, and these adaptive factors hold significance beyond just the technical and compliance aspects of the IDEA. This underscores that the work of educators is not solely driven by legal mandates but by a more profound and multifaceted commitment to educational equity and inclusion.

Voices and Stories from the Field

In this first story, told through the voice of a woman of color educator and leader, the educator's personal beliefs and lived experiences significantly influenced her professional trajectory and professional practices. She articulates how she entered the field with a commitment to student success, based on her identity and experiences, and this is what drives her to continue to advocate for what she believes in, even though the systems around her appear to constrain meaningful advocacy, reinforce patterns of exclusion, and hinder equitable opportunities:

> When I first entered the field of education as an educator, it was deeply personal. I wasn't the best student—hovering around Cs and B-minus grades—but there were a few teachers who truly made a difference in my life. They gave me the confidence to believe in myself, helping me realize that I could be someone capable of achieving greatness—using the words of one of my favorite teachers. That feeling of being seen for my potential stayed with me, and it became my mission as a teacher: to help every student see their own value and greatness, no matter where they started.

This is so important for me to hold onto because a lot of us are told we won't make it. I still remember being told by one of my professors in college, "You're not going to be a good teacher, because you're not a good writer." I was shy and barely spoke in class, and the professor basically suggested that I'd have to change who I was to succeed. Her words stuck with me, but they also fueled my determination. The people who didn't believe in me became my motivation. It was like being a diamond put under constant pressure; I could only shine brighter.

As a teacher, I never cared if a student performed poorly on their first test. I would always say, "This test doesn't define you. We're in this together, and we'll do better next time." I meant that, and I saw how that mentality brought kids along with me. If I believed in them, they believed in themselves in my classroom.

As time went on and I progressed in my educational career, my perspective began to shift further toward a more holistic and systemic lens. I started noticing the deep-seated issues in education, particularly around race. I began to ask, "Why is this student always being written up while that one isn't?" It didn't stop there.

When I had children of my own, things hit even closer to home. At just five years old, my son was almost expelled from kindergarten. I'll never forget the phone calls I received. That experience opened my eyes to the disparities in ways I hadn't seen before. As my son entered school, the problems only escalated. I could no longer ignore the systemic failings—not just for my son but for many students, particularly students of color.

My own educational experiences gave me the lens to understand these disparities on a more personal level. I started sharing my story, and through these conversations,

I began to uncover the deep flaws in the system. This became even clearer when I took on the role of an assistant principal, where I was deeply involved in special education. I attended meetings where students were being evaluated for special education services, and I began to notice a disturbing pattern. These meetings often focused on the deficits of the students, as though something was inherently wrong with them. The meetings were dominated by tests and evaluations, and it felt like the parents and teachers were disconnected from the child's true needs. It made me uncomfortable, but at first, I didn't ask too many questions. I observed and wondered where the problem lied.

However, as I spent more time in that role, I saw the patterns emerge more clearly. It was always the same students—those who were Black and multilingual—who were being labeled with issues like poor academic performance and bad behavior. But I knew that wasn't the real issue. These students spoke English just fine; their accents were different, and that was being misunderstood as a deficiency. Difference seemed to justify disability.

It was in this moment of realization, as an assistant principal, that I truly understood how deeply entrenched racial and systemic inequities were in our schools. It was a turning point, and I knew I couldn't stay silent anymore. The system needed to change, and I was determined to be a part of that change and I have focused on that in my career moving forward. This realization has pushed me to confront the system and my colleagues as I gained more confidence and authority. I am no longer afraid to ask my colleagues why these students were being treated differently.

* * *

In this next story, a white woman special educator reveals a pervasive tension around her need to reconcile how the special education systems and structures in which she is embedded are often at odds with what she believes is truly best for her students. Despite these tensions, she also expresses her commitment to seeing her students succeed, seeing her students for who they are, and advocating for their growth. She makes clear that her work as a special educator is not merely about following procedural requirements but also about recognizing students' humanity. But the systems around her can feel constraining and nonresponsive to this desire:

> As I sit back and reflect on my journey in special education, I realize that I'm constantly balancing several conflicting forces: the strict requirements of the IDEA and the deep, individual needs of the students I work with.
>
> When I studied the IDEA in graduate school, the message was crystal clear: students with disabilities should be placed in the least restrictive environment that allows them to learn and grow alongside their peers. That was and is my mission, too. I want to assure that students get what they need, every day, and I want to protect their rights. I know people with disabilities, and I do this work for them and for my students.
>
> What I found out when I started teaching, though, was that as much as the IDEA sounds good on paper, putting it into practice often feels like a task that doesn't quite match the messy reality of my students' lives and experiences and what I actually do as a teacher.
>
> I've seen it time and time again—when a student is labeled "special ed," parents often panic, fearing that their child will be put into a small room where their days will be spent doing nothing but basic tasks like coloring or counting. They

worry that their child will be stuck, isolated, and limited. Part of my job is to debunk that myth. I'm the final stop before kids are sent to out-of-district placements, which are the most restrictive options in our district. So I have to work hard to ensure that the students in my classroom still have access to the same academic experiences as their peers.

That doesn't mean it's easy. In fact, it often means reteaching old skills to students while trying to introduce new concepts—finding the balance between meeting their academic requirements and exposing them to a broader curriculum that prepares them for mainstream classrooms. But it's not a simple task.

Sometimes I wonder if we're making the right call for each student: are we pushing them too hard to fit into a system that may not be working for them, or are we holding them back from reaching their true potential? The conflict between the rigid mandates of the IDEA and the more individualized approaches my students need is ever-present.

Take one student, for example. He's a kid who doesn't quite fit anywhere in this district. What I mean is that he's not fully a behavioral student, and he could benefit from the typical behavior-focused special education classrooms in the district, but he also struggles in those because it is too restrictive. He fits, but he doesn't fit. But the fit is based on the programs we have available here in the district, not necessarily on his needs. That feels bad sometimes because it is not aligned with the spirit of the law.

In moments like these, I find myself questioning whether the out-of-district placements might actually be the best fit for him. These placements can provide the more tailored support he needs before he's ready to transition back to a general education setting. But these decisions are far from straightforward. They mean a more restrictive setting, and that is not always good, but sometimes it is good for the student. These decisions go beyond simply following IDEA's mandates. Sure, we can move the kid to a new placement, but I also know him. Nothing of what is actually available seems right. These decisions require a deeper understanding of what's going to actually help the student thrive in the long run rather than making sure he is in the least restrictive environment. It is really complicated, and it takes time to figure out these things, especially when I see him languishing in his current environment, but there is not a clear answer for what is best for him in law, in practice, or in conversation with his parents to be honest.

Another complication comes with the accuracy of diagnoses for students like the one I am talking about. While the diagnoses we receive from psychologists seem mostly accurate, they're often based on brief check-ins—snapshots, really—of who a student is. It is not right. I'm with my students all day, seeing them at their most vulnerable and seeing who they actually are when they are challenged. Sometimes I wonder if a more thorough, continuous approach to assessing these students would provide a clearer picture of what's truly going on. This would help us really identify the correct placement for them.

And building relationships with parents and making clear to them these decisions about a student adds another layer of complexity. By the time these students make it to my classroom, many parents have already been worn down by years of negative phone calls about their child's behavior. I'm conscious of not adding to that negative cycle. I don't want to be just another call about bad behavior; I only reach out when it's truly necessary. I focus on the positive, trying to reframe how parents see their children's progress.

When a student runs out of the classroom, for instance, I don't just document the behavior, call the parents, and punish the student. I work with the student to help them understand that asking for a break isn't a bad thing—it's a coping skill. In my experience, it leads to better outcomes because it fosters trust and helps students develop skills they'll use in the real world.

I just can't do this work thinking it is about getting through the day and checking boxes to move along. I am not OK with just being a teacher who shows up to work. It is deep in me to see my students for who they are and to meet them where they're at and advocate for them.

The real work, for me, is in those moments where what I have to do, what I actually do, and what I actually care about—which is my kids and their futures—is where I feel tension. I want to offer them a safe space for growth and help students find their way, even when the system doesn't always make it easy to do so.

And while it's exhausting at times, it's the work that I know is necessary. This is the reality of special education, and it's what drives me to keep pushing, even when the path forward isn't clear.

Reflections

This chapter explored the historical dimension of the paradox of compliance, examining the tension between the technical mandates of the IDEA and the historical and adaptive realities that gave rise to these provisions. The fundamental struggle to secure the right to be heard and to live fully as a disabled person in the United States is reflected in the development of federal disability policy and law. This struggle goes beyond the development to the EAHCA and the IDEA, and it is deeply rooted in a long history of exclusion, discrimination, and isolation shaped by the institutionalization of disabled people, eugenics, and other factors that systematically marginalized disabled individuals from full participation in society.[38] These systemic factors and their lasting historical legacy on present-day practices underlay an adaptive reality that impacts educators and the decisions they make in schools—whether explicitly or implicitly noted.

The chapter also makes clear that it is necessary to employ an intersectional lens when understanding disability rights history and when understanding the paradox of compliance. An intersectional lens helps give context to the political, sociocultural, and historical realities surrounding disability rights attainment and the legal and legislative impacts of these rights on the lived experiences of people in schools. These intersectional realities and lived experiences can be hard to uphold when the IDEA is implemented and thus impact adults and students in different ways.

As seen in the two stories and voices from the field, the educators describe a clear disconnect between their personal convictions and connections to education and special education, on the one hand, and the actual practices enacted within schools on the other. The gap between the technical provisions of the law and the lived experiences of educators and students reveals an element of the paradox of compliance, where strict adherence to the law can lead to dehumanizing practices that ignore the intersectional context of lived experiences and mandated rights. The stories of the woman of color who drew on her personal experiences and understanding of systemic inequities to advocate for inclusive education and the white educator who grappled with balancing the IDEA's strict requirements with her students' unique needs illustrate how the lived experiences of educators and students alike often clash with the technical demands of compliance. These tensions highlight how having a connection to disability or deep personal empathy for students and varied schooling experiences can be a powerful asset when envisioning a more holistic and equitable approach that is responsive to both technical and adaptive realities. Moreover, when we are connected to our practice, our students, and our communities—whether through lived experience, interpersonal relationships, or proximity to the systems we seek to change—we are more likely to maintain a deeply human dimension to compliance.

Critical Questions to Consider

- In what ways do the core provisions within the IDEA, while designed to protect the rights of students with disabilities, inadvertently perpetuate inequities and silence intersectional experiences when they are applied to educational practice?
- In what ways does the focus on technical compliance with the IDEA, without addressing the broader adaptive sociocultural and historical contexts of an intersectional disability rights history, hinder the achievement of true equity for students with disabilities at their intersections?
- How can educators draw on their own experiences or proximity to disability—whether personal or professional—to raise awareness and advocate for systemic changes that better support students with disabilities and that address existing inequities in education?

CHAPTER 2

Organizational Enactment of the IDEA

In the United States, millions of students receive special education services and supports under the IDEA, yet these services are not equitably distributed across disability and racial categories.[1] While some research indicates that special education services can improve outcomes in specific and localized contexts, other data illustrate that the overall benefits of special education are less positive.[2] For example, research indicates that English language learners do not experience sustained academic growth once in special education, and there are persistent racial and ethnic disparities in long term outcomes for students with disabilities.[3]

While special education research has traditionally focused on compliance with the IDEA to promote equal educational opportunity, there is no clear evidence of improved outcomes over time for *all* students despite IDEA protections.[4] IDEA noncompliance remains a significant issue across state education agencies (SEAs), with many states failing to meet some form of compliance with IDEA mandates.[5]

The federal government has for decades recognized the pervasive nature of IDEA noncompliance and the stagnant outcomes for students with disabilities, and it has employed various accountability measures and approaches to address the problem. In the most general sense, IDEA monitoring and enforcement is overseen by the federal government and through SEAs. The oversight is primarily carried out through the Office of Special Education Programs (OSEP). In accepting federal IDEA funds, states are obligated to establish a system of general supervision to monitor local educational agencies (LEAs) and their public schools, maintaining a balance between monitoring outcomes for students with disabilities and assuring procedural compliance. However, the IDEA does not prescribe an exact model for monitoring, each state's system must ensure enforcement of the legislation and promote ongoing improvements.[6]

According to the National Council on Disability, early monitoring under the IDEA primarily consisted of on-site visits (approximately every five years), during which federal reviewers conducted interviews, examined policies, and reviewed student records; states then received a letter from OSEP outlining any compliance issues and required corrective actions.[7] However, it became increasingly clear that these traditional compliance reviews were not translating into better outcomes for students with disabilities. In response, both states and OSEP began to adopt a focused monitoring strategy in the late 1990s alongside the changes introduced by the 1997 IDEA amendments that required states to set performance goals and measurable indicators for students with disabilities.[8] These efforts signaled a growing federal emphasis on educational results.

The 1997 amendments introduced the continuous improvement monitoring process (CIMP). CIMP aimed to shift oversight from a narrow focus on procedural matters to a more dynamic, outcomes-based model emphasizing collaboration between SEAs and OSEP.[9] The CIMP was designed to foster a continuous cycle of assessment, improvement planning, and monitoring that centered on improving results for students with disabilities. However, despite the introduction of CIMP, many SEAs chose to continue using self-assessment models rather than fully adopting the continuous improvement cycle.[10] As a result, by the early 2000s, nearly every state in the United States was found to be out of compliance with some aspect of the IDEA, irrespective of the 1997 reforms.[11]

Regardless, the 1997 reauthorization of the IDEA required that students with disabilities be included in state and local accountability systems—something that was not previously required—marking a shift toward greater accountability around outcomes for students with disabilities, even though students with the most significant disabilities were still exempt from this mandate.[12] The 2004 IDEA reauthorization further refined the accountability approach, resulting in a more direct shift from compliance-driven monitoring to results-oriented accountability systems.[13] It also introduced key changes to the field, among factors such as requiring that "highly qualified" teachers work in the field, improving transition planning services, revising disability identification procedures, and updating disciplinary policies and regulations.[14]

The 2004 reauthorization also included the establishment of state performance plan indicators (SPPs) under Part B. The SPPs were designed to monitor state and local educational agency (SEA and LEA) progress in ensuring equal educational opportunity for students with disabilities across various outcomes. They are aligned with the IDEA's core features, and they measure factors such as academic performance, least restrictive environment, and postsecondary outcomes for students with disabilities and IDEA compliance. They also include the monitoring of dimensions of racial disparities in special education outcomes, specifically across classifications, placements, and disciplinary outcomes.

The presence of these policy indicators has not substantially improved outcomes for students with disabilities over time, though.[15] Etscheidt et al. noted that effective accountability measures must not only align with policy goals (the technical aspects of policy mandates) but must also be responsive to the needs of local contexts (the adaptive mechanisms of educational practice) and meaningfully integrate quantitative and qualitative data to identify gaps to improve practice that are responsive to intersectional lived realties.[16] A multifaceted accountability approach is necessary to assure that short-term fixes are not pursued at the expense of longer-term sustainable solutions.[17] Regardless, the SPPs remain the dominant approach for assuring results-based and programmatic accountability with the IDEA. The SPPs are listed as follows (adapted from the US Department of Education):[18]

Indicator 1: Percent of youth with individualized education program (IEPs) graduating with a regular high school diploma

Indicator 2: Percent of youth with IEPs who exited from special education due to dropping out of school

Indicator 3: Participation and performance in statewide assessments for children with IEPs

Indicator 4: Rates of suspension and expulsion for youth with IEPs

Indicator 5: Percent of youth with IEPs placed in various educational and restrictive settings

Indicator 6: Percent of youth with IEPs enrolled in preschool programs and in early childhood programs across various educational and restrictive settings

Indicator 7: Percent of youth ages 3 to 5 with IEPs that show improvement in preschool children's skills (social-emotional, knowledge, behavior)

Indicator 8: Percent of parents with a child receiving special education services and supports that report schools facilitated their involvement in improving services for children with disabilities

Indicator 9: Percent of districts reporting disproportionate representation of racial and ethnic groups in special education and related services that are the result of inappropriate identification

Indicator 10: Percent of districts reporting disproportionate representation of racial and ethnic groups in specific disability categories that is the result of inappropriate identification

Indicator 11: Percent of youth who were evaluated in a timely manner for initial evaluations

Indicator 12: Percentage of youth who are referred from early intervention (Part C) before turning age 3, determined eligible for special education services under Part B, and who have an IEP in place and services started by their third birthday.

Indicator 13: Percentage of youth with IEPs that have post-secondary goals and services aged sixteen and over

Indicator 14: Percentage of youth who had IEPs and post-school outcomes

Indicator 15: Percent of hearing requests that went through resolution through settlement agreements

Indicator 16: Percent of mediations that resulted in agreements

Indicator 17: State's systemic improvement plan to improve outcomes for children with disabilities

With respect to racial disparities in special education, SPP 4 (rates of suspension and expulsion for children with IEPs), SPP 9 (disproportionate representation of racial and ethnic groups in special education and related services), and SPP 10 (disproportionate representation of racial and ethnic groups in specific disability categories) are relevant, along with a related mechanism within the IDEA known as significant disproportionality. SPPs 9 and 10 track racialized patterns in special education classifications and placements, while indicators 4a and 4b under the IDEA section 618(d) require SEAs to assess the frequency, duration, and nature of disciplinary actions—such as suspensions and expulsions—among students with disabilities. LEAs may be flagged for racial disparities in classification, placement, or disciplinary outcomes if SEAs identify racial disparities through numerical thresholds, often measured using risk ratios. This means that a state sets what it deems to be an acceptable level of disparity or inequality, as compared to all other groups. When a district exceeds that level in relation to the SPP focus (e.g., disciplinary outcomes), the district is flagged as being disproportionate and must reduce racial disparities and, in some cases, illustrate full compliance with the parts of the IDEA associated with that SPP (e.g., correctly filled out IEP, evidence of a manifestation determination meting being held).[19] For example, a state can set a 2.0 risk ratio for an indicator. If a district exceeds this value, indicating that a particular group of students has twice the risk of a particular outcome, then there is evidence of an inequity, and depending on the indicator, a review of policies, practices, and procedures related to the IDEA would be necessary.[20]

The theory of action behind these accountability mechanisms, again, is that IDEA compliance along with accountability monitoring can lead to improved outcomes for disabled students.[21] Ironically though, when states are faced with numerical evidence of racialized inequities in special education—or racial disproportionality as measured by the SPPs—IDEA compliance has proven to be less vexing of an issue. Research indicates that SEAs have been able to report compliance with the IDEA procedural protections related to the SSP racial disproportionality accountability mechanisms (e.g., evidence of a correctly filled out IEP) while simultaneously maintaining numerical disparities by disability category and racial group (e.g., higher number of Black students having an IEP as compared to all other students in a district).[22] These contradictions highlight how individualized compliance efforts may not lead to equity in educational outcomes or to systemic changes that increase educational opportunity and access for *all* students.

The accountability challenges outlined here are exacerbated by the individualized-service nature of special education, which is a global phenomenon shaped by a dominant special education discourse centered on individual rights and entitlements to increase educational opportunity and access.[23] Across different educational systems, this framework emphasizes personal accommodations and legal protections, reinforcing an individualistic approach to addressing the needs of students with disabilities. Special education has become an "atomization of needs politics," because disability policy is no longer concerned with a collective social justice agenda but caters to individual needs and individual parental advocacy.[24] This atomization of needs politics diffuses the impact of inequality and further reduces it to an individual issue, replacing the need to interrogate systems for their equity impacts while inadevertently highlighting student "failures" to succeed or behave in school as the primary issue.

The civil rights intent of the IDEA is weakened when attention shifts primarily to individualized and technical measures aimed at improving student outcomes. This narrower focus reduces the law's historically civil-rights-based foundations to a series of procedural requirements, such as ensuring that parents and caregivers can access their child's educational records through an IEP. Although these legal safeguards are important for protecting the rights of students and families, they operate primarily at the individual level and are embedded in the technical and dense legal structure of the IDEA. This highlights a crucial distinction; while the IDEA has roots in civil-rights-inspired policies, legislation, and judicial alignments as occurred in *Brown v. Board of Education*, its implementation often centers not on the animating ideal of systemic equality but on a more grinding adherence to procedural compliance. *Brown* aimed to dismantle racial segregation broadly through the constitutional principle of equal protection and strict scrutiny standards. In contrast, the IDEA seeks to guarantee equal educational opportunity for students with disabilities by ensuring individualized services through procedural means, without applying the same heightened level of judicial scrutiny.[25]

As a result, educators face significant challenges in meaningfully addressing adaptive realities when administering and implementing the IDEA at the local level via individualized and technical mechanisms in relation to broad-scale and transformative practices that center educational equity. This is only heightened when procedural mechanisms are siphoned into narrow accountability and compliance measures.

Organizational Enactment of the IDEA

The narrowing of the IDEA's core provisions to accountability measures, such as the SPPs, along with its heavy procedural, individualized, and technical focus, amplifies the administrative burdens of implementing policy to practice.[26] These administrative burdens are the result of the interplay between the manifest and latent functions of policy.[27] Manifest functions, such as districts gathering data for the SPPs, reflect intended policy outcomes, while latent functions, like the additional time required to generate these reports for state and federal officials, highlight the unintended consequences of policy.[28] The unintended effects of policy implementation dynamics help generate a disconnect between policy goals and actual outcomes, which leads to the loose coupling between policy intent and action taken on the ground.[29] Loose coupling highlights how the written and stated text of law, legislation, or policy becomes loosely coupled form the actual way in which it is implemented in practice. It is the slow unraveling of written policy intent (technical) in response to local needs (adaptive).

Loose coupling in schools is influenced by factors such as individual discretion, which is shaped by professional expertise and experience, personal beliefs, vague policy mandates, and organizational constraints.[30] Loose coupling is a defining characteristic of social service oriented professionals, such as teachers, police officers, and social workers, who navigate their roles and the associated organizational constraints by balancing policy compliance, personal beliefs, and situational or institutional factors rather than strictly adhering to policy rules—essentially acting as street-level bureaucrats.[31] For example, in the case of special education, loose coupling can occur with the implementation of the IDEA when broad requirements, such as providing a free appropriate public education (FAPE), are satisfied through procedural and technical factors, such as a properly completed IEP, even though the term FAPE itself remains loosely defined. The IEP becomes the mechanism through which FAPE is illustrated, but *how* the IEP is created and enacted in practice is at the discretion of educators. Again, the adaption of policy to practice is important, but it can also weaken the intent of law, legislation, and policy through loose coupling.

Thus, the interplay between manifest and latent functions, unintended consequences, and loose coupling highlights a critical tension. The tension exists at the intersection of the technical demands of policy and the ability of individuals to adapt and translate policy into practice within their local context. These policy interpretation processes shape how educators comply with and implement the IDEA's individualized procedural protections to ensure equal educational opportunity for students with disabilities.

Research shows that since the IDEA is so procedurally dense, procedural compliance can supersede substantive compliance.[32] When adhering to procedures and technical mandates becomes the central focus of policy implementation dynamics, legal endogeneity emerges.[33] *Legal endogeneity* means that law, legislation, and policy gain organizational meaning when managerial or educator needs take precedence over the substantive intent of law, which ultimately preserves existing systems that can weaken a policy's intended goals—another facet of loose coupling. When legal endogeneity occurs, acts of IDEA compliance can also become symbolic, where something like a correctly filled out IEP can serve as sufficient evidence that the intent of the law was enacted in practice even if it was not actually implemented in the way it was written.[34] This is the proverbial dotting i's and crossing t's phenomena where things may look good on paper but not in practice. Thus, the relationship between process leading to legal endogeneity—for example, symbolic compliance rather than substantive compliance—contributes to a sociological phenomenon known as *legal deference*, whereby symbolic acts of compliance are accepted as meeting legal requirements regardless of whether intended outcomes (e.g., educational equity) are achieved.[35]

The burdensome and compliance-oriented climate in special education allows for scripted technical organizational processes to persist that fail to support best practices that improve outcomes for disabled students.[36] Research consistently shows this phenomenon in action; when educators perform functional behavior assessments and behavioral intervention plans superficially, reducing them to mere procedural tasks done to satisfy IDEA compliance requirements, student needs are left unaddressed and student outcomes suffer.[37] Moreover, there is little sustained investment in organizational support structures related to IDEA compliance beyond SEA audits of LEAs, which can further contribute to barriers to implementing special education services effectively.[38] The rigid compliance framework around special education service delivery and acts of symbolic compliance undermine efforts to improve student outcomes by focusing more on regulatory obligations than on fostering effective, student-centered educational practices.

What becomes evident is that in many districts, compliance with the IDEA is handled by a small team of professionals, but there is minimal support to ensure that these individuals have the critical, substantive, and adaptive training, resources, and time needed to actually implement the IDEA effectively.[39] This creates a system where the pressure to comply is intense, given accountability and compliance needs and from litigation if the IDEA is not complied with, and where compliance is also nonnegotiable given the morally and ethically situated obligation to comply with the IDEA.[40] Without the necessary support systems and resource necessary to shift from compliance to equity, schools may prioritize short-term fixes, such as meeting deadlines or completing paperwork, over actions that could genuinely address students' needs.

While IDEA compliance enacted through bureaucratic and organizational routines may appear to be relatively neutral and morally sound, acts of compliance do not occur within a neutral cultural or historical reality, as discussed in chapter 1. Acts of compliance are shaped by historical and contextual factors that influence its application and impact. Oppressive ideologies and conditions—for example, racialized and ableist social forces–remain ever-present. Thus, when the organizational enactment of compliance is not critically interrogated for its equity impacts, acts of compliance can perpetuate harm, contributing to the racialization of compliance and reinforcement of ableism via IDEA implementation dynamics.[41]

The racialization of disability and the presence of ableism become embedded in educational practice when educators engage in symbolic compliance with the IDEA and do not actively work to address or name these social forces.[42] *Racialization*—the process by which racial meanings are assigned to resources, institutional practices, and individuals—directly influences access to education and shapes long-term student outcomes, thereby perpetuating systemic inequities.[43] Similarly, ableism, which systematically disadvantages individuals with disabilities, intersects with racism to exacerbate educational disparities.[44] When these forces are unacknowledged in educational practice, they can become even further obscured through acts of procedural compliance with the IDEA, allowing harmful and inequitable practices to persist under the guise of compliance.[45]

As a result, rather than driving systemic transformation, acts of compliance can reinforce the very disparities that the IDEA was designed to address. The hyper-individualized nature of special education service delivery can obscure the opportunity to develop broader, systemic improvements that could elevate collective outcomes for all students and be more responsive to intersectional inequities. To reiterate, a focus on individual needs as isolated cases rather than collective needs can shift educators' time and attention away from developing more holistic and systemic approaches to education that address the needs of *all* students.

The following stories and voices from the field show how educators' experiences with IDEA organizational implementation dynamics reflect the paradox of compliance. The educators describe how procedural, technical, and individualized compliance efforts are often coupled with an acute struggle to address deeper systemic inequities and harmful practices related to local realities and the enactment of special education policies, procedures, and practices at the school level. They also reveal the adaptive challenges of special education service delivery, such as staffing shortages, inconsistent evaluation practices, and the lack of culturally and linguistically responsive assessments, that can undermine the equitable implementation of the IDEA.

Both stories come from long-time educators working in school districts that were under constant state oversight and pressure to improve student outcomes. Their districts were repeatedly flagged for racial disproportionality across SPPs 4, 9, and/or 10. This reality influenced how district administrators approached IDEA compliance in their context and thus influenced the educators' willingness to speak up in relation to the organizational culture and related pressures.

The stories also highlight the danger of narrowly interpreting the IDEA and complying symbolically with the tenets of the act. Uncritically following the letter of the law risks perpetuating the very disparities that the IDEA was designed to rectify. They make clear how a narrow focus on procedural compliance can transform educational decisions and special education service delivery into administrative exercises rather than substantive acts of compliance that are responsive to student needs, family and caregiver concerns, technical mandates, and adaptive challenges. As a result, discriminatory practices can continue, masked by apparent compliance. Focusing solely on compliance-related tasks also risks reducing students' identities to procedural categories and missing the broader complexity of their experiences.

The stories also make clear the dichotomy related to the organizational enactment of the IDEA and the paradox of compliance. On one hand, the hyper-focus on individual cases or narrowly defined compliance can create solutions that are too small, limited to isolated interventions that are disconnected from larger systemic issues. On the other hand, attempts to address these challenges at the system level without considering specific needs can result in solutions that are too big, overlooking the lived experiences of students and educators and meeting the academic, social emotional, and behavioral needs of students. The challenge, therefore, lies in finding a balance by developing solutions that are both broad enough to create systemic change and specific enough to meet the diverse individualized needs of students. The educators indirectly and directly speak around these challenges in their stories.

Stories and Voices from the Field

In this story, a woman of color special educator expresses deep conflict, and a growing sadness, about what it felt like to be a special educator in her school district. She discusses how low expectations, particularly for marginalized students at the intersection of race and disability, were pervasive and intersected with IDEA procedural mechanisms. Her narrative also highlights the dehumanizing tensions between needing to follow the norms and routines of a system that is not aligned with her personal beliefs and professional expectations. She expresses how following along with the professional culture, norms, and processes and procedures in her district seems to hurt both her sense of agency and her student's capacity to succeed.

> The isolation of working in a special education program situated in its own wing in my school building often feels overwhelming for me as an adult. I feel like I have a minimal support system and limited collaboration opportunities around me because I am so isolated.
>
> I find myself facing the immense responsibility of crafting IEPs, balancing academic and social-emotional goals, and confronting conflicting observations about student behavior all of the time. But I do not have anyone to really talk to about these things and the district has not really created trusting communities of practice to voice these concerns. It feels like I am in a constant struggle to bridge the gap between my belief that students are capable of more

than my colleagues and the system tells them they are capable of. Special education here, in this district, it means that special education students are not always seen as capable. I think there is a pervasive mindset here that too often sets the bar low too low for my kids.

For example, this year, I've had to write IEPs for students who haven't been in my class long, relying on past notes and observations. I have gotten to know these kids through these first couple months of school though. I see the huge discrepancies between what others report on paper about my students and what I see. This also makes this process, being a special educator in this district, even harder to accept.

I'm often faced with differing opinions and assessments of a student's behavior, making it hard to create a cohesive plan for moving forward. I have one student who is discussed frequently in meetings, with emails flying back and forth about how to manage his needs, but no one seems to have the answers. At this point, I'm not even sure of his diagnosis. Some might say ADHD or other health impairments, but I wonder if these labels capture the full picture of who he is. I know I see and experience more success with him than his files indicate. But, because of how we fill out IEPs and then how we just move on, I'm left with one constant feeling, tension.

It's difficult to make sense of how my experiences with a student and the perspectives of others who've worked with them can differ so widely. I often find myself questioning: Should I trust my own observations or defer to others? This uncertainty can feel overwhelming, especially when there are multiple professionals involved in a student's care, all with differing views on their behaviors and needs.

I have been thinking about this a lot, and, again, being isolated from my peers makes me really think that is the biggest challenge. And the one that feels insurmountable sometimes, is that this district can talk the talk, but they don't walk the walk. What I mean is that there's an underlying assumption that my students, disabled students, can't handle a significant cognitive load, and while this may be true for some, it's not true for many. And that they cannot behave like the general ed students. And again, this may be true for some, but it is not true for all. I just think, more often than not, we kind of let down students and families with these beliefs, with the way we have systems set up that don't really uplift kids for who they are. And then we have these narratives of the kids in their IEPs that have the data to support the academic, behavioral, and social goals, but I really feel like the way we fill them out and are told to get them done just keeps a low bar for who students really are and what we all think they can and cannot do. I try to change this in whatever way I can, but again, it feels so overwhelming sometimes.

Some of my students have told me that they self-identify as "the bad ones," and they talk about how many schools they've been kicked out of, how many fights they've been in. It's heartbreaking because they don't see themselves as learners. They don't understand that they can achieve. Why or how am I complicit with this?

This mindset is difficult to undo in a child too if the school keeps telling them this in some shape or form, on paper or in person or in IEP meetings. And for me, it's particularly hard to ignore the systemic factors that contribute to these perceptions. Most of my students are students of color, and I can't help but see how their experiences are shaped by forces beyond their control. The isolation, the labels, the low expectations. Every day, I try to balance my hope for their growth with my growing frustrations.

For years, my whole life, I've been taught to maintain high academic and behavioral standards for myself and for the people I care about. This includes my students. But in special education, here in this district, I feel like those standards have to be lowered because of district pressures driven by compliance requirements.

I am sometimes startled by myself when I find myself questioning what my students are truly capable of, especially when I first read their files. This is not who I am to think like that, but it also is who I am because I work here and I take part in these systems.

Sometimes, you would be startled by our IEPs. They look so good on paper in terms of what supports, interventions, and related services kids are receiving, but then you have to really wonder: Why are so many kids doing so poorly and staying stuck in special education? And truly, are kids actually getting these services when in our classrooms? Or does everything just look good on paper?

Also, when students have behavioral challenges, or really long files and a reputation in a school, it complicates things further. One student had significant behavioral issues at the start of the year, but after months of hard work, we've made progress together. However, as he moves forward and to the next grade, I wonder: What comes next for him? What will happen to him when he leaves my classroom? Sure, his IEP is updated and I showed what we did and what needs to be done to keep moving him forward. But that is on paper. The real work is in the relationship. The space I created for him beyond his IEP goals. The space I created for him, the joy we create and created, will this be taken away? Will the next teacher he comes across see him like

I do? Will they narrow who he is and see him differently than me?

I am not sure others will see him like I have. And who can I talk to about this? We do not have that kind of professional community here. We move on to the next task, the next IEP, the next intervention, the next thing—but we do not really see the kids in all this moving on to the next thing mode. Everything is always done for the students, sure, but it is also true that it is a lot easier for us teachers to just move on and get the paperwork done for admin and the lesson over with. I think about these things a lot because it does not feel right.

This tension leads me to really doubt if I am in the right profession. The environment feels isolating—physically and emotionally—I can only imagine what it does to my students. My classroom is tucked away at the end of a long hallway, far from the activity of the rest of the school. Sometimes, if you want me to be honest, it feels like being in a little prison for me and my students.

* * *

In this next story, a white woman related service provider expresses a similar feeling in a different way, reflecting on how the disjointed, disconnected, and dehumanizing nature of following rules just to follow them, without truly connecting with students, families, and caregivers, is hard for her. While she doesn't blame anyone in particular, the context within which she works seems to justify complying with the IDEA in ways that supersede substantive intent, revealing a consequential systemic issue where the procedural nature of the IDEA is followed, but it is not used in ways that adequately meet the needs of students:

In my district, the push for IDEA compliance can really feel like a checking the box exercise rather than something that actually benefits the students. We have a lot of multilingual learners in the district, but we do not have enough people to help with translation services. We all adapt, because we have to, but I have seen time and again how this harms students. It also makes me feel really uncomfortable.

For example, our IEP meeting coordinator who does not speak fluent Spanish is always asked to translate during IEP meetings. On paper, it made sense. We can say we have a translator and that we are technically compliant. But when it comes to truly facilitating a meaningful conversation between us all, the parents, the related service providers, the students, and the educators, it falls short.

I get it, we do not have another option, and something is better than nothing, but there really is no room for deeper dialogue about a child's educational journey or challenges. Instead, we get through the meeting and move on to the next one. Partly because we have to, but also partly because I do not think we know how to do better given the resources we have available to us.

I cannot tell you how many times, both during an IEP and after, there are quiet murmurs amongst us all about how what we know about a student didn't actually get properly translated to a parent. A lot of us know a bit of Spanish, and we definitely know our students, and what information parents are given in these situations is not enough. But no one really unpacks what is going wrong or changes anything. Sometimes I feel like we are kind of just waiting to see if we get hit with a lawsuit and then maybe we will change, because we have to. In the meantime, we will all just continue to follow the proper procedural steps to get through the next IEP meeting and then move on to the next one.

> What really strikes me is how quiet we all are and, honestly, how emotionally hollow it all feels. We may be superficially complying with IDEA, like needing to have a translator present—and we are technically complying with IDEA, always—but we are creating little to no connections with our families. I work in a district that has at least nine different languages, and English is not the most common language, and we cannot do better? We can't actually try to talk to our families and get to know them and make that a priority?
>
> I think, with the leadership we have now and the staff that have been working in this district for decades, we are settled into a pattern of operating that feels like it is more concerned with following the rules than making a real difference in student's lives.

Reflections

This chapter examined the organizational enactment of the IDEA within the context of the paradox of compliance. It theoretically and practically demonstrated how there are many organizational challenges and pressures that can inadvertently undermine equitable outcomes for students with disabilities, especially for those from historically marginalized groups.

The chapter exposes how the paradox of compliance relates to organizational constraints and the capacity of educators to substantively comply with the legislation. It reveals how the IDEA's civil rights intent is often overshadowed by rigid procedural mandates and how its implementation can be more responsive to organizational needs rather than substantive intent or developing meaningful relationships with students that extend beyond one teacher or one classroom. It also highlights how IDEA accountability measures, such as the SPPs, operating in the background as policy pressure can further reinforce a compliance-oriented culture that limits transformative progress. This dimension of the paradox of compliance highlights the tension between the bureaucratic demands of special education service delivery and the pursuit of equal educational opportunity via the IDEA.

As the stories and voices from the field illustrate, the organizational enactment of the IDEA often reflects organizational patterns and expectations that can prioritize procedural and paperwork compliance, maintaining established routines that can be dehumanizing and demoralizing for both educators and students.[46] The educators describe feeling stuck or in a rut with respect to the way they engage with the IDEA and how it is organizationally enacted in their local context. This rut creates space between meaningful engagement with students and families and leads to alienation and burnout, especially in schools where symbolic compliance with IDEA is inadvertently prioritized and in those that do not have a strong and critical professional learning climate and culture. The stories also reveal a persistent tension between delivering individualized services, through IDEA mandates and expectations, and advocating for broader systemic improvements that can benefit all students outside of one teacher, one classroom, or one person's effort. Balancing these priorities—providing individual support and collectively advocating for the needs of students with disabilities within schools—remains a critical organizational challenge.

Critical Questions to Consider

- How does the paradox of compliance and the organizational enactment of the IDEA allow for procedural compliance to substitute substantive compliance efforts, and in what ways does this dynamic reinforce systemic inequities rather than disrupt them?
- In what ways do organizational needs and priorities (loose coupling, legal endogeneity) influence how the IDEA is complied with and the overall implementation of the IDEA within schools and districts? How do these processes contribute to or legitimize discriminatory and harmful practices despite paperwork evidence of compliance?
- Given the current structure of the IDEA, how can educators move beyond procedural compliance in ways that navigate the "too small" and "too big" dichotomy, developing approaches to the organizational enactment of the IDEA that balance the need for systemic change with attention to the individualized needs and lived experiences of students?

PART 2

The Logic of Compliance

Humankind emerge from their submersion and acquire the ability to intervene in reality as it is unveiled. Intervention in reality—historical awareness itself—thus represents a step forward from emergence, and results from the *conscientizacao* of the situation. *Conscientizacao* is the deepening of the attitude of awareness characteristic of all emergence.

—PAULO FREIRE

CHAPTER 3

Current Contexts

This chapter is rooted within the decades-old equity issue of racial disproportionality in special education.[1] Racial disparities in special education are evident in categories, such as specific learning disabilities (SLD), intellectual disability (ID), emotional disturbance (ED), speech or language impairment (SLI), other health impairment (OHI), and autism, and have persisted for decades.[2] Racial disproportionality refers to both under- and overrepresentation of a particular group for a particular outcome. This can include instances such as overrepresentation in special education classifications by race and disability category (e.g., Asian students and autism) and/or underrepresentation of a particular group in gifted and talented programs (Native students in gifted and talented programs).

For instance, in the 2022–23 school year, as a percentage of public school enrollment the percentage of public-school students served under the IDEA was highest for American Indian/Alaska Native students at 19 percent and Black students at 17 percent.[3] In contrast, the lowest percentages were seen among Pacific Islander students at 12 percent and Asian students at 8 percent. The most identified disabilities under the IDEA were specific learning disabilities and speech or language impairments. For Hispanic, American Indian, Alaska Native, and Pacific Islander students, these two categories accounted for more than 50 percent of those receiving services. In comparison, in the Asian demographic, autism was the most prevalent condition. Moreover, students with disabilities, and in particular Black students with disabilities, are more likely to receive punitive disciplinary outcomes.[4]

The disparities are the result of a multitude of interconnected and complex root causes.[5] Research shows that educator biases contribute to racial disparities, as student behaviors and achievements are interpreted more harshly for students of color than their white peers, which can lead to increased special education classifications and disciplinary actions.[6] Black students are particularly vulnerable to being referred for behavioral issues and typically face more frequent suspensions for similar behaviors compared to their white counterparts, with disability status compounding these disparities.[7] Moreover, structural factors, such as residential segregation, teacher and student demographics, and district-level poverty, contribute to these inequities.[8] Research also shows that districts with higher poverty rates, greater enrollment of students of color, and urban locales are more likely to experience racial disproportionality as defined under the IDEA, with urban districts facing repeated citations under the SSPs without significant improvements in outcomes.[9]

The IDEA accountability and monitoring mechanisms for racialized disparities in special education outcomes, specifically the SPPs and significant disproportionality regulation, do not fully engage with the complex root causes of the inequity. As outlined in chapter 2, these are technical measures that SEAs and LEAs use to report disparities and outcomes for students with disabilities at the local level. These measures are often numeric, and they can be procedurally intricate for both SEAs and LEAs to navigate with the disproportionality measures (see chapter 2) containing both quantitative and qualitative metrics to identify and address racialized disparities.[10] These indicators have been critiqued for their ineffectiveness and their lack of impact, with scholars noting that the accountability approach surrounding racial disparities in special education inherently "mathematize[s] social problems" like racial disproportionality, with its "deep structural roots," that cannot be accounted for in mathematical formulas. Such indicators, therefore, "are not likely to unearth historical precursors and ideologically laden processes that constitute them."[11]

The Salience of the Past on Current Contexts

The root causes of racial disproportionality are historically situated.[12] They stem from what Gloria Ladson-Billings describes as accumulated educational debts that continue to shape present-day disparities in education, specifically for Black students, Indigenous students, and students of color (BISOC).[13] Current educational inequities, such as the opportunity gap and racial disproportionality in special education, are in this case analogous to a budget deficit.[14] They represent present-day issues that are historically rooted. Given this, there is an educational debt owed to BISOC.[15] The education debt represents a long-term accumulation of inequities, like the national debt, that comprises historical, economic, sociopolitical, and moral factors.

The historic debt reflects structural racism and the systemic denial of access to quality education for Black, Latinx, and Indigenous populations. The economic debt encompasses racialized disparities in educational funding and the compounded effects of economic and housing segregation on schools. The sociopolitical debt highlights the exclusion of historically marginalized communities from civic participation and decision-making processes. The moral debt is conceptual, highlighting how deficit-based and discriminatory narratives about Black people, Indigenous people, and people of color have justified unfair and harmful policies and practices that continue to perpetuate structural inequities.

The components of the education debt are significant to special education and to racial disproportionality as the root causes of racial disproportionality emerge from historically situated intersections of racism and ableism, among other factors, across time and space.[16] Economic debts are compounded by ableism in employment settings, limited job opportunities for people with disabilities, and poor post-school outcomes for those labeled with a disability in schools.[17] Funding disparities for students with disabilities can also hinder educational equity, as many states fail to report on special education expenditures, despite evidence that increased funding can improve outcomes.[18] Additionally, moral debts persist due to the continued legacy of eugenics, forced sterilizations, and the lasting impacts of the institutionalization of people with disabilities on current lived realities.[19]

Within an educational space, sociopolitical debts have significant impacts on students, caregivers, and families. They are reflected in the exclusion of people with disabilities in relation to special education service delivery situations. For instance, Ong-Dean described how "parents who are most privileged—who have the most cultural and economic resources at their disposal—who can make the strongest claims to distinguish their children's particular disabilities and needs in an objective, scientifically and legally justified way" are able to secure more resources for their children via the IDEA.[20] And these realities perpetuate inequalities that are often classed and racialized.[21] The exclusion is amplified when educational professionals dominate IEP meetings and marginalize family and caregiver input with professional language, legalese, and complicated assessments of student progress.[22] These inequitable dynamics are intensified through the individualized nature of parental and caregiver advocacy enshrined in the IDEA.

Parents, caregivers, and families, "rather than acting as collective agents of a political movement," advocate for their children individually, and this then disadvantages structural changes when marginalized groups have been historically "reduced to passive cases in the special education process."[23] Sociopolitical engagement is thus muted when an educational need is addressed with a purely technical and procedural response (e.g., creating an IEP) rather than a substantive and relational approach.[24] Therefore, through acts of IDEA compliance, existing systems of marginalization can become legitimized, obscuring the underlying historical, social, and political forces that shaped the need for the IDEA from its inception and subsequently privileging some over others.

These educational debts relate to the decades-long inequity of racial disproportionality in special education.[25] This present-day educational "deficit" of racial disproportionality as measured by the SSP and significant disproportionality regulation are a technical metric that reflects the cumulative effects of the historical and systemic marginalization of disabled people at their intersections—something that policies like the IDEA were designed to address and redress but have not been able to do. The persistence of this educational deficit, despite the presence of the IDEA, brings to light how "ideological layers" connected to the historical realities behind the development of the IDEA (chapter 1) become embedded in bureaucratic systems (chapter 2) that inadvertently uphold and reify conceptions of ability, disability, race, difference, smartness, and so forth.[26] These ideological layers are deeply embedded within special education ecosystems as the intent behind the IDEA unfolds as it is taken up and implemented by educators at the state, district, and school level.[27]

It is important to reemphasize here that racial disproportionality and the broader educational debts it reflects serve as a historical and ongoing backdrop that shapes how both technical and adaptive forms of compliance with the IDEA are carried out in practice. This backdrop—historically universal yet locally specific as policy—is enacted within organizational contexts, and it is continually mediated through the implementation of the IDEA's core principles and statutes, such as FAPE and LRE. Notably, educational debts remain ever present and are also absorbed into the day-to-day operations of state, district, and school operations as they relate to special education service delivery and acts of compliance, whether they are explicitly recognized or not. And once again, as described in the introduction, these debts are mediated through a split educational system that delineates between a general and a special education system.

These boundaries and the associated "professional bureaucracies" that develop across SEAs and within LEAs "divide and coordinate" special education work amongst professionals "through specialization" (i.e., matching students with like needs to teachers with presumed complementary repertoires of practices) and professionalization (i.e., standardizing teachers' knowledge, skills, and practices through professional education), and in turn, further "screen out diversity" in factors such as students, teacher practices, and professional expertise "by removing it [diversity] from classrooms and containing it in decoupled programs like special, vocational, compensatory, bilingual, and gifted education (Skrtic, 1991, 2003)" systems.[28] This fragments the clarity within which educational debts are seen, felt, and understood by educators in everyday educational practice and within special education systems. This fragmentation further solidifies how the "ideological layers" of difference (e.g., ableism and racism) influence how educational deficits, such as racial disproportionality, manifest in education practice and are also obscured through the bureaucratic layers of compliance.[29]

In the following stories and voices from the field, educators describe how their current teaching and learning contexts feel inequitable, as these inequities relate to their positioning within special and general education systems. They describe how they experience and observe educational inequities, make sense of them, and link these to their work as someone working within and across general and special education spaces. In doing so, they make visible how educational debts and deficits coexist and influence IDEA implementation dynamics. Their narratives reveal harmful practices and norms that undermine the IDEA's original intent to secure equal educational opportunity for historically marginalized and disabled students. They place these descriptions within the reality of being educators working across general and special education spaces. They describe how the prioritization of procedural compliance and the need to address immediate educational concerns (deficits) in the current context, inadvertently neglects the broader systemic and social factors (debts) that are necessary for achieving educational equity. And they also describe how they can feel both stuck and energized to change inequitable conditions and how, sometimes, the IDEA is a protective factor in doing this while other times it is an undermining factor.

The educators also describe the need to both recognize and address the complex challenges faced by students. These efforts extend far beyond what IDEA compliance alone can do. They describe how systemic inequities impacting their students, such as the cumulative impacts of poverty and trauma, are adaptive realities that must be attended to just as much as the need to assure technical compliance with the IDEA. In this sense, the gap between the intended purpose of the IDEA and its real-world implementation in schools emphasizes how compliance-driven processes that serve institutional purpose more so than student needs can do more harm than good and also obscure the salience of education debts on current contexts. Both educators also express a sense of frustration with their current contexts, which seem to prioritize compliance and documentation of compliance over effective, student-centered, and culturally responsive teaching that is a necessity for rupturing broader inequities shaping their practice.

Stories and Voices from the Field

In this first story, a woman of color related service provider highlights how she thoughtfully, purposefully, and diligently worked to combat the broader structural inequities and challenges she and her students faced in her school. A special education related service provider is a professional—like a speech-language pathologist, occupational therapist, or school counselor—who offers targeted support to help students with disabilities make progress on their IEP goals.

This related service provider describes how she purposefully collaborates with families and like-minded colleagues, how she supports mental health support initiatives in her school, and how she creates personal connections with students to generate more equitable learning environments. She also acknowledges that the IDEA alone cannot resolve the larger systemic issues that she works to combat daily. She emphasizes the need for sustained advocacy and structural changes that extend far beyond existing systems across both general and special education spaces.

> I was drawn to this work because I wanted to make a meaningful difference, especially in communities that mirror my own experiences of being a person of color educated in an urban setting.
>
> The students I work with primarily Black and Latino students—connect with me on a deeply personal level. They see me as someone who understands their struggles, not just academically but also in navigating a world that too often overlooks their needs. This connection fuels my belief

that education goes beyond grades; it's about supporting the whole child and helping them overcome barriers that might seem insurmountable. I know this is important because they tell me this all of the time.

When I first joined this school, the staff did not reflect the diversity of our student body. Over the years, however, the school has made a concerted effort to hire more Black and Latino educators. I am glad about this because I know it matters.

But, you know, the effort to diversify staff has created some tensions over the years. Some of the white staff feel that their professionalism is being questioned in favor of meeting diversity quotas. This bothers me, but I stay focused on what matters. I remain committed to my school's vision as it is written on the door when you enter our building—all kids will learn here. Every student deserves the opportunity to thrive. I will continue to work for that mission and to advocate for that chance for all of my students.

And what keeps me going, to be honest, and what is aligned with what I believe in is that we have no other choice, and I have found educators here who believe this along with me. We have built a strong team spirit here among our special education team. With three psychologists, three social workers, and three counselors, we share a progressive mindset, and we talk about this mindset all of the time and remind each other to stay focused on what matters—the kids—and not the noise of our colleagues or the things that distracts us from the important work.

However, it's not always easy to convince everyone outside of this tight circle, *my* tight circle I have created over time, about the importance of pushing forward in a way that truly engages and respects *our* community and *our* students.

My circle, we've all been in the trenches. We are a diverse group, and we are honest about that. We talk about who we are. We lean on each other. We learn from each other. We push each other. We share strategies. We support one another in ways that are vital to staying focused on our students. Sometimes, though, we have to close our doors and just do the work we believe in because our kids need us and what we are being told to do doesn't always protect our kids or fortify us as educators.

For example, some long-time staff members resist new approaches, especially in recognizing the impact of trauma and poverty on learning. Our kids have been and are impacted by poverty and trauma. This is real.

Several years ago, I introduced a responsive classroom approach focused on social-emotional learning and supporting the whole child through a culturally responsive framework. For those that use it, I have seen kids feel more connected to their learning. Yet not everyone has embraced it. Some teachers remain entrenched in outdated methods, handed down through decades of a "this is what we have always done" mentality, that ultimately hurts and devalues our Black and Brown kids. It's tough to change long-standing mindsets, but I remain hopeful that, with time and continued effort, we can make progress. We have to.

It is also hard, too, within the context of our district. We are a poor district and, like I said, our kids have trauma. But that does not mean we devalue them or look at them in a patronizing way. We just have to do better for them and with them, because let's be real, poverty and its impact on our kids is a significant challenge.

Don't get me wrong. I see and hear people using poverty as an excuse to disparage our students sometimes. But that is not what I mean when I highlight poverty and trauma.

What I mean is that we can't just do whatever we used to do, expect kids to succeed, and then punish them if they don't. I know I cannot change everyone's mindset that our kids, Black and Brown kids with disabilities, are capable of amazing things and that who they are matters and is beautiful. I cannot always counter deficit mindsets that blame poverty and families for kids not doing well in school, but I can adapt. I can change. I can learn and grow and accept truths for what they are and then find ways to change what isn't working instead of blaming our kids.

It is so frustrating too, because everyone in this school and district knows that we have racial disparities on almost every outcome you can imagine. This is for both our special and general ed kids. Our data always shows it, for years! We know what next year will bring, and we know who will likely not do well, and with this knowledge, we still want to keep doing the same thing? If we aren't willing to change, then of course the kids and families will be the problem, not us.

We have data meetings all the time about this. They always tell us, "Your data say we have racial disparities blah blah blah." Then we get technical, especially when it comes to IEPs and when the special ed department is leading a professional development. I can barely stand it. I hear it over and over again: "Our data always show this and this, so we need to make sure we are adhering to IDEA and providing mandated services blah blah blah." That doesn't and hasn't worked! And frankly, all of it feels short-sighted, disconnected from the realities of our kids.

Do you know how many perfectly filled out IEPs I can show you? But the real question is, what actually happens to the kid in our schools and our classrooms? I can show you a perfectly filled out IEP and I can also show you how this kid has not made growth with almost every teacher since kindergarten—he seems to always be failing. That is his narrative. The data is clear on this, but what we do about this knowledge as a district does not make sense to me. Are we actually using the IEP or do we just have a pretty document? Are we actually talking to the student and his parents and getting to know what he needs and wants? Do we know what the families are dealing with outside of these four walls of the school? Not really.

To be clear, and don't get me wrong, those data points we always talk about *are* important but they also *feel* useless because we do not *use* the data to change what we are doing in a really meaningful way. Like, what are we actually doing and thinking about and changing? What are we doing to help our kids? Are we doing anything to go beyond compliance?

Within my circle, my friends and colleagues, we talk about how as a district we are good at passing state audits, IDEA compliance, but none of that really addresses who kids are and some of the harsh realities that shape the lives of our students. What we do with what we have—the tools and resources in front us—what we believe is possible and how we love our students, is what can help a kid move forward like they need to.

Many families in our community, and especially at this school, they face frequent housing instability, evictions, and ongoing food insecurities. We have to recognize that in our daily practice. And you know what? Our kids are different from the kids in this same district who live in the wealthier part of town. They have different opportunities and they have had different life experiences. What they do over there in that part of town may or may not work over here. And that is okay. And we should adjust what we do.

But if we pretend like these differences don't exist, we are only harming our kids HERE.

Again, don't get me wrong. While the district leadership often speaks about equity, it falls short in providing the resources necessary for schools like ours to thrive. Basic funding gaps make it challenging to address the needs of our students and families. That is it. We do not always have what we need, and that is structural.

Fortunately, though, we do have two agencies that provide therapy within my school. My tight-knit group and I have worked hard to make that a reality. You can make things happen if they need to happen. You kind of have to work around things to build the supports our kids need.

This therapy agency, I think it has been an invaluable resource for our students. I work closely with our families, helping them decide whether to seek outside therapy or use the services we provide. This collaboration is essential, especially when addressing the mental health issues that many of our students face. I also work closely with the principal, especially around bullying, anxiety, and peer conflicts. He is responsive to this. We talk about mental health and recognize how important it is and how we have to support our students in really responsive ways.

In many ways within this school, my tight-knit group and I have become a central point of contact for teachers, parents, and students to ensure that everyone is aligned and that students get the support they need here at this school. I like this. I make it a point to build personal connections with students—greeting them in the morning, visiting the cafeteria during lunch—so they know I'm there for them and that they can come to me whenever they need someone to talk to. I am here to listen and help.

I truly believe that when we work with students—not against them—we can help them navigate challenges and find their way forward. Naming inequities is a start, but it's not enough. IDEA offers important protections, but it wasn't built to address the deeper, systemic issues our students deal with every day. That's why we need a both/and approach—one that ensures compliance with IDEA while also recognizing and responding to the broader realities shaping students' lives, so we can truly support them.

In this second account, a white woman special education teacher describes how she has to push against a variety of barriers to assure that her students get what they need. She also expresses how the compliance tools at her fingertips (e.g., behavior intervention plans) feel misaligned with student needs and can also be used to justify further segregation and marginalization of students. She makes clear that while the IDEA is meant to safeguard students' rights, in her experience, it can become a mechanism for institutional self-protection rather than an instrument of equity. She also makes clear that it takes someone within the system to advocate for and shift conditions of inequity that go beyond compliance.

The more I think about it on paper, the IDEA is a lifeline for ensuring that students with disabilities receive the support they need in the least restrictive environment. But in practice? It often feels like a tightrope walk between annoying things, like all of that compliance-driven paperwork and then getting my students what they need.

I had a student last year who brought a knife to school. He immediately realized it was a mistake, handed it over to me when he arrived at school, and then we went through the required manifestation determination meeting process. The administration pushed for him to be placed in a restrictive out of district setting because of this incident. Yet I know that in my classroom, with tailored support, he could and did and has thrived. I mean, maybe I should say he was doing okay—not perfect, but manageable. He didn't need an out of district placement.

I know it's a safety concern what happened, but I also know he immediately regretted what he did. He let us know he did it—he brought the knife for safety. He was being bullied, and he made a quick decision around this. It wasn't right and he needed help. He made a bad decision, and I do think his disability was related to this decision, but he needed more supports than we were giving him. And we can give him those supports here in the district. He is a white kid, does not have a lot of family resources, and the way we treated him, shows that

After a lot of advocacy on my part, he ended up getting a one-on-one aide rather than being sent away to a more restrictive placement. He also got more mental health supports and, to be honest, he has completely changed. He has learned to ask for and seek help in much more productive ways. This did not come easy though. We, us, his teachers and the administration, we had to fight for him. We had to get on the same page, align resources, and agree he could be helped. That is not easy. And honestly, we could have easily pushed him out and seen him fall even harder, but we didn't let that happen. I am proud of that. That is why I am here.

I often see how the system can be used to push kids out and create a record that justifies pushing them out. We can use an IEP and IDEA, frankly, to make a case to get a kid out of a school. No one really wants to admit that, but it is true. I see this all the time with behavior intervention plans [A Behavior Intervention Plan (BIP) is a proactive, team-developed plan designed to understand and address the reasons behind a student's challenging behavior and to teach positive, replacement skills that support learning and social success]. I've had students come into my classroom with BIPs that are so outdated or irrelevant. One student had a BIP written two years ago that didn't match her current behaviors at all. Another student, a Hispanic girl with severe autism and mental health needs, had a BIP targeting work avoidance, asking her to work for five minutes at a time. But her behaviors weren't about work avoidance—they were deeply rooted in her autism in ways that extended way beyond work avoidance. Of course, these students don't show progress—their plans are not tailored to their needs and someone at the school has to notice that and change that. If they don't, the student will act out, and it is a whole cycle of failure, all justified by paperwork and no one takes the time to understand the context on how our kids got to where they are. It is kind of a weird thing to say out loud, but it is true.

These plans, which should be tools for meaningful intervention, don't show any true knowledge of who a student is. But the fact that we have them, and if the kid does something they shouldn't, this document can be used to justify anything. I mean anything. Again, I hate to admit it, but it is true. To help a kid means you have to know them, work hard for them, and get the system to move for them. Sometimes, this is hard to do—and especially if they are not coming from homes where the parents know what their rights are.

And then there are the students who slip through the cracks entirely. I currently teach several students on the autism spectrum who weren't identified until middle school. One student was consistently labeled as defiant and frequently suspended because he couldn't transition from one activity to another without an incident. But once we reframed his behaviors through the lens of autism, the solution became clear: he wasn't being defiant. He was overwhelmed. Similarly, I have students with severe dyslexia whose reading challenges have never been adequately addressed in their IEPs. The IEPs show we are providing interventions and whatever else, but it does not mean it is actually what the kid needs to do better in class.

You have to take time to see these things. These students, the ones we fight for as a system and the ones we let fall through the cracks, don't always feel random either. Who a parent is—if they have connections to the school board, if they have access to lawyers and advocates, if they know their rights—we will move as a system to help them right away. If they don't have these things, we tend to just move along and let things keep going unless someone like me, and I mean it, unless someone like me tries to create trouble to assure everyone can get what they need.

I grapple with this all the time. I truly do think my colleagues want to do right by kids, and many are so well intentioned, but sometimes I think we work to preserve ourselves in a difficult profession. This means we can lose sight of the bigger impact on our students.

Reflections

This chapter sheds light on the first element of the logic of compliance, that of the importance of *current contexts.* Drawing on Ladson-Billings's educational debt framework, I demonstrate the ways in which historical inequities—economic, political, sociocultural, and moral—continue to shape special education service delivery and, by default, racial disproportionality.[30] Local contextual factors, including school and district demographics, residential segregation, educator mindsets, and resource availability, significantly influence how IDEA compliance is enacted and how student needs are addressed in the current context. Technical acts of compliance remain far removed from the adaptive factors that shape how special education service delivery decisions are made in current contexts.

In summary, the current contexts that shape teaching and learning conditions are a powerful reminder of the salience of the past on present-day outcomes. Factors such as local school demographics, district dynamics, and residential segregation play a crucial role in shaping how IDEA compliance is understood and implemented, because they shape what resources are or are not available to meet complex student needs. They also influence how educators make sense of their workflow and the beliefs they hold about their students and the communities they work within. These factors, while rooted in historical inequities, are directly tied to present-day realities and practical needs and thus influence special education practices and, ultimately, student outcomes.

These structural conditions also reveal the layered and often overlooked factors that shape how students with disabilities are supported—or left unsupported—in ways that go beyond the IEP, procedural safeguards, or technical compliance. The educators' stories illustrate how a confluence of factors, such as limited training on using data to guide instruction, technically focused professional development, and widespread burnout, can lead to flawed or uneven implementation of the IDEA. In these cases, IDEA paperwork may be filled out, but the way in which this paperwork is enacted—for example, through IEPs or BIPs—can be in conflict with the IDEA's stated and intended purpose. This contradiction reveals a significant gap between what is documented on paper and how student needs are addressed in practice. Bridging this gap requires a critical examination of how IDEA compliance—both technical and adaptive—functions within broader structural constraints alongside a sustained commitment to strengthening educator and system capacity.

Critical Questions to Consider

- How do the historical, sociocultural, and political contexts of today's education system relate to the concept of the educational debt, educational deficit, and IDEA implementation interpretation dynamics?
- In what ways can the concept of the educational debt be used to guide policy reforms that address systemic inequities in special education, ensuring that both the historical and current impacts of intersectional inequities are fully considered in educational decision-making processes?
- How can critical and thoughtful communities of practice help educators navigate the interplay between technical compliance and the structural realities of schools and districts while also building the capacity to identify and implement adaptive, equity-driven solutions?

CHAPTER 4

The Status Quo

The implementation of laws and policies aimed at addressing historical inequities is complex, especially when they disrupt long-standing practices and societal beliefs, such as the exclusion of students with disabilities from educational contexts.[1] Moreover, organizational routines and the people sustaining these routines are hard to change.[2] Thus, both people *and* organizations perpetuate inequalities via a tacitly agreed on organizational inertia that maintains a status quo. This is especially true when laws and policies are procedurally dense, are layered onto complex organizational environments like schools, and contain subjective and social justice ideals.[3] It is here, where people interpret and make sense of law and policy in complex contexts, that a consequential space emerges for the status quo to take shape in relation to IDEA compliance.

To clarify how the status quo emerges, I first leverage the concept of fragmented harm to center people, and then I place their actions within a neoinstitutional framework to highlight how organizations become powerful drivers of inequality.[4] Neoinstitutionalism is a sociologically grounded theoretical framework that emphasizes how social norms, cultural meanings, and taken-for-granted routines and practices within organizations influence how they function just as much as formal rules and structures.[5]

Payne's theory of fragmented harm examines how educational inequalities are perpetuated within schools through daily microactions, decisions, and interactions between individuals who in the aggregate perpetuate the status quo or systems of harm.[6] A critical feature of this concept is that key contributors of inequality come from everyday decisions that adults make across and within organizational units. The perspective shifts drivers of inequality from a deficit perspective where families, students, and/or communities are blamed for unequal outcomes to the aggregate impacts of adult actions and the ways in which they do or do not create opportunities to learn.[7]

The idea of fragmented harm also highlights how adults, simply by their organizational positioning, can distance themselves from the consequences of their actions. Their daily microdecisions, like an administrator assuring that IEPs are in regulatory compliance, remain a well-intentioned act that is based on their professional expertise. However, if assuring regulatory compliance is of utmost importance due to policy pressures and organizational needs—and not necessarily the substantive monitoring and enactment of the IEP in classroom contexts—then the microdecisions made around this are enactments of fragmented harm. Their sphere of influence, in relation to other actions and decisions made by adults in a school or district, can compound in ways that allow for inequities to persist, such as racial disproportionality in special education outcomes, despite evidence of compliance with the IDEA.[8] Therefore, through the lens of fragmented harm, we can see how individuals can distance themselves from accountability for the impact of their microactions on aggregate outcomes by simply performing their job—in this case, complying with IDEA. Here, a seemingly neutral act can inadvertently contribute to educational harm. Educational inequities, like racial disproportionality, persist not because individuals seek to intentionally cause harm but because systemic inequities continue when people follow existing structures without challenging practices that are sustaining irrational or outdated practices that can be harmful to students.

I place this understanding of inequality within a neoinstitutional perspective to directly link it to IDEA compliance within an organizational context—again, linking to concepts highlighted in chapter 2.[9] Neoinstitutional theory provides a framework for examining the *legalization of education*—the way in which legal, legislative, and procedural mandates are used to dictate how education services should be delivered or how student rights should be protected in schools—allowing for a critical examination of why the legalization of education occurs and how this legalization shapes the structure of schooling.[10] Like fragmented harm, the theory underscores how unexamined norms, routines, and customs within organizations perpetuate social actions that take on a life of their own via habitual actions that may not achieve their intended aim but continue to persist, typically through acts of symbolic compliance.[11]

For example, the IDEA mandates an annual review wherein an IEP team (including parents and caregivers) revisits a student's IEP to assess and discuss student growth, progress, and goals. The need to conduct annual reviews creates a time pressure for educators that is layered onto an already complex workflow. If a district has a large case load, staff is overextended, and annual reviews are scheduled in a compressed period at a particular time of year. Research has shown that these meetings under these types of conditions can be perfunctory and decontextualized, limiting meaningful discussion of a student's progress.[12] On one hand, the taken-for-granted nature of organizational conditions and constraints assures that annual reviews are conducted in a timely manner, but on the other hand, the prioritizing of compliance can lead to compliance that is symbolic only, deficient in substance and impact and not aligned with or responsive to student needs.

Here and as described in chapter 2, loose coupling and symbolic compliance are interconnected concepts that contribute to fragmented harm. Loose coupling, as described in chapter 2, refers to the disconnect between the goals of policies and their actual execution on the ground.[13] *Symbolic compliance* occurs when individuals symbolically demonstrate that they are following legal requirements without needing to enact transformative organizational changes.[14] A focus on symbolic compliance can serve as a protective factor for organizations and for the adults working in them.[15] Symbolic compliance protects an organization's reputation and the professionals within it and also minimizes the risk of legal issues, fines, and/or reputational damage. It serves the adults and the organization's legitimacy. With this lens, we can see that there is a clear, vested interest in maintaining the facade of compliance even if actions that are taken within an organization do not lead to substantive changes.[16]

Acts of compliance under this framework, then, are understood to help cultivate a culture of integrity and accountability within organizations. But these acts of compliance can evolve into a self-perpetuating process where technical actions are reduced to ineffective symbolic gestures.[17] Rather than complying to transform systems, organizations and the people within them become *coping organizations*, managing compliance issues rather than solving the issues that the compliance actions are targeting.[18] When this happens, people do not disrupt entrenched routines and ultimately activate and reinforce a status quo.

As highlighted in the annual review example, this dynamic around the status quo and the persistence of taken-for-granted organizational routines that do not achieve their intended aim is particularly salient in special education. The IDEA has numerous procedural safeguards that necessitate mechanisms for monitoring and implementation, which can increase administrative oversight at the state, district, and school levels.[19] As a result, specialized roles emerge that are dedicated to monitoring mandates, ensuring regulatory compliance, and facilitating their implementation across states, districts, and school systems.[20] In this sense, the legal and policy interventions of providing FAPE in the LRE via the IDEA can take on a bureaucratic life of their own. Mandates frequently lead to a proliferation of internal rules and procedures intended to ensure compliance across all organizational levels, but these can become unwieldy and ineffective when they are not substantively and critically engaged with in practice due to organizational constraints and professional capacity, among other factors.[21]

A bureaucratic system of this type develops its own momentum around assuring regulatory compliance. Organizational operations become depersonalized, prioritizing technical and legal order over emotional and personal connections to the work at hand or, in this case, to students.[22] The self-perpetuating organizational inertia stems from deeply embedded organizational and professional cultures, structures, routines, and systems that begin to resist change.[23]

Organizational inertia in special education can reinforce entrenched norms and practices, allowing systemic inequities to persist not necessarily through intentional bias but through institutional inaction. This inertia solidifies and preserves existing structures, or a status quo, that can prioritize compliance over equity and innovation.[24] And as special education systems expand to serve more students, using a neoinstitutional perspective, they become increasingly resistant to transformative change.[25] The entrenchment in what already exists stems from the sociological reproduction of norms that may provide stability in a chaotic educational environment but also serve as a significant barrier to progress when systems need to evolve and adapt.

There is a body of research in special education that highlights this dynamic and how special education professional cultures are often resistant to significant changes.[26] These professional communities tend to respond to external challenges by intensifying their existing practices rather than reforming them, which deepens inequities.[27] For example, Harry et al. found that Black families made consistent and proactive efforts to support their children's schooling.[28] However, over time, their engagement waned, not due to a lack of interest but rather as a response to systemic barriers that included the isolating effects of special education placements and the absence of meaningful opportunities for parental influence in special education decision-making processes. The focus on compliance and professional norms alienates parents and underscores the need for more reciprocal family and school communication. This professional rigidity within special education systems contributes to the perpetuation of the status quo and the harms associated with the resulting dehumanizing nature of compliance. Moreover, there is often little to no space for special education policies, procedures, and professional expertise to be meaningfully challenged without legal counsel or well-informed parents and caregivers about special education advocacy and rights.[29] The bureaucratization of special education processes and the resulting professional insularity helps ensure that the status quo, the way things always operate, remains a significant factor in the logic of compliance, which is all rooted in the inertia of everyday educational practice. When the status quo does not work for everyone or promote equitable outcomes, challenging the resulting inequities as a caregiver or parent can be an especially difficult task. Moreover, proving discriminatory intent is particularly arduous when institutional structures are assumed to be neutral and serve as evidence of nondiscriminatory practices.

In the following stories and voices from the field, the educators' stories highlight how the status quo is maintained in their contexts. They explain how assumptions about the role and function of IDEA compliance are so routinized and unquestioned that blatantly problematic practices persist without much disruption. The entrenched routines they describe appear to persist with little to no pushback, allowing the status quo to remain unchallenged. The very systems that are meant to support students with disabilities, in fact, are also used to inadvertently maintain inequitable practices. They provide situated and lived experiences where educators describe how the gap between policy goals and actual implementation sustains the status quo. They also illustrate how the microdecisions made by these educators and their colleagues contributed to an organizational inertia that does not always prioritize student needs, absent of malintent. The stories also show how fragmented harm takes shape and contributes to ongoing inequalities. Small, everyday actions, though informed by professional expertise, uphold existing systems when they are not critically challenged or examined for their equity impacts.

This pair of stories and voices from the field also further illustrates the dynamic of legal endogeneity, first introduced in chapter 2, where the enactment of law, legislation, and policy are shaped by the everyday practices and priorities of organizations.[30] As mandates are implemented, they are often interpreted in ways that align with organizational routines and needs—such as meeting timelines or documenting compliance—rather than advancing the broader social justice goals the law was intended to promote, leading to practices that satisfy legislative and legal requirements but fall short in meaningfully supporting students.

Stories and Voices from the Field

Here, a white woman general education building administrator describes how the unquestioned routines she was complicit in sustained the status quo rather than meaningfully addressed student needs. The meeting she describes appeared to prioritize efficiency, needing to move things along and so forth. This allowed flawed practices to persist. The microdecisions she exposes in her story illustrate how inaction seemed to be the complacent norm—the status quo. She also recognizes how her own complicity sustained harmful practices that potentially denied critical educational opportunities and resources for students who may have benefited from more careful attention. She also expresses how, looking back, she wished she had challenged these entrenched practices and advocated for meaningful change instead.

> I am an administrator now, but I'll never forget one particular meeting that really brought home how the system can fail our students when I was a teacher. The meeting reminds me that I have to advocate for our kids much more than I used to in the past and now that I am a leader.
>
> We were all in a pretty typical meeting—kind of informal—and discussing students in our middle school who were not necessarily doing too well and not necessarily failing either. Kind of these middle-of-the-way students. In some cases, we were reviewing students who had already been identified for special education services, and in others, we were considering whether to recommend a student for evaluation to determine eligibility.
>
> In this meeting, it was me along with several teachers working across the middle school, the school psychologist, and the assistant director of special education. We were

reading notes on students, drinking coffee, reading student files, eating donuts, looking at student test scores—that kind of mundane stuff.

I can't ever forget, though, when the conversation shifted to a multilingual sixth grader. We all started talking about how the student had been getting ESL (English as a second language) services for many years but wasn't really progressing academically. He also had never been evaluated for special education or been classified as having a disability. His case was kind of typical, to be honest. We had a lot of kids like that in our district—these kids who seemed to sit forever in ESL programs and not really make any kind of progress. It was like we had created a space in the district, a weird space, where we did not know if these kids had something like a speech and language impairment or if they just couldn't really make academic progress in their current programming. We never really questioned why there were so many students like this, it just was that way.

Anyways, his homeroom teacher was in the room, and she talked a lot about how much the student was struggling in his classes. She said that he had a lot of issues around language retention and around language vocabulary. I remember she wondered if he might be severely learning disabled. I also remember she was genuinely concerned about the student, and you could feel it in the room. But as the discussion went on, it also became obvious that we were not going to really address his needs or talk about the fact that this student was not an anomaly in our district.

I remember flipping through the student's file when his teacher was talking. I knew a little bit about the student and his family, as I had taught his older brother. His brother had similar issues. I remember I wanted to bring this up, and I wanted to mention that we might need to think more critically about his capacities to learn and what services and supports he was receiving. But I didn't.

The school psychologist in the room did, though. She was known for trying to disrupt things a bit. I remember that she kind of casually stated that in her professional opinion, the student was not being served well by his teachers, or the ESL program, or frankly, the district. This did not sit well with people in the room. It was uncomfortable because, in some ways, I think we all kind of knew that was the truth.

The silence after her statement lingered for a while until our assistant district special education administrator asked, "Is he SIFE [students with an interrupted or inconsistent formal education]?" I remember that no one answered immediately, because honestly, I don't think any of us really knew the answer, which is embarrassing. She then asked something like, "Has he had any reading interventions?" Again, I remember that no one could really answer that question in the room, and his files were sparse. I also remember that the tone of our meeting really changed then.

His ESL teacher spoke up loudly. She was so frustrated and exasperated, and I think she might have felt like a target. She said that the district's reading interventions, the ones she had access to, didn't work for ESL students and she worked around that. She also made it clear that the assessments she had access to were based on phonics, which just do not work well for kids who aren't native English speakers. She then added that she didn't have tools to help him and then sat back quietly.

His homeroom teacher, who would see him every morning and also was supposed to be a key connector to the family, I remember her really lamenting that she felt like she always sees the ESL kids falling through the cracks in the district and that they never really get what they need in the district. Again, I just remember silence and no one really reacting to any of this. We kind of just sat there. I will never forget that. I felt so uncomfortable and I also just sat there.

At that point, I remember the assistant director of special education looking really frustrated. She told us to move on and called the student a "mystery kid." That term has stayed with me to this day. Our conversation didn't go any deeper after she said that either. We just moved on. And frankly, that is what we always did. We moved on to the next case, the next fire to put out, the next meeting, and the next task at hand.

I left that district the following year. I got my administrative license. But I will never forget how we made a decision for that student through indecision. We did nothing. Nothing—that was our decision.

I cannot shake the memory of that meeting. It wasn't about understanding that student's struggles; it was about not rocking the boat.

A few years later, I found out he dropped out of school.

The boy had stayed in the ESL program, where he was still struggling. The system didn't change for him. We didn't reflect on our failures. This is why I can't stop thinking about that meeting. The complacency of it all kind of haunts me. I guess I also contributed to those failures by not speaking up loud enough.

* * *

In the next story, a white male special educator expresses how he feels professionally isolated when he tries to disrupt the routines and procedures that do not support what he believes are best practices for meeting student needs. He also expresses a deep frustration with how disabled students appear to be an afterthought when understood within broader district operations and initiatives. He expresses a disdain for the mundane and the comfort in routines that do not prioritize his students.

> I'll be honest with you—it's hard being a special education teacher. My job is to serve these students, and I absolutely love doing it, but there's a part of me that struggles with it. I don't want to say it out loud, but the truth is, it's painful to work in a system that doesn't fully support the kids it is designed to support. It's easy for teachers to turn off their brains, and sometimes, even their hearts. I see it every day with some colleagues.
>
> Everyone says they love their students, right? But let's be real—there's a limit. This limit shows up when it starts to feel uncomfortable, when we're asked to step outside our routines or go the extra mile for a student.
>
> I've worked with so many incredible colleagues who inspire me, who go out of their way for these kids. But I've also seen plenty of teachers who just draw the line at certain things. They'll say things like, "That's not my job" or "Why should I change the way I teach to meet this student's needs?" It's frustrating.
>
> I have also realized that people do not like it when I speak up. There's a lot of people who don't even want to talk to me anymore because I'm the special education teacher that is advocating for my kids. I am loud, but I am often alone when I am loud.
>
> I think they don't want to adjust their thinking or their practices—they're comfortable with the way things are, and they don't want to be pushed. But I'm not like that. I thrive on being uncomfortable. I want to be challenged, even if it

means rocking the boat. But how much change can I actually make alone?

It doesn't help that I often feel like special education students are an afterthought in our district. The way we do things—the way we've always done things—doesn't prioritize these kids. Let me give you an example that kind of puts a spotlight on our district and school leaders. At the high school, we don't have a designated space for testing accommodations. Students with IEPs—federally mandated IEPs, mind you—need a separate location for their tests. But there's no dedicated room for that in the whole district! Classrooms are filled, schedules are set in the summer, and we are left scrambling—we being the special education teachers who are on the line to comply with IDEA. This is a choice about scheduling that has been made over and over again over the years. So guess who has to find the rooms? Me. People like me that want to do right and who don't want to be held liable for anything illegal!

Every time a kid needs to take a test—a student with an IEP—they don't even know where they're going to be taking it. It's up to us, their teachers, to scramble and find any available space in the building we are working in. And let me tell you, it's a frustrating game of "Where can we fit them?" Sometimes you find a room that's a ten-minute walk from your classroom. That is ten minutes taking out of testing time. And then there's the whole issue of different types of accommodations—some IEPs require completely separate locations. Where am I going to find all the rooms to accommodate all these needs? Why didn't administration prioritize this?

Do parents know this reality? No. Why? Because the accommodations are on their IEPs so they must be happening, right? No. Do the students and I know the truth of it? Yes. Am I afraid someone is going to catch us and we will face litigation? Of course. Everyday. But until then, we keep doing it.

It makes me really upset. This should be the first thing we think about when building a schedule, but it's treated as an afterthought. We plan everything else first for everyone but the special education kids, and then, when it's too late, we scramble to make these accommodations work for students with IEPs. It shouldn't be left to individual teachers or caseworkers to solve this problem. But that's what happens. It's just another burden added to our already overloaded plates.

And then there's the data-driven focus that's completely taken over how we are told to make IEPs and monitor student process. The emphasis on numbers, benchmarks, and scores has pushed the real needs of students to the sidelines. We're supposed to track every little detail, that is what our administration tells us. But it feels like the goals we set for our students are so detached from what they actually need. We are making really nice goals, that is for sure. I may have them written down right on paper, but that doesn't mean a thing in practice. We spend professional development hours making these perfect goals, and we do not talk about instructional practices, differentiated instruction, or whatever that lies behind actually achieving these goals. Behind every discrete, measurable, and attainable IEP goal is an instructional practice. Maybe we should also be talking about best practices and how to actually meet these perfectly written IEP goals. Like, how do I become a better teacher so my students can succeed?

Every meeting with administration is about data now. What's your data? Are you collecting data? Where's your data? Did you use the data to write an IEP goal?

It's exhausting. And the worst part? Like I already said, most people don't even understand the data they're talking about or putting in a child's IEP or how that data relates to the way we teach and what we teach and how we teach our students. But don't worry, we have the data if someone wants to see it.

A perfect example? The reading fluency tests we have to give once a week to struggling readers. I have to give my students this one-minute fluency test every week. EVERY week. Fluency is important, sure, but it's not a reliable measure of a student's reading ability. And honestly, it drives me wild. So instead of spending time teaching, my coteacher and I are spending thirty to forty-five minutes each week administering this test to numerous students so we can write the numbers on their IEPs. This kind of stuff makes me feel like we've lost focus.

The truth is, sometimes I want to close my door and just do what makes sense to me. This way, I can pushback against all the noise out there. When my door is open, it feels like I have to do what everyone tells me to do even if it doesn't make any sense to me. It is all just about fulfilling expectations, ticking boxes, gathering data, reporting data.

The focus on data and outcomes without any real understanding of the student behind the numbers is only perpetuating this chaos around special education here. Just go with the flow, do what admin tells us to do, but that keeps real change from happening. And the ones who suffer the most are my students. They're the ones who are left behind. I make this clear with my colleagues all the time, but to be honest, I am an outlier and I feel like no one listens to me anymore. I will keep saying it though, because I have to.

Reflections

This chapter highlights the second dimension of the logic of compliance, that of the status quo. While IDEA compliance is essential for protecting students' rights and ensuring consistency in how these rights are upheld, organizational inertia and the routinization of IDEA compliance can lead to taken-for-granted ways of operating that depersonalize educational practices and do not sufficiently serve student needs. As a result, status quos develop that are maintained via institutional inertia and allow for entrenched, and often ineffective, practices to prevent transformative change.

The educators' stories in this chapter reveal deep tensions that arise when professionals are expected to act responsibly and competently within systems that often feel contradictory, confusing, or misaligned with student needs. The educators make clear that while they are committed to following policies and procedures to meet student needs, they are often stymied by limiting professional and organizational cultures that are also sustained by structural barriers, such as inadequate training and professional development, limited resources, lack of time, and so forth. Collectively, these factors undermine their ability to effectively support students in an efficient and responsive manner. Under these conditions, compliance becomes a form of self-protection for the organization and the people within it. Paperwork may be completed, but lasting improvement remains out of reach when forms are filled out for the sake of compliance and data are collected without purpose. These practices reinforce the status quo and can ultimately harm rather than support students. Educators may do everything right on paper, yet students can continue to be underserved. Disrupting this dynamic requires more than procedural fidelity; it demands intentional efforts to build professional capacity, foster collaboration, and create space for adaptive, equity-driven practices. Ultimately, it means challenging the taken-for-granted assumptions and status quo that underpin existing systems. The assumptions about the effectiveness of current laws and policies must be challenged, and disrupting entrenched norms, procedures, and institutional frameworks is necessary to meaningfully address racialized disparities.[31]

In summary, this chapter highlights how organizational inertia and the status quo can perpetuate practices that do not serve adults or children well. The status quo, a key element of the logic of compliance, is a harmful social force because it depersonalizes acts of compliance through extreme loose coupling of policy intent from action taken on the ground. The status quo is a powerful social force because while teachers and staff fulfill their duties, the system, as a whole, discourages challenges to entrenched practices, which need collective effort to rethink and transform. And while resistance to the status quo exists, established organizational structures, norms, and routines can overpower individual efforts to drive change, which will ultimately harm students.

Critical Questions to Consider

- How can the balance between technical and adaptive compliance mechanisms be achieved to ensure that compliance genuinely contributes to equity rather than reinforcing the status quo?
- In what ways can cultural and structural inertia within educational organizations be disrupted to encourage

meaningful change, challenge symbolic compliance, and address systemic inequities?

- What are the mechanisms and processes that allow for the status quo to take root within an organizational context?
- What underlying assumptions about students, educators, and learning conditions sustain the status quo, and how might we address these assumptions to build trust and foster more collaborative environments that lead to more equitable practices?

CHAPTER 5

Good Intentions

Compliance with IDEA procedural protections is based in legal, moral, and ethical necessity. It is also dependent on the good intentions of those tasked to protect the rights of disabled students in schools. Good intentions often guide educators' efforts to comply, but those intentions alone are not enough to disrupt persistent inequities. When routines and practices are shaped more by the need to follow policy than to challenge the assumptions underlying policy enactments, well-meaning actions can reinforce the very disparities they aim to resolve.

When educators comply with the IDEA's procedural requirements, for example, disparities like racial disproportionality can be framed as external to their actions. This is not to say that they are openly or explicitly discriminating against a particular group but rather that, in these actions, they are providing legally mandated services via the IDEA.

Thus, rather than examining how structural barriers and institutionalized biases may contribute to these disparities, this logic can shift the blame for unequal educational outcomes onto students and their families—a deficit-based perspective.[1] With this move, compliance with IDEA policies and procedures can coexist with persistent disparities, yet no one within a school system is to blame or has bad intentions. The sources of and solutions for addressing racial disproportionality remain elusive because no matter what educators do, no matter how well intended their actions are, no matter what interventions or supports are in place, certain groups of students continue to fare worse on academic and behavioral outcomes. The problem is not ours, as educators, under this line of reasoning.

Disability critical race theory (DisCrit) can help us better understand the mechanisms behind the tension between good intentions and compliance. It helps us look beyond intent to consider how everyday acts of compliance can mask deeper forms of exclusion.[2] It can also help us better see how ideological forces tied to whiteness and able-bodiedness remain intact despite the well-meaning actions of people and the associated educational policies, procedures, and practices they enact.

DisCrit draws directly from critical race theory (CRT) to link disability discrimination to racial discrimination and to law.[3] Critical legal and race scholars have long argued that laws based on the principle of equal treatment often enable systemic inequities to persist under the illusion of fairness.[4] Because legal protections guaranteed under the Constitution's Fourteenth Amendment require proof of explicit intent to discriminate, proving systemic discrimination is nearly impossible unless people are openly violating the law.[5] DisCrit brings to light the ways in which discrimination related to disability and race and other identities can be masked within special education policies, practices, and procedures.[6] It also highlights how racism and ableism function both explicitly, through exclusionary policies and practices, and implicitly, through factors such as beliefs about racial superiority and disability as a deficit.[7]

To fully understand how these ideological forces shape educational systems today, we must first view their influence through a historical lens that accounts for the roots of intersectional disability discrimination—also discussed in chapter 1. From the early twentieth century, eugenics framed both disability and racialized difference as threats to societal progress.[8] Black, Indigenous, immigrant, and disabled populations, among other groups, were subject to forced sterilizations, institutionalization, and exclusion from public life under the guise of protecting the social order.[9] These systems of exclusion were codified into law and justified intersectional oppressions.[10] With the civil rights movement, the pendulum of disability rights shifted away from these exclusionary practices and toward rights-based protections.[11] However, many scholars have argued that disability laws, both within the United States and internationally, continue to reinforce a medical and psychological model of disability while sandwiched between civil and human rights discourse.[12]

The persistence of framing disability as an individualized problem in policy and law as something embodied within a person that must be remediated can neglect the broader historical, social, and structural factors that have shaped disability oppression and discrimination locally and globally.[13] This highlights how the paradox of rights discussed throughout this book allows for educational inequalities "to persist under the guise of legal protections" because current legal frameworks "do not adequately recognize the constructs of ableism and the intersectionality of culture, affect, language, race, and ethnicity within special education law," which leads to a "misguided focus on technical compliance and procedural monitoring of dis/ability rights that is dismissive of the lived experiences, emotions, feelings, and affects of students."[14]

To this point, Artiles stated that the "unit of analysis" for racialized disability discrimination "has been grounded in the so-called 'medical model' in which the unit of analysis is the individual, completely devoid of social or historical influences," further elaborating that "the medical model fragments the individual, focusing either on race or on disability, rarely examining the interplay of race and disability with other key dimensions such as social class and gender."[15] By nature, then, people employing disability legislation like the IDEA to protect the rights of students with disabilities in schools do just that—they protect a person based on their disability, without the need to fully consider how the full nature of their human experiences and identity, which are culturally, historically, and contextually situated, influence schooling experiences.[16] Thus, when educators use the IDEA to provide special education supports and services without recognizing these factors, the lived experiences and intersectional identities that students embody are not always accounted for in meaningful ways in educational practice.

The implicit nature of continued disability and intersectional discrimination through the enactment of law, legislation, and policy to practice is rarely explicitly named or disrupted in educational spaces unless people are intentionally pushed to do so through professional development or technical assistance efforts.[17] These social forces of discrimination often remain intact in varied ways.

Recently, scholars have pointed to the racialization of organizations and bureaucratic structures and the way in which ableism also functions organizationally through bureaucratic and organizational routines.[18] Ray, for example, proposed a theory of racialized organizations that has been applied empirically across a variety of fields.[19] The theory illustrates how organizations are not neutral entities; they are fundamentally shaped by racial hierarchies that are embedded in the rules, routines, and resource distributions of organizations in ways that consistently advantage whiteness and disadvantage people of color. Ray contended that seemingly race-neutral bureaucratic practices reproduce societal and racial inequities whereby organizational processes themselves uphold systemic racism. The same type of logic can be applied to disability discrimination and ableism, as organizational processes, routines, and structures are built in ways that sustain disability discrimination and marginalize disabled people. In essence, then, we can comply with law, legislation, and policy without having to name, see, or confront these organizational processes. When we do this under the guise of good intentions, we can reify the very mechanisms that antidiscrimination laws and rights based legislation were designed to address and redress.

It is here, where a DisCrit lens is once again useful. Ableism, or disability discrimination, does not exist in isolation from other discriminatory forces.[20] The core tenets of DisCrit highlight this reality and the need to understand educational inequities through an intersectional frame in law, legislation, policy, and practice. The mechanisms designed to protect people with disabilities do not adequately recognize how race, class, language, and other identities intersect with disability to sustain inequities.

This is an important point to note because a focus on disability alone can promote a color-evasive approach to special education service delivery that is rooted in a seemingly benign, compassionate, and benevolent intent.[21] Kathleen King Thorius called this a cloak of benevolence in special education that perpetuates harm.[22] The cloak of benevolence is steeped in good intentions and "niceness" in education that obscures the historical, contextual, and organizational conditions that shape the structure of schooling. Niceness serves as a societal mechanism "for maintaining the status quo" that functions as "both an institutional norm within schools and an embodied practice among educators" that glosses over rather than recognizes difference, the harms perpetuated, or impacts on students.[23] Being nice, in relation to something like a historically situated and intersectional inequity like racial disproportionality, will not lead to more equitable outcomes, because being nice does not adequately address unequal structures of educational opportunity and access or the reality of the multifaceted lived realties of students.[24]

The concept of niceness, or having good intentions, also glosses over the impact of harmful ideologies that DisCrit makes visible. Although niceness and good intentions are rooted in benevolence, such beliefs neglect the deeper ideological and structural forces that uphold inequities in education and society. Longstanding institutional norms, policies, and practices, while often framed as neutral or objective, disproportionately disadvantage historically marginalized communities when implemented.[25]

For example, Skiba and colleagues found that perceptions of student behavior are racialized, leading to disproportionate disciplinary actions against Black students as compared to their white peers.[26] They found that Black students were more frequently referred for subjective disciplinary infractions, such as "disrespect," "excessive noise," "threat," and "loitering," which rely heavily on individual interpretation of behaviors. In contrast, white students were more often referred for objective, clearly defined disciplinary infractions such as "smoking," "leaving without permission," "vandalism," and "obscene language."[27] This empirical evidence suggests that Black students are disproportionately disciplined for subjective behaviors that, when combined with institutional norms framed as neutral but applied inequitably, can reinforce racialized inequities. Similar findings emerge at the intersection of race, disability, and discipline.[28]

When niceness and good intentions dominate how academic and behavioral systems are structured and enacted across educational systems without explicitly addressing how race and ableism influence IDEA implementation dynamics, systemic barriers can remain in place that limit educational opportunities for historically marginalized students. For example, surface-level expressions of diversity and gestures of kindness are often prioritized in schools over deeper, more meaningful efforts to drive systemic change that discuss the impacts of racialized or ableist student policies and practices.[29] These dynamics also fail to recognize the historical and structural roots of cultural conflicts that shape long-standing inequities in education.[30] Researchers have noted that being nice and having good intentions enables individuals to maintain a sense of moral virtue while undermining the self-determination and agency of marginalized groups by glossing over harms that are or have been perpetuated.[31] Therefore, beneath seemingly well-meaning policies and the illusion of fairness, harmful ideologies remain deeply embedded within educational systems, shaping decision-making processes and reinforcing systemic inequities. These forces influence policies, institutional practices, and professional attitudes in ways that disproportionately harm disabled students, BISOC, and historically marginalized learners, sustaining racial and ability-based disparities in educational access and outcomes.[32]

Addressing Structural Inequities Through Culturally Responsive and Sustaining Pedagogies

As shown, special education policies and practices, often framed as altruistic and individualized, can emphasize procedural compliance while obscuring the systemic inequities at the intersection of race and disability under a cloak of benevolence.[33] This emphasis reinforces a core point of DisCrit, where the entanglement of racism and ableism remain unquestioned and embedded within discriminatory structures that influence everyday educational decision-making.[34] By normalizing these inequities under the guise of neutrality and fairness, special education systems can perpetuate disparities with tangible consequences for students.

In response to these limitations and the inadequacy of good intentions alone, culturally responsive pedagogy (CRP) and culturally sustaining pedagogy (CSP) have emerged as critical frameworks for challenging entrenched educational inequities.[35] These approaches recognize the necessity of affirming students' cultural identities while actively confronting structural barriers that disproportionately affect students of color and disabled students. By integrating CRP and CSP into special education, educators can move beyond procedural compliance toward transformative practices that address the root causes of racial and ability-based disparities.

CRP emphasizes incorporating students' cultural identities and lived experiences into teaching practices to validate their identities and connect home and school cultures. CRP can be used to leverage students' cultural knowledge, experiences, and learning styles to enhance educational effectiveness.[36] Building on this, CSP seeks not only to affirm but also to expand students' cultural identities in education by promoting multilingualism and multiculturalism while challenging assimilationist norms and encouraging dynamic cultural expression.[37] These frameworks challenge the marginalization of student identities and recognize cultural diversity as a valuable asset in learning.[38]

Therefore, when special education policies and practices prioritize compliance-driven interventions and remediation, harmful and limiting practices can persist despite the good intentions of educators. Yet one mitigating factor may be the use of culturally responsive and sustaining practices to enhance educator criticality and responsiveness to diverse student needs.[39] In the following story and voice from the field, the educator describes how this very tension manifested in her practice. She describes how she grappled with the tension between following the IDEA's procedural requirements and responding meaningfully to the complex, intersecting needs of her students. In doing so, she makes visible how, when, and where she realized that her good intentions and technical proficiency within the special education realm alone cannot dismantle systemic inequities. Through her reflection, she also shares how she began to recognize her own role within institutional structures that narrow student identities and experiences within the special education system. What becomes clear to her is that good intentions, while necessary, are not enough to disrupt systemic inequities, and she begins to articulate how culturally responsive and sustaining pedagogies can potentially provide a pathway for moving beyond compliance.

Stories and Voices from the Field

The white woman educator describes how her good intentions and knowledge of culturally responsive practices did not sufficiently infiltrate into the way she served students with disabilities. She expresses an unexamined initial belief that special education was inherently culturally responsive but then realized through dialogue that when complying with the IDEA, she was not applying what she knew about culturally responsive practices to her IEP writing. Her well-meaning intentions intersected with liming policies and practices that emphasized individualized interventions and compliance with IDEA requirements, but she expresses a willingness to grow, reflect, and learn how to be more responsive:

> I know there are so many teachers in this district who care deeply about our students. We work long hours, spend our own money on supplies, and we do it because we truly care

about these kids and their futures. But too often, the district gets a bad reputation. People outside the community often express pity when they hear where I work, saying, "Oh, I'm so sorry" or "That must be really tough." And I always respond the same way: "Please don't feel sorry for me. We have great teachers and amazing kids, and we work hard to make a difference every day." I think when people say that, they mean well, but they do not really understand either how much effort goes into teaching in a district like this. They don't see how much we sacrifice—time, energy, and money—to give our students what they need to succeed. And how much we care.

When I first started teaching, a colleague of mine used to joke that I was like a pristine white woman who could never succeed teaching kids who are not like me. She thought there was no way someone like me, with my background, would thrive in such a diverse environment. But the truth is, I've always loved working with diverse kids.

The kids in this district are amazing, and despite the tough, sometimes heartbreaking, challenges they face at home, they're really good kids. I often say that they're fun, funny, and full of potential. Even though their lives can be filled with drama and hardship, they have this incredible ability to brighten up a room.

And here is a hard and real truth about teaching in this district. If you do not learn this quickly, it will become clear, fast: if you don't truly like the kids, if you don't have a heart for them, they'll know immediately. And when that happens, you're done—you'll lose them. You have to genuinely want to be there, to be invested in their lives, and if you're not, it shows and they know it. We may be different, but what remains the same is the heart. The students here—they know I care about them.

Now, because I have worked here for decades at this point, I have realized that I have to also change as our students and our community change. I've started to pay more attention to the impacts of race and culture in my classroom, because I have to, I want to, and I need to. I have to evolve as an educator.

Over the past few years, we have learned so much about culturally responsive practices. We have been pushed to engage in culturally responsive practices, to speak with each other about race and difference explicitly, and to be reflective.

I try so hard to be culturally responsive. I have a long way to go, but wow, I know I have learned so much from just being exposed to new ideas and ways of teaching through professional development and just in conversation with the newer generation of teachers that work here now.

For example, I think I am becoming more culturally responsive as I've moved away from teaching the classics—those books filled with white, European characters. There's nothing wrong with those stories, but they don't speak to my students' lives. Now, I'm more intentional about choosing books where my kids can see themselves, not as stereotypes but as real, complex people. And when they do, it's like a light switches on. They're more engaged, more confident. But I'll admit, this didn't come naturally to me. I had to learn how to do this, and I had colleagues help me with this. I make a lot of mistakes as an educator and as an older white woman, but I am trying, and all of this comes from a place of love too. Love for the work and for the kids.

Here is another hard truth that I recently realized with the help of a colleague—a Black teacher and a critical friend of mine—that never occurred to me before: I kind of have not brought this culturally responsive lens to my IEP writing.

This happened after we were talking about an IEP meeting that felt off. The conversation with the parents felt combative, and they were not happy with the services their child was receiving. This was with a family of Afro-Caribbean descent.

My good friend and colleague asked me after that meeting (he was in it too), "Why don't you write goals that tie into that student's cultural background?" I could not answer his question. I had no good answer, and to be honest, I did not really understand what he meant when he asked me that, because I have always thought that I have included their culture and who they are. Their IEP goals *do* represent their social emotional, academic, and behavioral needs. That is what I was trained to do! To write good goals!

But his question really got me thinking more after some time. What if, instead of writing the usual "the student will be able to compose a five-paragraph essay," I connected the assignment to something meaningful in the student's culture? I don't really understand what that means though. I grapple with that a lot and I try to think of what this would authentically look like. Seriously though, what *would* that look like? How would adding their culture not just come across as a superficial move? Am I supposed to change the goal to say something like "the student will be able to compose a five-paragraph essay that draws upon their family and cultural experiences?" Is that the answer? I have no idea! But I feel like I just have not really connected what I do in special ed and with IEP's enough to the critical frameworks I have been reading about and learning about.

It is really complicated. I mean, when I moved away from teaching the classics, my same colleague and friend reminded me, I could still teach the classics if I wanted to, but I had to put them within a critical historical context.

I still didn't quite understand that either, but now I get it a little more. Like, when I teach the *Scarlet Letter* or something, I can contextualize the story within a broader history of colonization or something. Or maybe I can teach some of Thomas Jefferson's writing in the context of enslavement. I am still trying to figure this out. But I would have never thought of this if I didn't have colleagues to think through this with. I just was never taught this in my own life, my own teacher training. I have to really stretch myself to try to understand all of this.

Anyways, this brings me back to the IEP meeting. What did I write in that IEP, and what happened in that meeting that went so off script? What did I possibly do that made the family feel slighted? How did I describe the student? What language did I use? I think I ask myself these questions now, instead of saying the parents are combative or whatever, because of what I have learned from my colleagues through professional development and honestly, my own self work.

It is odd too, because the more I thought about that meeting, the more I realized that I have always seen culturally responsive teaching happening in other areas, like English and social studies. My colleagues talked about doing this all the time in gen ed. But it didn't necessarily live in a special education space, in an IEP, even though I guess it could and should. Kind of like what I was saying before–isn't an IEP goal already responsive to a student's needs? By definition, aren't IEPs inherently culturally responsive? We are supposed to write goals that reflect a student's social, emotional, and academic needs and goals. It is the whole child.

Let me try to clarify my thinking some more. Sometimes I'll get an IEP for a student I haven't met yet, and it's just this list of stuff, all important stuff, but nonetheless, it is stuff—accommodations, scores, goals, metrics. I used to take these as fact and go from there, plan instruction, get to know the student and family throughout the school year, and then move on.

But the more I think about it, the more I talk with others about these ideas, I realize I've never pushed myself to think deeply about culture and context when writing IEP goals or evaluating an IEP. I do not know if I fully understand what this means. What is a culturally responsive IEP? I keep wondering, how did I fail to do this when I have committed to being a culturally responsive educator?

Like, when I sit down to write an IEP, my brain goes straight to academics. Where's the student at now? Where can they realistically be in a year? It's all about ability, progress, and measurable goals. Then I think about their social, emotional, and behavioral needs. What does the student need to function appropriately in a classroom? What accommodations or related services will help them achieve their social, emotional, and behavioral needs?

Our district tells us to focus on these areas too. Oh, and we are told the state will look for it if we are ever audited. We need to make compliant and thorough IEPs that are data driven. This way, we can show we are making measurable progress with a student. This makes sense to me. It is the right thing to do too. I always focus on the individual, the student and their specific needs, when I do this. We have to, right? That is the essence of special education. What does this specific student need on an individualized level to succeed?

You know, I would say that in general, I am really good at writing IEPs. My admin always asks me to share what strategies I use when writing them. I have even presented at conferences about writing really thorough and detailed IEPs. But honestly, when I look back and reflect on things, I have to ask myself again; have I actually shown who a student is in their IEP in their totality? I do not think so. Well, I am just not sure. I am figuring this out.

The more I reflect too, I realize how segmented I have been in my work around all of this. Culturally responsive practices, and the talk about them in our district, are widespread. I have been to so many book clubs and trainings on this. I love it.

In the special education department, we talk about this stuff too. We also talk about avoiding racial disparities and reducing racial disproportionality. We have casually and informally talked about being antiracist special educators and being more culturally responsive teachers. So yes, these conversations exist in our special education department meetings. But, when it comes to special education policies, procedures, and processes, we have not really figured out how to make all of those parts of the special education system culturally responsive, beyond adding the word "culturally responsive" or "antiracist" to an already established process or procedure. Like, that is what I meant before—how do you make an IEP goal more culturally responsive without making it feel like a superficial add on? Is a culturally responsive IEP, in name, truly culturally responsive?

At this point in my career, I think a lot about the two parallel worlds I am traversing. I am an expert in special education, and I am growing in my practice through culturally responsive professional development opportunities. But when I try to merge these two parts of me, I feel like I am operating in parallel worlds instead of overlapping worlds, if that makes sense.

> For me, it's aways been about addressing the student's individual needs, and those individual needs are hard to connect to antiracist and culturally responsive pedagogy. And it is even harder to think about what this would mean in a SMART [specific, measurable, attainable, realistic, and time bound] IEP goal. But now, I wonder: What is possible? Can all of this "stuff" really be tailored to who the student is in a culturally responsive way? Can I find a better way to do all of this? I think the answer is yes, but I need a community of practitioners to actually unpack what this means with me. I need help with that. That is it. I need help doing this.

Reflections

In this chapter, I discuss how the third component of the logic of compliance, good intentions, does not always translate to improved equity outcomes. I make clear how educators may aim for equity, but their focus on procedural compliance under the "cloak of benevolence" can unintentionally reinforce systemic harms.[40] This is especially true when cultural and racial considerations are excluded from acts of procedural compliance with the IDEA. The altruistic practices and policies operating within special education, which prioritize individuality and procedural compliance, can obscure underlying structural inequities at the intersection of race and disability, reinforcing the connection between racism and ableism.[41] These forces subtly normalize discrimination and tacitly permit educators to neglect the cultural and racial dimensions of students' identities when complying with and using the IDEA, as seen in the featured story and voice from the field.

Moreover, a focus on IDEA compliance and the good intentions that are wrapped within providing educational opportunity and access via the IDEA does not require educators to intentionally connect and emphasize students' cultural identities and lived experiences to the enactment of special education polices, practices, and procedures. The absence of this critical lens means that achieving equity requires moving beyond individual intentions to critically noticing, challenging, and addressing the institutional policies and practices that sustain these disparities. Thus, while good intentions are important, they are not enough to dismantle systemic inequities; real progress requires equity-centered actions that address the root causes of complex intersectional inequities.

The educator's story also reveals how procedural compliance—embedded within FAPE and LRE within the IEP process—is often assumed to guarantee student needs are met. In practice, however, technically compliant approaches can overlook students' lived experiences and intersecting identities.[42] She also described the challenge of figuring out how to apply culturally responsive and sustaining principles within the confines of special education policy and practice. These tensions highlight how technical and adaptive aspects of schooling, as they relate to IDEA administration and implementation, interact in ways that can perpetuate racial and ability-based marginalization, as rigid educational structures privilege normative conceptions of intelligence and behavior while not meaningfully engaging with diverse ways of knowing and being.[43]

Stories like hers also point to the need for sustained professional learning that helps educators respond both critically and compassionately to student needs and for systems that enable, rather than restrict, transformative work. When educators are equipped and supported to align their intentions with equity-driven action, special education can become not just a tool for access, but a pathway to meaningful inclusion. Therefore, it is necessary for educators to shift away from a reliance on good intentions and procedural compliance under the IDEA and toward embracing equity-centered actions that directly confront systemic inequities. Equity-centered approaches demand that schools invest in sustained professional development that deepens educators' understanding of racism, ableism, and their intersections; create space for critical reflection and collective problem-solving; and prioritize the voices and experiences of marginalized students and families in decision-making processes. It also means aligning resources, staffing, and supports in ways that challenge, rather than reinforce, existing hierarchies and disparities. By intentionally designing systems that center cultural responsiveness, student dignity, and structural change, special education supports and services can move beyond a system of compliance into one of more responsive possibility.

Critical Questions to Consider

- How can educational practices shift from relying on good intentions and IDEA compliance to actively addressing systemic inequities rather than reinforcing the status quo and perpetuating harm for marginalized students?
- How can educators critically assess how they comply with the IDEA, particularly in relation to IEP development, to move beyond individual student deficits and address the underlying ideological, systemic, and

structural factors that contribute to disparities in special education outcomes?

- How can educators create space for culturally sustaining, adaptive practices that truly respond to the diverse identities and lived experiences of students within existing special education structures?

PART 3

A Framework for Transformation

For apart from inquiry, apart from praxis, individuals cannot be truly human. Knowledge emerges only through invention and re-invention, through the restless, impatient, continuing, hopeful inquiry human beings pursue in the world, with the world and with each other.

—PAULO FREIRE

CHAPTER 6

Praxis and Transformation

In this chapter, I show how the insights gleaned from parts 1 and 2 can be placed within an actionable framework to move beyond technical acts of compliance and toward the adaptive components of practice to better move systems toward equity. I first summarize the main ideas from part 1 (the paradox of compliance) and part 2 (the logic of compliance). Then I leverage the insights from these chapters to demonstrate to readers how they can develop locally and contextually responsive pathways for transformation. I frame the discussion within praxis so that the technical, adaptive, and thematic questions explored in the previous chapters can be placed within a dialogic process, inspired by Freire's culture circle and critical cycle process, to reimagine and reshape how IDEA compliance can be approached in educational practice.[1] I use the term "adapted critical cycle process" as it is applied to IDEA compliance.

The culture circle and critical cycle process is a transformative framework that emphasizes dialogue to raise critical consciousness through the sharing of lived experiences. It requires individuals to engage in dialogue as they critically analyze their own realities and cocreate knowledge to pursue transformation—building *conscientização* or critical consciousness. As El-Amin and colleagues described, *critical consciousness* is a developmental process that requires understanding structural barriers, building a sense of personal and collective power to make change among these barriers, and engaging in deliberate efforts to transform oppressive realities leading to critical action.[2] This is praxis—the merging of theory with practice and the ongoing cycle of reflection and action—where individuals not only analyze injustice but also act on that understanding in ways that disrupt and reimagine oppressive systems.

Through parts 1 and 2 of this book, I attempted to make visible how the limiting aspects of compliance function in educational practice. This understanding helps readers begin to critically understand their limit situations to promote critical consciousness and lead to the transformation of the systems we work within that do not promote educational equity for all students. Chapter 6 then serves as a roadmap for finding ways to drive meaningful change by fostering active reflection, encouraging multilevel community and participant engagement, and building strategies to identify and address inequities within the educational system. It also emphasizes purposeful action planning at both personal and systemic levels to disrupt harmful practices associated with entrenched logics of compliance.

The chapter ends with practical guidance on how to work together, with other like-minded colleagues, using an adapted version of the culture circle and critical cycle process to develop locally relevant solutions that lead to meaningful action and change. It asks readers to take the insights from parts 1 and 2 related to the paradox and logic of compliance not just as critiques of the system but also as illuminations of the conditions that limit educators and marginalize students so that these conditions can be named, questioned, and ultimately changed.

In part 1, I examined the evolution of the Individuals with Disabilities Education Act, highlighting its emergence in response to the historical neglect and exclusion of students and people with disabilities in the US context across various identities. I also showed how the IDEA was shaped by the civil rights movement, when disability rights advocacy efforts drew upon the legal precedents of *Brown v. Board of Education*, and which eventually led to the passage of the Education for All Handicapped Children Act (EAHCA) and later the IDEA. I also made clear that although the IDEA is not a civil rights act, it works alongside Section 504 of the Rehabilitation Act and the Americans with Disabilities Act to protect against disability discrimination across both federal and private entities, and that it is responsive to a history of intersectional inequities.

I also outlined how the IDEA's core principles—free appropriate public education, appropriate evaluations, individualized education programs, least restrictive environment, parent participation, and procedural safeguards—are monitored through various compliance and performance-based metrics like the state performance place indicators (SPP). I described how results-driven accountability efforts can promote superficial and symbolic compliance responses that can lead to the prioritizing of regulatory compliance over meaningful educational improvement in schools. I also highlighted how the technical provisions of the IDEA do not adequately account for intersectional disability rights history and the continued inequitable outcomes for people with disabilities, especially at the intersection of race and disability, thus limiting adaptive realities surrounding acts of IDEA compliance.

In setting up this historical account in part 1, I provided the context for understanding how the paradox of compliance and IDEA protections can coexist. The paradox of compliance highlights the tension between the IDEA's civil rights inspired history, its procedural mandates, and the realities of its application in schools.[3] It makes clear how, historically, disability policies rooted in medicalized frameworks have amplified inequities that have disproportionately impacted marginalized groups and communities. I showed how while the IDEA provides access to essential resources for students with disabilities, it also perpetuates stigma and exclusion.[4] The IDEA functions as both a source of educational opportunity and a contributor to harm, underscoring the intersectional nature of disability rights and the limitations of IDEA compliance to achieve substantive equity outcomes.[5] Therefore, part 1 establishes how compliance with the IDEA can coexist with persistent documented inequities.

In part 2, I unpacked the components of the logic of compliance, situating it within broadscale historical inequities in special education, like racial disproportionality.[6] I also described how the logic of compliance operates through three interconnected dimensions that can uphold inequities. First, I describe how the current contexts of educational practice reflect legacies of societal and educational harms using Ladson-Billings's concept of the educational debt—a framework for understanding how present day racialized educational inequities are historically situated and relate to historical, economic, sociopolitical, and moral debts.[7] Second, I described how organizational inertia and the status quo reinforce inequitable practices by maintaining existing power structures and ignoring the root causes of disparities, such as systemic racism and ableism that influence inequities in special education. Third, I highlighted how the good intentions of educators can perpetuate harm when filtered through compliance-focused frameworks that remain race and ability neutral. I also showed how good intentions are insufficient to disrupt inequitable systems and instead can lead to fragmented, surface-level solutions that leave oppressive structures intact. Therefore, part 2 makes clear that moving beyond compliance requires addressing complex historical and systemic barriers in ways that also challenge entrenched norms and ideologies that allow for the paradox and logic of compliance to persist.

Also, throughout parts 1 and 2, I framed the systemic challenges explored in each chapter with stories and voices from the field. These narratives reveal how technical adherence to the IDEA can obscure adaptive challenges and hinder transformative change. They also show that while procedural protections are necessary, they often conflict with the need for equity-driven, adaptive solutions or with educators stated ideals and professional competencies.

Therefore, parts 1 and 2 prepare readers for the penultimate goal of this book, which is to provide educators and leaders, working across both general and special education spaces, with the insights and tools necessary for identifying the paradox of compliance and for disrupting harmful logics of compliance that allow for educational inequities to persist under the guise of compliance. Each chapter thus far has juxtaposed technical and adaptive mechanisms as they relate to IDEA compliance—both theoretically and practically—and has asked readers to reflect on these mechanisms via critical questions at the end of each chapter. These questions were designed to help guide readers to begin to develop contextually situated themes, understandings, and interpretations of the paradox and logic of compliance that can be eventually leveraged in an adapted culture circle and critical cycle process to foster more equitable transformation and change.[8] An adapted culture circle and critical cycle process can help disrupt the paradox of compliance and the associated harmful logics of compliance that can lead to more meaningful change on the ground for both adults and students. The process is firmly rooted in praxis.

Imagining an Adaptive Critical Cycle Process Related to Compliance

Central to Freire's work is the focus on changing the conditions of the oppressed, including people at the intersections of class, race, ethnicity, age, religion, citizenship, and disability.[9] Freire advocated for moving education beyond the technical "banking" model of education and toward more critical practices.[10] This involves not simply absorbing knowledge as it is given to us but actively working to investigate, question, and critically understand our own context. This call for critical pedagogy emphasizes that learners should not just know things—in the context of this book, IDEA legal literacy is not enough—but rather that they should humanize, critique, and commit to the becoming of transformation.[11] This entails critical inquiry and letting go of the idea that there is one way to be, think, or act. In this case, it is thinking expansively to understand that IDEA compliance can be both limiting and freeing, but it must be understood for its complexity as a mechanism of harm and educational opportunity.[12] And as noted previously, a central facet of this type of critical pedagogy is rooted in a critical cycle process of inquiry and investigation, which is designed to increase *conscientização*—loosely translated as "critical consciousness."[13] Freire's critical pedagogy has been applied to varied contexts and typically focuses on students.[14] Its power as an analytic frame and method are well known. Giroux described the purpose of Freire's critical pedagogy as follows:

> For Freire, pedagogy is not a method or an *a priori* technique to be imposed on all students but a political and moral practice that provides the knowledge, skills, and social relations that enable students to explore the possibilities of what it means to be critical citizens while expanding and deepening their participation in the promise of a substantive democracy. Critical thinking for Freire was not an object lesson in test-taking, but a tool for self-determination and civic engagement. According to Freire, critical thinking was not about the task of simply reproducing the past and understanding the present. To the contrary, it was about offering a way of thinking beyond the present, soaring beyond the immediate confines of one's experiences, entering into a critical dialogue with history, and imagining a future that would not merely reproduce the present.[15]

This powerful way of understanding the world and engaging with it can extend beyond students. As Collins and Bilge have argued, there is great value in the transferability of Freire's ideas to varied contexts.[16] Although his critical pedagogical approach is grounded in the needs of oppressed people, its methods have value for many groups of people.

> Freire clearly grounds his analysis of critical education in the needs of oppressed people . . . [but] the value of critical education is open to everyone. Everyone benefits from a better understanding of the dynamics of intersecting social inequalities, as well as the kinds of critical thinking and problem-posing skills that can remedy them . . . moreover, developing a critical consciousness about how intersecting systems of power are organized within and across the structural, disciplinary, cultural, and interpersonal domains of power can result in new and powerful perspectives on social inequity.[17]

Therefore, while educators using and complying with laws like the IDEA are not oppressed in a conventional sense, Freire's core concepts are still applicable in building critical consciousness about the oppressive nature of compliance and its potential to undermine equity outcomes.

It is also important to note that by applying a lens of critical pedagogy to adults for adults, I am naming a space where the process can begin but should not end. Freire's dialogical, or transformational methods rooted in dialogue, and critical approach emphasizes a dialectical relationship between those in positions of power and the oppressed; both are essential participants in a collective process of cocreation, where those in positions of power can learn from the experiences of the oppressed while offering critical knowledge in return. Central to the process is dialogue, not to be understood as a tool or procedure but as engagement with each other to collectively shape the world.[18]

It is also important to be very clear that there is not and cannot be a concrete method associated with the culture circle and critical cycle process. Therefore, in this book, I do not provide a concrete method for unpacking the paradox and logic of compliance. I only provide suggestions that give readers the opportunity to combine theory (e.g., fragmented harm, neoinstitutionalism, DisCrit) and practice (e.g., insights from the stories and voices from the field) to shift educational practices through a dialogic process. Because, to be clear, there is no singular definition of what constitutes the process for raising critical consciousness, and there is no prescribed method for engaging in a critical cycle process of inquiry and transformation.

According to Souto-Manning, Freire asserted that the "method should not be exported or imported," because the process is generative, contextually bound, and locally situated.[19] For readers of this book, this means that there is not a specific intervention, timed inquiry cycle, or other such prescriptive process associated with the adapted culture circle and critical cycle process. Rather, as participants engage with the themes raised in this book, the insights they gain can serve as a starting point for a collaborative process of inquiry and action linked to real-world experiences related to IDEA compliance and the technical and adaptive challenges surfaced in parts 1 and 2 of the book. Participants can unpack these experiences together and analyze the deeper social forces at work behind them. By engaging in this process of collective sense-making, individuals can better understand how their personal experiences connect to broader social dynamics and the experiences of others. Ultimately, this process of shared reflection can lead to informed action, where participants begin identifying and implementing contextually relevant changes that can promote systemic transformation. This book asks readers to be vulnerable and to be critical of themselves and their practice, to come together, to be willing to discuss the themes that arise across the chapters of the book, and to be willing to collectively discuss and identify the oppressive issues impacting their practice in order to create more equitable school systems for historically marginalized students. Such conversations can take place in a range of settings tailored to local needs and norms, including but not limited to professional learning communities, book clubs, and informal discussion groups.

Given the flexible and responsive nature of the culture circle and critical cycle process, I present loose guidelines on the process here, drawing from Freire's and Souto-Manning's body of work related to the culture circle and critical cycle process. Souto-Manning offered a loosely structured framework for transformation that I have reframed to specifically challenge the limitations of the paradox of compliance and the components of the logic of compliance.[20]

Step 1: Participants create and engage with generative themes that are "codifications of complex processes in the lives of the participants."[21] These codifications are rooted in participants' experiences and are gleaned with the help of a researcher's/facilitator's guidance. The facilitator brings the codified theme to the group in the form of a representative story, a photo, or an object. The questions at the end of each chapter in parts 1 and 2 were designed to lead to the formulation of these codifications. The facilitator can be a colleague who has looked at a series of responses from the reflective questions offered in this book and who identifies a common pattern across responses, then codifies this pattern into something concrete for the group to discuss. This can be an object (e.g., a representative IEP that exemplifies how these documents are commonly written or prepared within a particular context) or a word or phrase that reflects a common sentiment across participant experiences (e.g., "We are data rich but data poor," implying that there is a plethora of data collected but the data are not used to inform practice in meaningful ways, a theme we saw in many of the voices and stories from the field). These codifications are often politically significant and will lead to dialogue and transformative action.[22] These dialogues and actions occur because the codification is meaningful to the participants—it comes from them. It is socioculturally and historically situated in their lives, social realties, and experiences. According to Souto-Manning, the "artifact resulting from the codification represents the very issues experienced by participants without exposing the individual(s) experiencing the situation. . . . It represents a collective experience which includes details of many situated representations as opposed to details of one case study."[23] These codifications are an important part of the dialogic process that ensues.

Step 2: Participants engage in problem posing, which requires that participants work to collectively destabilize engrained assumptions, values, orientations, explanations, and understandings of the theme or codification. Sample problem-posing questions adapted from Souto-Manning are listed following this step.[24] The questions are purposefully open-ended. They are designed to bring to light oppressive or taken-for-granted values and orientations to a theme or codification. The sample questions are in response to the codification suggested previously (that a school may be "data rich but data poor"). The series of questions can begin with the facilitator but can move to include all participants as they unpack what the codification means to them through dialogue.

- Why do you think the school has a pervasive "data rich but data poor" practice?
- What is the significance of the statement "data rich but data poor" to you?
- Who or what could help you with moving away from a "data rich but data poor" practice?
- How did a "data rich but data poor" climate take shape, and why do you think this has happened?
- Who benefits and who is harmed by a "data rich but data poor" approach?
- How does a "data rich but data poor" practice relate to your workflow?

Step 3: The meaning-making process related to the codification happens in dialogue. The facilitator or researcher is not more knowledgeable than the participants, and job rank and experiences (professional hierarchies) are not significant either. Rather, the dialogic process allows for mutual learning and unlearning to occur. This creates the conditions for a broader goal for the group to be established during the dialogic process. Participants not only unpack oppressive conditions, they also problem solve as they unpack and identify pressing issues that stifle their progress in a collective goal defined by the group in the dialogic process. Souto-Manning described possible conditions for shaping the space where this iterative and dynamic dialogic process can occur.

- Participants are seated in a circle so that they can look at each other and engage with each other without an imposed physical hierarchy.
- The researcher/facilitator is just as much a part of the group and the dialogic process as the participants are.
- All participants act as learners.
- The facilitator is flexible, not knowing exactly "where the circle is headed," but the dialogue is driven by the themes and codifications.[25]
- Participants are central to the dialogue. They drive the discourse, the flow of the conversation, and the direction of the circle.
- The dialogical process pushes participants to problem solve and identify pressing issues that stifle their progress in achieving a particular goal, which is defined by the group.
- In the adapted culture circle and critical cycle process that is relevant to the content of this book and the example provided in steps 1 and 2, it may emerge that the group wants to shift how IEP meetings are run and to also provide parents and caregivers with data that are meaningful to both educators and families, with the ultimate goal of creating more equitable special education service delivery processes and procedures.

This goal has the potential to begin to rupture the "data rich but data poor" codification and transform practice.

Step 4: Through the dialogue around the codifications and the development of shared goals through dialogue, participants engage in a problem-solving process that leads to action, or praxis. *Praxis* is a productive reflection about and action upon the participant's world that leads to transformation.[26] Through dialogue, participants connect their individual lives and experiences to broader social constructs and collectively make plans to transform their social realties in the pursuit of a more just world. The transformative process occurs through "self-empowerment," which is locally situated, constructed and fostered throughout the critical cycle process.[27] During this transformative phase, new issues may emerge that the group takes up on their own, which are then codified, and the critical cycle process begins again.

The four steps of the adapted critical cycle process, as outlined previously, provide guidance on how people can collaboratively engage in a dialogic approach that generates contextually relevant solutions. They also provide the contours for understanding how a pathway for transformative praxis can occur through dialogue that is situated within a critical understanding of the limits of IDEA compliance. As a loosely structured framework, the adapted culture circle and critical cycle process described here is thus designed to challenge the paradox and logic of compliance by asking practitioners to think critically and creatively about their current context. It asks them to see, name, and reflect on how procedural compliance with the IDEA can be used in ways that can both maintain and disrupt inequities for historically marginalized students. Through the dialogic process, the adapted critical cycle process also provides educators with the opportunity to see how the IDEA is currently being used and to also reimagine how the IDEA can be better used to provide educational opportunity and access.

Imagine a professional learning community composed of educators, school psychologists, and family advocates engaging in the adapted culture circle and critical cycle process. A shared codification emerges that is represented as a booklet of the IDEA regulations that is handed out at every IEP meeting for parents and caregivers. The group unpacks why they do this, and they determine that it is done to increase transparency on parental and due-process rights through the IDEA, but they also discuss the fact that it is rarely used. They begin to consider how it is inaccessible and exclusionary due to the heavily technical and legal language in the regulations, especially for families who do not speak English as their primary language. They identify that the codification represents an exclusionary and overly technical response to an adaptive equity concern—the sometimes-limited parent engagement and meaningful discussion with culturally and linguistically diverse families during IEP meetings. Through dialogic reflection and the problem-posing process, the group develops a new approach for sharing the regulations at IEP meetings that is centered on relationship building. This includes restructuring meetings to begin with family and student input, better explaining how the focus of the meeting aligns with the overall purpose and scope of the IDEA, simplifying technical legal language, and offering interpretation and advocacy support to parents and caregivers in every meeting. This represents a first step in a larger, transformative process that would require significant shifts in how IEP meetings are run. It also represents an opportunity to reimagine how the IDEA can be better used to provide educational opportunity and access in a more equitable manner.

Significantly, the adapted culture circle and critical cycle process also provides a framework for educators to identify, name, and disrupt harmful logics of compliance by generating contextually situated and creative pathways rooted in a reflective process that challenges taken-for-granted practices in educational practice. Moreover, the transformative approach is inherently iterative, meaning that the adapted critical cycle process can be and should be revisited as new issues arise. Educators can engage and reengage with the dialogic process numerous times to address emerging challenges and further transform practice. What is required though, is a shared commitment and belief in the process.

At the heart of this process, and in line with Freire's work, is a desire to liberate people from oppressing conditions and realities. With dialogue, limit situations related to how the IDEA is complied with and how it is utilized in practice can be identified and acted upon to break cycles of oppression. This can be done only when the necessary components for authentic dialogue (love, humility, faith, trust, hope, and critical thinking) are honored so that oppression does not become repurposed into another form. In relation to IDEA compliance, this requires, for example, that the components of the logic of compliance are consistently pushed back on and not repurposed to harm or limit educational opportunity.

It requires vigilance, a resistance to routine, and a commitment to reimaging what is and what is possible to transform policy and practice in the service of educational equity. In the example provided previously around family engagement, it means that the work is not done when the IEP meetings were restructured to be less technical. That is just the first step in the process of transformation, as continuous reflection is necessary to continue to improve practice, make IEP meetings more democratic, and assure they are not exclusionary or privilege some groups over others.

In the last chapter of this book, I provide a real-world example of how this adapted culture circle and critical cycle can be used as a powerful framework for guiding educators to think critically about the limits of IDEA compliance and to determine what contextually situated systemic changes are necessary to better achieve educational equity. I show how the dialogic process can inspire change to make visible to readers how adults in positions of power can begin to shift systems toward equity and transformative change.

CHAPTER 7

Developing Just Systems

This chapter contains a story of transformation rooted in an adapted culture circle and critical cycle process as described in chapter 6.[1] In it, two colleagues, both of whom are district-level leaders, joined me to reflect on their journey of professional and personal transformation. We engaged in a loosely structured adapted critical cycle process over a prolonged period of time and used codifications and themes to unpack how their use of multitiered systems of support (MTSS) in their school district were leveraged to improve student outcomes. I first frame how we engaged in the work, and then I briefly define what MTSS is. Then they tell their story. They describe how they came to "aha!" moments through the dialogic process, with and without me, that they reflect on and how these sudden moments of insight led to personal and systems level transformation in their local context. They also articulate how they were able to identify oppressive issues to further develop a critical sociocultural and historical understanding of their environments to foster meaningful change. Their story provides a powerful example for how the dialogic process, responsive to technical and adaptive realities, can begin to shift practice.

Using the Adapted Critical Cycle Process

To begin this chapter, I asked my chapter coauthors, Rebecca (Becky) and Erika, to provide a collaborative positionality statement, much like the one I included in the book's introduction, as this is also part of the work and an honest engagement with the adapted critical cycle process as outlined in this book. Following the statement, I describe how we worked together using an adapted critical cycle process. Their statement is as follows:

> Very often, when writing—both as practitioners and in response to research—we do not reflect nor highlight how our own identities intermix with our body of work. As Boveda and Annamma asserted, "Positionality statements must be more than a listing of identities or a claim on authority through the naming of professional proximity to marginalized communities."[2] We would be remiss if we did not discuss both our positions about how public education serves or does not serve historically marginalized groups. We would also be remiss if we did not also recognize who we are as individuals and the impact that intersectionality has had with our work.
>
> As white, cisgendered, heterosexual women without accessibility issues, we cannot ignore the influence that these categories have on our experience and the ways in

which we both influence and experience our work. There is also power within our degrees that interplays with our relative perspectives and interacts with our work on a day-to-day basis. Patricia Hill Collins reminds us that "challenging power structures from the inside, working the cracks within the system, however, requires learning to speak multiple languages of power convincingly."[3] Recognizing our positionality means understanding how to navigate these structures to create real, sustainable change within educational institutions.

To not firmly stand on the fact that we know that we are awarded certain privileges based not only on our skin color but also on the alignment of our gender identity with biological sex and our positional titles would be to exclude a piece of a puzzle of our work. As Boveda and Annamma cautioned, "Positionality, as it has been taken up, often recenters the powerful or uses researcher proximity to marginalized communities as a rationale for why we are an authority."[4] This reflection pushes us to interrogate how our identities influence our engagement with the work and the power structures within which we operate.

As you read through the practical applications of what we have cocreated and continually refine as an approach, you will clearly see the ground in which our beliefs are rooted and that our creation of systems are meant to disrupt the disproportionate marginalization and segregation of students of color and students with accessibility needs—and most assuredly with those who have an intersection of both. Collins warned, "Suppressing the knowledge produced by any oppressed group makes it easier for dominant groups to rule because the seeming absence of dissent suggests that subordinate groups willingly collaborate in their own victimization."[5] It is imperative that our systems not only acknowledge this but actively center the voices of historically marginalized groups. We actively seek out those who can push our own personal ideologies that may be subconsciously rooted in our positionality, and that stands in contrast to our positions.

The level of privilege that we hold can be counterproductive to the actual work that we are attempting, to the changing of educational systems from within. It is only through the marrying of both, the recognition of our personal identities and personal beliefs, that we can see the relational interplay with each separate school we work in and understand how to leverage the relational processes that we have built so we can step outside of this paradox.

It is incumbent upon all of us to recognize not only our own internal identities but how our identities are perceived by those within our sphere of influence, and to see the complicated intersectionality of the identities and experiences of those we work with and for. One of the key pieces to our success, or at least to our continued devotion to creating equity through a multitiered system of supports, is to continue to bring to the forefront that we reflect on our positionality, our personal identities, and how the context is receiving those perceived identities. Collins stated, "Most activism is brought about by us ordinary people."[6]

True transformation in public education requires the commitment of every stakeholder—students, educators, and community members—to push together for systemic change. We believe that this change is incumbent on our never coming from a place of "saving" public education or anyone whom it serves. Instead, we should be comfortable with acknowledging our power, even as we relinquish leadership to those of a historically marginalized group. It is only through this critical lens that we find contextual space to unpack how to adjust our practice within the school's context while upholding what we are there to do. There is no way to truly honor the intended outcome of our work without keeping our privileged positionality at the forefront and to acknowledge the uncomfortable fact that can come with some of our intersected identities. We must embed them within our didactic reflectional processes in order to continuously push our goals and desired outcomes in this work.

We are both successful products of the public education system, most assuredly a privilege awarded by our perceived identities, and this too has influenced and continues to influence us as we grapple with the best way to adjust and support practices within public education. Being able to hold multiple truths at the same time allows us to use this to our advantage, to ensure we hold up others in the work with us who have not been awarded our privilege of positionality due to their own perceived identities found within those historically marginalized communities. This in turn gives us a small chance at pushing our positions forward by leading sometimes from behind, sometimes in front, and sometimes alongside those colleagues, students, and families.

Our Collective and Transformative Process

Becky, Erika, and I engaged in an adapted critical cycle process intermittently over the course of four years. During this time, I got to know their context and hear their stories, and I was able to develop themes and codifications from these conversations that I then brought to a structured space. I spent a considerable amount of time learning about their context, reading documents, and paying attention to news stories coming from the district. I did this through the lens of compliance and its limits, drawing from some of the frameworks outlined in parts 1 and 2 of this book. Through this lens, I developed codifications that I brought to them. Some of these included reflections on documents they relied on in their educational practice (e.g., MTSS plans). At other times, it included quotes and images compiled from our dialogues that represented reoccurring themes and limit situations in their work. Through the dialogic process, it became clear that the codifications were relevant to their systems-level work developing MTSS to mitigate persistent racial disparities across both general and special education spaces. Our dialogic discussions were conducted over Zoom because of the global pandemic. We talked over Zoom and reflected together, making sense of the world and of the themes and codifications.

One codification that generated significant conversation was related to the following image (figure 7.1). In sharing the image, I relied on the metaphor of standing in quicksand. What I consistently noticed in my work in their district was that there was a plethora of initiatives, mostly grounded within an equity lens—which I characterized as solid ground

Fig. 7.1 Codification

or a shared understanding of purpose and mission—that was also tenuous, like quicksand, because there was literally too much going on around the educators. This diluted their capacity to feel agency and to make substantive and lasting change. On the left and right of the image, I placed words I had repeatedly heard, and together we made sense of this codification. As the facilitator and a participant, I brought the codification to the group, and we talked about it; the sense-making of the codification was established in dialogue. Through open-ended and critical dialogue, we unpacked how both technical and adaptive barriers related to this codification. The transformative work emerged from the dialogic process as Erika and Becky made sense of the codification in relation to their work around MTSS. The dialogic process led to "ah ha!" moments rooted in transformation and possibility, further described in the words of Becky and Erika later in this chapter. This focus was not imposed on the group; rather, it arose organically from our collective learning and reflection around the codification.

Through the dialogic process, I documented emerging insights about our intentions as a group and their educational practices, and I shared reflections with them, in vivo and after the structured dialogues. I also recorded these meetings to ensure that I captured what was happening through dialogue and so that I could translate how the adapted critical cycle process unfolded to others. Through dialogue, and evident in these transcriptions, was the consistent surfacing of "aha!" moments. These "aha!" moments were captured in our transcripts, and I also used these as an opportunity to create a codification again. Erika, Becky, and I would further reflect in dialogue and in alignment with the responsive and iterative nature of the adapted culture circle and critical cycle process. When we engaged in conversation around these "aha!" moments, both Erika and Becky would share a new insight or limit situation related to their leadership, teaching, and learning context and, again, around the use of MTSS to change systems.

The stories and voices from the field that they share discuss how these "aha!" moments extended far beyond our more structured dialogues. Their testimony is a powerful example of how dialogue, rooted in vulnerability and love—for their work, for their students, for their community—can be used to transform practice. I situate their stories within the literature on the purpose, scope, and limitations of MTSS to address broadscale educational inequities.

Multitiered Systems of Support

Multitiered systems of support are a comprehensive framework designed to address the diverse academic, behavioral, and social-emotional needs of students. MTSS is a proactive framework designed to deliver high-quality instruction and interventions tailored to students' varying needs across large systems.[7] MTSS relies on data-driven decision-making, evidence-based interventions, and continuous progress monitoring to ensure that all students receive appropriate and timely supports and services.[8]

MTSS typically refers to response to intervention (RtI) or positive behavioral interventions and supports (PBIS). RtI is academically focused and designed to provide early, systematic support to students who are struggling to meet academic demands.[9] PBIS are focused on promoting positive behavior systems and creating supportive school climates. PBIS are designed to use data-driven decision-making and tiered interventions to address students' varying needs, with a primary focus on behavior and social-emotional well-being.[10]

MTSS are typically structured into three tiers when implemented in schools.[11] Tier 1 represents universal supports provided to all students, including high-quality instruction and proactive classroom management strategies. Tier 2 offers targeted interventions for students who need additional and more specific supports. Tier 3 provides intensive, individualized interventions for students with the most significant needs. If a student does not respond to the tiers of intervention, then a special education evaluation may be appropriate. One of the strengths of MTSS is its potential as an intervention system to promote equity in outcomes, by systematically addressing both academic and behavioral challenges through a tiered approach,

MTSS can mitigate disparities that historically have disproportionately affected students from marginalized communities, including those with disabilities and students of color.[12] However, implementing MTSS is not a simple task. It requires collaboration across all levels of a school system, from district leadership to classroom teachers.[13] Effective implementation also requires adequate professional training, resources, and consistent practices across schools.[14] Without sufficient supports for the tiered intervention framework, schools may struggle to deliver high-quality interventions, exacerbating existing inequities, whereby systemic biases and resource disparities further hinder its effectiveness.[15]

For example, research indicates that Black and Brown students are more likely to face punitive measures for the same behaviors that are overlooked or addressed less harshly than their white peers, even within PBIS frameworks.[16] Many interventions under MTSS, RtI, and PBIS are developed without adequately considering the cultural and linguistic diversity of students, which leads to a failure to resonate with or meet the needs of students from diverse backgrounds.[17] The reliance on data for decision-making in these frameworks can unintentionally exacerbate inequities if the data systems themselves are biased. For example, disciplinary records and standardized test scores often reflect systemic inequities rather than actual student abilities or behaviors, which can lead to inappropriate placement or support decisions.[18]

Therefore, maintaining fidelity to evidence-based practices and ensuring consistent application of interventions across tiers and different classroom contexts is a critical concern.[19] To combat these issues, research indicates that it is necessary to address structural inequities, such as training educators to recognize and mitigate biases when providing interventions and supports to students, to assure more equitable supports.[20]

Given this context, I asked Erika and Becky if they were interested in writing their story of transformation as it related to our process. They agreed and wrote a reflective and insightful piece that highlights the power of dialogue to transform. Their story reflects how dialogue spurred transformation both in our structured space, and more often, they did so with each other organically and independently. Their story, which follows, is a combined voice from the field that makes clear that these two authors and colleagues push each other both professionally and personally with a spirit of love, humility, faith, trust, and hope and through critical thinking.

Stories and Voices from the Field

Becky and Erika's reflection highlights the importance of iterative dialogue and reflection, whereby dialogical discussion rooted in praxis can lead to transformation. It also highlights the tension between technical and adaptive mechanisms embedded within systemic change efforts. Their story underscores the importance of engaging in critical reflection to move beyond surface-level policy compliance and, also, how hard that work is.

> There is an element of serendipity in how the two of us came to work together in a district at the time that we did, with the particular leadership that was in place. We often reflect on our fortune to have the impetus of true equity work in our organization spearheaded by the leaders at the very top of the organization who were, in some ways, openly tackling disproportionality, bias, and racism within education before many others in the field. Working under the superintendent leading the organization at the time, we were given the opportunity to deliberately push the thinking of the organization away from simple compliance toward understanding the historical marginalization of our students and their families and what it could mean in relation to our current educational practices.
>
> Over time, we have seen turnover in leadership, both at the superintendent level and cabinet level, as well as at the building level. There are fewer of us who remain from the beginning of this work that was overtly directed at addressing systemic racism and disproportionality. We grounded ourselves in research to do this, but overtime, words such as antiracism and even bias have been replaced within the organization by equity and inclusion. For the two of us, living and working within the organization through four

superintendents and a cabinet and school board that has turned over twice-fold, the evolution for us has occurred slowly over time, and it continues to feel as if we are within that snowball effect, gaining momentum and evolving, as the two of us continue to learn through reflection and our open dialogue with one another that allows us to remain grounded in the work.

Today, we continue to root our work in research and learning from experts. However, the biggest change for us has been that our learning and leading is not driven by experts delivering professional development to us but is instead found within the dialogue we are having with those with whom we work directly, at both the highest levels of the organization and down into the classrooms themselves. By listening and by engaging in dialogue, we have been able to build an understanding of the context and perspectives of others, which in turn has allowed us, over time, to build and deepen relationships, where space is created to have brave conversations and where we can unpack the *what* and *where* in the system inequity is occurring.

If we were to attempt to create something akin to a formula for other leaders to replicate, a formula that creates space for one to test just how rigid their systems are in terms of upholding inequity in the name of compliance, it would begin with multitiered systems of support.

For us, MTSS has been the foundation on which we have built all of our work. It has helped us initially identify places in our system where adhering strictly to compliance has actually reduced or even eliminated opportunities for our most vulnerable students. In the beginning, we knew that to change our system from one that reacts after a student had "failed" to one that prevents failure through the structures of MTSS, we first had to build a foundational knowledge of what MTSS is and concurrently stop focusing solely on individual student stories. This required a shift to a focus on the system of educational failure we had inherited and were, in fact, perpetuating. We knew that this would not be an easy lift, as the very system that we were questioning is the same one that had produced, and continues to produce, the same teachers and leaders who work in schools with children that often look nothing like them—white teachers and white administrators produced by a system that was created to produce the results that were being produced. Our journey consists of the knowledge that disproportionality lives not just in the student outcomes as it relates to literacy and math but also in the very image of the white teacher standing in that room of Black and Brown children and that compliance is not only the name of the game but often the only way to "win," or at least to stay off a state list for not meeting accountability measures.

An example of this would be how we used to review student outcome data to identify supports for students, such as Tier 2 or Tier 3 interventions. We now understand that we are making an assumption that it is the students who are not responding rather than the adults who are not providing. Our dialogue, when looking at data, has shifted to include the requirement that whenever we look at student outcome data, we must also look at the actual fidelity of intervention that the adults are providing. We understand that our students come to us as they are, and it is our responsibility to understand not only their needs but their strengths as well, and it is us, not the students, who must adapt and design the supports needed. We do this by looking at the whole child within our MTSS framework.

However, if we lived only within the framework of MTSS and did not develop the understanding that it is simply that, a framework, we would not still be engaged in true organizational change. Simply following a process, even one as evidenced based as MTSS, cannot adequately address disproportionality and inequity.

Our journey and work are not just about system change, they are actually about us growing and changing along with the system. Unbeknownst to us, we were engaging in dialogue with each other and learning from our mistakes. Part of our formula has been to not only reflect on the structures we have outlined in what MTSS in our district looks like (engaging the minds of those we are leading and working alongside) but also reflecting together and with those with whom we are engaged in the work (changing hearts). At first, it was a question of moving away from compliance only as a tool for change. But through our own conversations, we have learned that it has become a fine balancing act between compliance of federal, state, and local laws with the integrity of what research tells us and what we know is best for our students. To an extent, compliance is necessary to ensure consistency of practices and procedures. Compliance without deep understanding, though, does not work. Simply asking educators to complete a referral form for a student with evidence of multiple iterations of intervention backed by data is not effective unless the educators understand that the most reliable way to identify a learning disability is by looking at the many approaches used to support and teach that student, and then they can compare their outcome data to like peers to demonstrate that it is a true lack of growth and progress, despite intensive interventions delivered with fidelity.

We have discussed the importance of reflection and dialogue as a way to continuously review the work, our thinking, and the outcomes we are producing in order to ensure that we are actually shifting the data and hitting our goals. Over the past six years, some of the biggest breakthroughs that we experienced have occurred because we have moved beyond just engaging in that reflective dialogue with each other and have purposefully started to engage in it with others. We have used the leverage of our roles as leaders of MTSS to pull a chair up to every single table within our district, whether it is a teacher-led professional learning community or a superintendent cabinet meeting, to present information, ask the right questions, model a conversation between each other in front of those groups of how to build off of ideas, generate new ones, or even admit that something isn't working and deciding to reverse course. It means we have intentionally and openly, and at times with true vulnerability, admitted when we missed something (for example, not providing enough professional development around the purpose of MTSS prior to rolling out the first version of our manual). It has created a synergy between the two of us as educational leaders that we can bring into other teams and have it be cocreated within their teaming.

If we were to sit with the idea of a formula to address systems change that improves outcomes for our most vulnerable students, we would lift the recognition that the systems within general education need to be adjusted to address inequities before we could address inequities in special education. We would also address the importance of understanding context. Had we not had the initial leadership nearly a decade ago that began the work in systems change, inequality in education, and disproportionality, our work would be in a very different place. Having a framework that is grounded in research, such as MTSS in our organizational context, is also another key piece of this formula. Finally, learning how to engage in meaningful conversations with other leaders—and with those you lead—requires creating space to recognize ideas, acknowledge both spoken and unspoken agreements, and navigate disagreement with respect. These kinds of dialogues encourage people to take risks, fostering the trust and patience needed to embrace the uncertainty and complexity that come with building something new. It is through these very discussions where we continue to have our "aha!" moments, those moments where something is said and we understand in that very moment where we have failed in our own communication or where the system is flawed and needs to be adjusted or sometimes even subverted. These discussions provide us with the important qualitative data we need in order to understand where we must shift and adjust at a contextual level.

Even if you are building something as simple as a behavior response protocol within a building, you are simultaneously tearing down previously held beliefs, behaviors, and systems that were held by the people running the building as a collective and hoping to help them understand the roles they may hold in maintaining the disproportionate or inequitable outcomes the data are showing. Even when systems do not work for students, or even adults, it is important to acknowledge that it is naturally uncomfortable when making a change. Once you've engaged in that dialogical process with a team and they start to make changes, leaders cannot just end there. They must continuously reengage with the team, its conversations, and the system process that is happening in that particular context. They must be clear on the change they are intending to create and to then closely monitor the impact of that change through data. It is an ever-evolving, organic process that needs to be nurtured and never abandoned. Otherwise, everything, once again, simply becomes an act of compliance rather than an effort to improve a system and its outcomes.

In developing this level of continuous improvement, there come opportunities for what has evolved for us. This is having another leader to reflect on the system within the system and to push each other to keep reflecting, refining, and readjusting our approach as the different contexts demand. Other leaders can find their coconspirators within these authentic experiences in conversation about what is seemingly a simple plan. Those are the people who can continue the work when you are not there, and you begin to do what we have done, which is write a manual, then intentionally ignite others with the ideas of how to work within the zone of compliance but work in a manner that still challenges whether or not compliance is the goal or if what we are doing to get to compliance is working. We may not be able to change a law, but we can change the way we move toward fulfilling a requirement, as compliance is nothing more than meeting a mark. And true educational equity means you can check a box but continuously question how we check that box.

This next "aha!" moment is one that is somewhat hard to swallow, as it shows our own ignorance and narrow focus that was serving to perpetuate inequities. This can be illustrated by our initial hyperfocus on only racial disparities in education to such a degree that when our own leadership changed, we felt the chafe of someone introducing how complex the intersectionality is of race, ableism, sexism, and classism is and their role in disproportionality. We did not acknowledge our exclusion of the concept of intersectionality, and, to the detriment of students, our mistake led to the exclusion of other historically marginalized identities and how MTSS supported their interface in our educational organization. This was never more apparent than most recently, when we began engaging in conversations at the building level with teams about multilingual and/or English language learners (MLLs/ELLs) student outcome data. This data in turn caused us to talk about our own procedures around identification of MLLs/ELLs as potential students with disabilities where we found significant disproportionality. Because MTSS plays a crucial role in the identification of students with disabilities, we knew we had to go back to our guidance document in the MTSS manual and our current systems, the lack of our own knowledge on this topic, and what we had not yet addressed for this student population. We had created a MTSS guidance manual, outlining a system we felt addressed inequities but where the mention of anything about the specific needs of MLLs/ELLs and second language acquisition, its development, and impact on learning was nowhere to be found.

In our most recent iteration of our MTSS guidance manual, there have been several additions that have come from digging into the research around what we needed to know specifically around MTSS and supporting MLLs/ELLs. This was paired with continued reflective dialogue between just the two of us and other leaders outside of the organization with a particular expertise around MLLs/ELLs, language acquisition, and how the phases of language acquisition can in fact mirror characteristics of speech and language delays or learning disabilities.

Another huge "aha!" moment occurred during one conversation that we were engaging in as we were working on cocreating professional development for our positive behavioral intervention and support teams. As mentioned previously within our discussion, we realized quite suddenly that you cannot review student outcome data without also reviewing fidelity data. As soon as measuring fidelity of intervention was discussed in our planning, it was as if a lightbulb went off, and we realized that we had missed a huge piece of our system's puzzle. We could not reliably measure our student outcomes, even at an aggregate level, if we did not also measure and review the fidelity within which we were delivering instruction and interventions. In other words, we could not just use measurement of student proficiency. Rather, first, we must ensure that there is a level of adult proficiency. How could we say that our student outcome data was both valid and reliable if each adult in the system was delivering instruction or providing services differently across our classrooms and buildings? Over the past two years, we have delicately engaged in discussion around fidelity of implementation around curriculum in programming, instruction, and even processes designed within MTSS. The tricky part is that we are asking for adult compliance from within the organization in the form of nonnegotiables and clearly laid out processes that are designed to ensure fidelity of MTSS processes and adult behaviors. The fine line we are continuously walking is ensuring that the leaders and staff within the organization are not just engaging in the processes simply to get through the process or to get to the Committee on Special education (CSE) table but rather that they understand that, by following these processes and procedures outlined in our MTSS process, they are in fact creating a more effective and efficient system that will ultimately result in better, and hopefully proportionate, outcomes for all students.

If we did not continuously return to our dialogical process to identify problems or inequities in the system and reflect with each other on our product and process, we would remain static, thus perpetuating inequities for both general education and special education students. One must stay diligent in creating that time to return to your original work and to sometimes lay it bare for others to reflect on too.

So where do we, personally as leaders, go from here? One thing that holds constant is that context matters. In our context, this means we are still in the thick of our work on implementation of MTSS and in confronting all the barriers that continue to exist in changing hearts and then minds. For our organization, change happens when proof of effectiveness is provided, at least initially. Our organization is an interesting mix of externally viewed positional authority that masks the true relational power that affects any change of our systems and practices. Without trust from those that do the work with those that think up the work, there is no change for our organization. Over time, the two of us have been able to build trust and relationships with upper leadership to help them understand the change we have been trying to implement with the staff with whom we work to put these changes into action. We have learned that simply stating the research or rolling out the processes and procedures of MTSS is not enough. We must often sit side by side with those with whom we work and engage in dialogue that allows us to understand each other's perspectives and come to a collective agreement on how to move forward. We remain committed—perhaps even more today—to addressing the inequitable educational outcomes for historically marginalized groups, for continuing the conversation related to disproportionality in general and special education, and, to tag a line from our first year together in our organization, to be true "guardians of equity and access." We do this through questioning, through reflection, and through continuous dialogue with each other and those who are in this work with us.

Reflection

This chapter demonstrates how codifications and themes can serve as catalysts for transformative changes to practice when they are grounded in the localized knowledge and expertise of practitioners. The sustained and iterative process that I engaged in with Becky and Erika, rooted in deep listening, contextual inquiry, and mutual trust, allowed us to surface systemic constraints and collaboratively envision how more equitable use of the policies, practices, and procedures surrounding IDEA implementation and MTSS could occur. The process honored and built on Becky's and Erika's lived experiences, professional expertise, and leadership. The sustained and recurring reflective process allowed themes and codifications to continue to emerge from their expertise and to continue to influence the reflective and transformative process that lays the groundwork for sustained, systems-level equity shifts.

Throughout their narrative, the "aha!" moments also functioned as *codifications*—concrete realizations that illuminated systemic challenges or contradictions within current practices, beliefs, or leadership approaches. A critical moment that they articulate and that had a significant impact on their practice was expanding their understanding of intersectionality and how these understandings relate to the educational inequities they were working to address. The "aha!" moment opened space for them to reconsider the limitations of their existing equity framework and approach. Similarly, the discovery that their MTSS manual lacked any attention to the specific needs of MLLs/ELLs exposed another "aha!" moment, prompting further critical reflection on how such omissions contribute to patterns of misidentification and exclusion across intersecting identities. These "aha!" moments arose through the adapted culture circle and critical cycle process and our collective dialogic engagement and reflection grounded in their local expertise and organizational and contextual realities. In summary, this process empowered them to challenge assumptions, surface systemic barriers, and take targeted action, providing a powerful foundation for continuous engagement with equity-driven change.

* * *

Looking Forward

The need to rehumanize compliance—and, more importantly, to rehumanize one another in the process—is a critical step toward building relationally rooted educational systems that can disrupt the harms related to the paradox and logic of compliance. Rehumanizing compliance requires us to move beyond a technocratic understanding of the law and instead view compliance as a practice of care, dignity, and mutual accountability. Thie requires that the *need* to comply is destabilized and reframed, not as a bureaucratic requirement, but into a more humanizing practice—one that rebuilds trust and one that can meaningfully address the deep harms caused by historically situated systems of exclusion that continue to influence the structure of schooling. Moreover, working to rehumanize acts of compliance that rupture the binary between technical and adaptive mechanisms can further promote collective efficacy and shared responsibility for systems change. It can encourage educators to reflect on how their own perspectives influence their interpretation of the IDEA. They can use this as a starting point for engaging in a critical analysis of their environments and to create systems that center relationships so that we can cultivate educational environments that not only meet legal requirements but also affirm the dignity, expertise, and agency of every person working, teaching, learning, and experiencing the impacts of policy enactments.

To move beyond the impasse and unproductive conditions surrounding the paradox and logic of compliance, compliance must be reimagined not as the ceiling but as a foundation of educational commitments. It also needs to be revitalized in a way that acknowledges everyone has a story and a lived experience that needs to be recognized and honored when we work to provide educational opportunity and access. Resisting constraining practices, systems, and structures, collectively, is one way to begin to recognize this in everyday educational practice.

Within this context, the adapted culture circle and critical cycle process described in this book can encourage meaningful reflection at the intersection of technical compliance (procedural compliance) and adaptive compliance, which considers the sociocultural, historical, interpersonal, and institutional factors influencing the implementation of laws and policy. When these two components are considered in critical dialogue with each other, educators have the capacity to name and transcend current limit situations to shift practices. By engaging in an adapted critical cycle process, educators can critically examine often overlooked dimensions of educational practice that profoundly impact student lives and schooling experiences as they relate to IDEA compliance. Ultimately, the critical dialogic process can help foster a contextually situated reimagining of IDEA compliance and the purpose of the IDEA.

This book is only a starting point, and it is framed in a way that begins with us, the adults, and our need to cultivate deeper reflection in our practices. But it must not end there. The adapted critical cycle process emphasizes intentional reflection, open dialogue, collective commitment to change, and strategies to reimagine the purpose and function of IDEA compliance. This transformative and reflective process must extend beyond the confines of the process outlined in this book and purposefully involve students and community members, centering the voices of those most affected by systemic racism, ableism, and other inequities present in school systems. It also must continue to evolve and prioritize collaboration to dismantle inequities. The transformative process is done in community with each other, and it must expand beyond us, the adults within schools, to foster systemic equity and inclusion.

AFTERWORD

I first came to know Catherine Voulgarides at a gathering she co-facilitated—a rare academic space where people were invited not just to talk theory, but also to interrogate power. The convening brought together scholars committed to confronting the intersecting systems of ableism and racism embedded in U.S. educational institutions. Catherine's scholarship does not simply reveal the persistent injustices that occur under the guise of compliance; it demands that we reimagine what justice can and should look like in schools. Since our initial meeting, our paths have continued to cross in ways that have deepened both our scholarship and shared commitments. It is no surprise that this book reflects the same intellectual clarity and thoughtfulness Catherine brings to every space she inhabits.

Reading this book is like sitting in on a series of urgent, vulnerable, and radically honest conversations about what it means to "do equity work" inside systems that were never designed for disability justice. Catherine offers more than critique—she makes visible the deeply entrenched logics of compliance that sustain inequities in special education, particularly for racially and linguistically minoritized students with disabilities. This book is especially timely. We are living in a moment when critical frameworks like Critical Race Theory and DisCrit are under coordinated political attack, all while the very inequities they expose deepen in our schools and institutions. The IDEA, though born of movements for equity and access, is now too often weaponized as a shield for bureaucratic inertia. Educators can perform compliance and be rewarded for it—even as students of color with disabilities are excluded, silenced, and misunderstood.

As a scholar grounded in Black feminist thought and influenced by Paulo Freire's emancipatory vision of education, I read these chapters with deep resonance. Black feminism has taught us to reject binaries—between intention and impact, between care and control, between legal compliance and transformative justice. Freire and bell hooks remind us that no transformation is possible without a dialogic, critical process rooted in hope and humility. Catherine's work stands firmly within that intellectual lineage, demanding we attend to how power, identity, and bureaucracy intersect in the daily decisions practitioners make. In my own work, I often say that intersectionality is not simply about checking boxes; it's about fundamentally rethinking systems. Catherine has done just that—interrogating the legal, structural, and emotional economies of special education with precision and care. She models what it means to be both critical and constructive. Hers is an invitation to pause our impulse to "fix" and instead to cultivate dialogue, vulnerability, and shared responsibility.

Among the most impactful aspects of this book is the way it situates educators—not as passive implementers of policy—but as agents with the capacity to interrogate, reflect, and transform. Through the adapted critical cycle and dialogic process, Catherine does not merely call for change—she scaffolds how to engage in it. This approach aligns with those of us who understand that professional learning and educational leadership must be dialogic, intersectionally conscious, and grounded in praxis.

Across these chapters, we are asked to confront the dissonance between what schools *say* they are doing—complying with IDEA, providing support, attending to disparities—and the lived realities of students and families. Catherine's conceptualizations, particularly around "fragmented harm" and "symbolic compliance," are not abstract—they speak to what actually happens in an IEP meeting that goes through the motions without centering the child. They name how compliance can function as a shield for adults while students continue to be disproportionately sorted, labeled, and denied access. For those who have walked through these chapters, I hope you have felt the productive discomfort that signals growth. I hope you've reflected on your own positionalities, as the district leaders in Chapter 7 did. And most of all, I hope you are compelled to move—beyond symbolic compliance and toward practices that are liberatory, humanizing, and sustaining.

This book refuses easy answers. Instead, it moves toward possibility, offering frameworks for adapted culture circles and dialogic critical cycles—approaches that echo the Freirean belief that systemic transformation begins with collective self-transformation. And I must underscore how powerful it is to see this praxis enacted with practitioners who hold privileged identities yet are willing to interrogate how their social positioning shapes the systems they lead. This is what Black feminism calls for: truth-telling, accountability, relational care, and centering lived experiences in our collective pursuit of justice.

Ultimately, what this book offers is an invitation. It calls us to move from compliance to criticality, from professional detachment to relational accountability—to acknowledge that "good intentions" are not enough. Policy without praxis will never be sufficient. Our students—especially those navigating the intersections of racism, ableism, linguistic discrimination, and poverty—deserve more than symbolic gestures.

So, what are our next steps?

We recommit. We expand our coalitions. We sit in circles. We read the codifications of our systems and reimagine them. We resist the comfort of procedural correctness—what I call "charm school social justice,"—and name discomfort not as a barrier but as an entry point into transformation. This book is not a conclusion but a provocation—and I am grateful to Catherine for having the courage to write it and refusing to accept compliance as a proxy for justice.

Let us now have the courage to respond.

Dr. Mildred Boveda
Associate Professor of Education, Special Education
The Pennsylvania State University

APPENDIX

Applying the Critical Cycle Process

In this appendix, I outline how the paradox and logic of compliance can be challenged at the local level using a dialogic process rooted in the insights gained from this book. At the heart of this process, and in line with the ethos of Freire's critical pedagogy, is a desire to liberate people from oppressing conditions and realities. With dialogue, limit situations can be identified and acted upon to break cycles of oppression. This can only be done when the necessary components for authentic dialogue (love, humility, faith, trust, hope, and critical thinking) are honored so that oppression does not become repurposed into another form.

In relation to IDEA compliance, this requires that, for example, the components of the logic of compliance are consistently pushed back upon and not repurposed to harm or continue to limit educational opportunity. It requires a vigilance and pushback to routine and a commitment to reimaging what is and can be possible to transform policy and practice in the service of educational equity. In the following sections, I provide some process steps and a roadmap of sorts for integrating theory and practice through reflection (praxis) by leveraging the themes presented in parts 1 and 2 of this book to challenge the paradox and logic of compliance through an adaptive and technical lens. It is important to note, again, that the process is not and should not be prescriptive, therefore these are just guidelines to get started.

Suggestions on Process

What is discussed here are not rigid directives but flexible suggestions that educators can adapt to their unique contexts and needs. I outline who can be potential participants in the dialogic process, and then I briefly outline a process for establishing the conditions to engage in an adapted critical cycle process.

Participants

Anyone can be included in the adapted critical cycle and dialogic process. In this book and with the framing of the content of this book, the work begins with the adults working in schools, but the work should not end there. It should extend to others and to a much broader community context.

I suggest that the first participants in the adapted critical cycle and dialogic process could be those whose work is directly involved with the IDEA compliance process, as these individuals are typically steeped in the technical components of compliance. However, drawing from technical assistance work focused on addressing racialized inequities in special education, the number and identity of participants can also be much more expansive and include individuals such as school and district administrators, educators from all disciplines and grade levels, related service providers, curriculum and instructional planners, students, families, and community members.[1] As more people with varying roles that extend beyond those whose work are directly involved with the IDEA compliance process are included, the nature of the technical and adaptive questions presented in this appendix will likely evolve in response to the needs and concerns of the community members engaging in the iterative and dialogic process.

The adapted culture circle and critical cycle process requires a diverse array of participants to foster collaboration as we work to reimagine how educational systems can be transformed as they relate to compliance and policy enactments. And while the process may start by being grounded in the limits of the IDEA, it is expected that it will extend beyond these confines, much like the example provided in chapter 7 that showed how Becky and Erika, in their own voices, moved through multifaceted and varied processes of transformation.

It is important to note, though, that the success of the dialogic and iterative process requires the capacity of participants to be vulnerable. Therefore, as readers consider how to engage in an adapted critical cycle process, it is important to understand the six conditions that Freire set forth as necessary for authentic dialogue to occur: love, humility, faith, trust, hope, and critical thinking. These can be difficult preconditions to establish for the dialogic process because they require a deep willingness of participants to commit to changing their conditions in ways that humanize and rehumanize people, policies, and practices and also require that they reflect on their own role in systems of oppressions.[2] As the "Stories and Voices from the Field" in parts 1 and 2 show, nearly every educator described some sort of disassociation from themselves or their professional expertise when complying with the IDEA or using the IDEA to support their students and/or enact special education processes and procedures guided by the provisions of the act. This reflection requires vulnerability. Therefore, the conditions and elements of authentic dialogue as outlined by Freire must be present, and people engaged in the dialogic and critical cycle process must be willing to learn from and with each other through the process of transformation.

Process

The process described here is rooted in the contents of this book. It assumes that readers are reading this appendix after having read parts 1 and 2. What is presented here is a more detailed account of how the questions and prompts at the end of each chapter can be acted on and can provide insight into the relationship between the technical and adaptive components of compliance.

Reflect on the Role of IDEA Compliance in Your Context

- Engage in exploratory work around IDEA compliance that is situated within your sociocultural, historical, and lived realities of your environment. Use the questions at the end of each chapter and outlined in this appendix to reflect on the tensions between technical and adaptive realties when pursuing educational equity and record your thoughts.

Generate Themes and Codifications and then Represent the Codification

- Based on your reflections and answers, generate themes that are deeply connected to your lived experiences and social reality within your school. The themes can and should be open ended, should engage with the particulars of your context and your experiences, and should be framed in a way that you can share them with peers if you so desire. If you plan to engage in the critical cycle process with colleagues, a facilitator must be designated to cull the themes from individuals that can be turned into a codification that represents some kind of meaningful representation of the collective experiences of you and your peers as it relates to IDEA compliance. The themes, in response to the content of this book, should build on each other and intersect across components of the paradox and logic of compliance. They should be understood in the aggregate and lead to codifications that do not represent an individual narrative or experience but rather represent some kind of collective experience across responses. The codification can be something such as a small composite story, a photo or series of photos, an object like an IEP compliance manual, or a due process complaint. Most importantly, the codification should reflect an aspect of your peers' shared experiences and should resonate with their cultural and social context, understandings, and experiences with the IDEA, ultimately serving as meaningful tool to support contextually grounded dialogue and reflection. The group should agree that the artifacts and codifications brought to the group resonate with the participants' cultural and social contexts so they can be used to generate contextually situated conversation.

Bring Together and Engage a Group

- Bring together a group of peers who can engage with the themes and codifications related to IDEA compliance gleaned from parts 1 and 2 of this book. This can be a formal or informal gathering, but it is important that everyone is welcomed and willing to engage as an equal participant in the dialogic process. While the facilitator may have helped develop the codification, they will also learn with and from the group as they help build dialogue around the codified themes and tangible artifacts. A designated facilitator can present the codified theme to the group using the prepared artifact(s). They, along with the group, should then build conversations that delve into the participants' shared experiences and collective understandings of the artifact and the challenges or limit situations they note in relation to the codification. Knowledge is coconstructed through the dialogic process, with dialogue always remaining at the center of the meaning-making process. This requires that the group remain cognizant of and committed to the core conditions of authentic dialogue as described by Freire (humility, faith, trust, hope, and critical thinking).[3]
- As the group is engaged in dialogue over time, there can and should be variability in how participants are physically organized. The dialogic process is flexible.

One suggestion is that participants are seated in a circle. This can foster a sense of equality and mutual engagement that eliminates physical, relational, and professional hierarchies during the dialogic process. In chapter 7, I describe how the dialogic process took place over Zoom, highlighting how this space can be flexible. One of the most important factors in setting up the group is that all individuals are active participants in the process, including the facilitator. And as previously highlighted, the conversations and dialogic flow should be flexible and adaptive to the group's dynamics. Moreover, participants must take ownership of the dialogic process, fostering a collaborative environment where everyone actively contributes to and shapes the direction of the conversation.

Movement Toward Transformation

- As the dialogic process unfolds, whether in one session or across multiple sessions, the facilitator, with the support of the group, can build understandings of the codification that move from critical sense-making to an action-oriented frame that is geared toward addressing the systemic issues reflected in the themes represented in the codification. This can be done through the dialogical process as participants identify and name pressing issues, brainstorm solutions collaboratively on how to address these issues, and define actionable goals related to the codification. Importantly, participants should feel as though they can take ownership of the dialogic and transformative process. And participants should assure that all action plans or discussions are firmly rooted in their collective shared experiences.

Reflect and Reengage

- As the adapted culture circle and critical cycle process unfolds, new issues will constantly emerge through dialogue and reflection. The themes, codifications, dialogue, and action planning process will recur multiple times. The concluding chapter of this book highlights how integral the ongoing nature of the dialogic process is for sustaining transformation. The group can reenter the adapted culture circle and critical cycle process numerous times as new issues emerge and lead to continuous reflection, raised consciousness, and, ultimately, transformation.

Enacting Praxis

The themes and insights from the first two parts of the book are intended to highlight vulnerabilities within individual practices and the systemic issues that persist despite efforts to address them. These insights should be shared and discussed with colleagues, sparking collaborative action to transform practices into approaches that better serve everyone. Therefore, here I provide critical prompts rooted in the content of each chapter. The prompts are intentionally designed to juxtapose the technical and the adaptive components of educational practice. They are also the foundation for developing pathways for transformation that can disrupt the paradox and logic of compliance through a technical and adaptive framework. These prompts serve as critical tools for deepening understanding, encouraging reflection, and equipping educators with actionable strategies for systemic change rooted in the content of this book. Far more than simple prompts, they are also integral to internalizing key concepts related to the paradox and logic of compliance.

It is important to note again that the prompts listed here are nonexhaustive and serve as a starting point for reflection and transformation within an adapted culture circle and critical cycle process focused on IDEA compliance as outlined in this book. They are designed to draw from our understanding of technical compliance, which refers to adherence to IDEA mandates, and to adaptive compliance, which refers to the conditions (e.g., contexts, belief systems, personal and professional experiences) surrounding technical acts of compliance. Moreover, through these prompts, readers can explore how the convergence and divergence between technical and adaptive realities offer opportunities for praxis, allowing readers to better understand how their localized experiences connect to broader themes of equity and to transformation.

Enacting the Themes of Chapter 1

Chapter 1 invites educators to critically examine the historical foundations of IDEA and the paradox of compliance, assessing how its civil rights origins continue to shape educational practice. By engaging with an overview of the IDEA's key provisions, readers have access points for analyzing how broader societal ideologies have shaped the development of the IDEA and the pursuit of equal equational opportunity through it. Applying an intersectional lens, readers are also encouraged to explore the ways in which systemic structures influence their professional decisions, encouraging reflection on how personal experiences related to disability and difference shape their perspectives and how these perspectives interact with, or are constrained by, institutional realities. The following critical prompts are offered to guide readers in evaluating the intersection of the IDEA's legal framework, the adaptive realities of implementation, and their own beliefs about disability and educational equity.

Technical Compliance

- Outline your technical knowledge of the IDEA and what you understand to be its central purpose. Connect these answers to the core provisions of the IDEA (2004).
- Describe how you see and experience the way the technical aspects of the IDEA are enacted in educational practice daily. Consider what, for example, FAPE, LRE, and IEP development look like in everyday educational practice.

Adaptive Compliance:

- Define your own personal vision and/or mission for education and special education. Consider how this vision and/or mission developed and critical factors influencing it.
- Articulate your "why" for being an educator. Consider what connects you to the work you do from a personal and a professional standpoint and what drives you to persist in the field.

Theme Generation for the Adapted Critical Cycle Process

1. Compare and contrast your technical and adaptive responses either alone or with colleagues.

2. Reflect on how your personal biography, vision, and mission towards education relates to how special education functions in your work setting.
3. Reflect on any moral and/or ethical tensions that arise for you between your technical and adaptive responses.
4. Note the gaps, convergences, and divergences in your reflections.
5. Generate an overarching theme that is responsive to the gaps, convergences, and divergences. The theme can start with a statement as simple as "I notice. . . "
6. Consider an object, picture, or artifact that embodies the theme you notice. Consider bringing this "codification" to the adapted critical cycle process.[4]

Enacting the Themes of Chapter 2

Chapter 2 examines a key dimension of the paradox of compliance: how the broad goals of the IDEA are directed into technical accountability measures known as the state performance plan indicators (SPP), which are designed to monitor outcomes for students with disabilities across a variety of domains. Readers are asked to grapple with the need to balance procedural compliance with their commitment to providing equitable student supports and services under the highly proceduralized and individualized nature of the IDEA and the associated accountability measures, revealing how organizational pressures stemming from the need to comply with the IDEA can constrain educator efforts to achieve meaningful change. The following critical prompts are designed to spark inquiry into the organizational impact of IDEA compliance leading to critical inquiry into the gap between policy intent and implementation dynamics. They are also designed to prompt readers to consider how professional discretion and systemic constraints influence special education service delivery decisions.

Technical Compliance

- Outline who you communicate with most often when making educational decisions for students with disabilities and when implementing the IDEA (e.g., administrators, teachers, related service providers, caregivers).
- Describe who (e.g., related service providers, teachers) and what resources (e.g., certain departments, academic and behavioral interventions) you rely on to serve students with disabilities and why these people and resources are important when implementing the IDEA.
- Describe how special education service delivery decisions are made from the district to the school level. Consider what processes and procedures are followed and articulate why these choices are made.

Adaptive Compliance

- Describe what IDEA compliance looks like and feels like on a daily basis in your context. Add details about what you feel, see, and experience when you comply with the IDEA. Provide insights into and reflect on why you have these reactions to IDEA compliance.
- Describe which aspects of the special education process demand most of your time and attention (e.g., completing IEPs) and how this relates to your articulation of what IDEA compliance looks like and feels like on a daily basis.

Theme Generation for the Adapted Critical Cycle Process

1. Compare and contrast your technical and adaptive responses either alone or with colleagues.
2. Reflect on how your understandings of the purpose and function of the IDEA relate to your experiences with IDEA administration and special education service delivery and how these factors unfold in your professional settings.
3. Reflect on any moral and/or ethical tensions that arise for you between your technical and adaptive responses.
4. Note the gaps, convergences, and divergences in your reflections.
5. Generate an overarching theme that is responsive to the gaps, convergences, and divergences in your reflections. The theme can start with a statement as simple as "I notice. . . "
6. Consider an object, picture, or artifact that embodies the theme you notice. Consider bringing this "codification" to the adapted critical cycle process.[5]

Enacting the Themes of Chapter 3

Chapter 3 examines the first force shaping the logic of compliance: current contexts. It analyzes how contemporary schooling conditions are rooted in historical inequities that continue to shape IDEA implementation dynamics. Drawing on Ladson-Billings's concept of the educational debt, the chapter provides readers with deeper understandings into how accumulated systemic disparities across moral, economic, sociopolitical, and historical dimensions influence the provision of special education services in current contexts and especially for BISOC.[6] By making these connections between the past and the present, the chapter allows readers to understand how past injustices inform present-day constraints and educational inequities. The prompts provided below are designed to push readers to analyze how historical and structural inequities continue to shape their professional decisions, relationships, and approaches to special education service delivery. They also encourage readers to identify and ultimately challenge situational inequities and counterproductive compliance practices that weaken IDEA's mission and their own personal convictions. Furthermore, the prompts are designed to push readers to interrogate how a reliance on technical compliance fails to address deeper structural issues affecting special education service delivery, necessitating reflection upon the root causes of educational disparities in their own contexts and the consideration of how their professional practices either reinforce or disrupt these patterns.

Technical Compliance

- Describe the larger community within which you work, demographically. Include factors such as the racial, ethnic, and linguistic characteristics of the students and families in the community, the teaching workforce, migration and immigration patterns, dominant languages spoken, and so on. Use data to support your descriptions of these factors.
- Collect and disaggregate data to identify which groups of students, by various demographic factors, have access to various programs and supports (e.g., gifted and talented, special education self-contained classrooms).[7]

Adaptive Compliance

- Describe any common narratives, histories, or assumptions about your work context (e.g., LEA or school level), the community, and its students. For example, consider: is there a right and wrong side of the track in the community? Is there a housing development that a particular demographic or group of students come from? Is there a particular image of who a successful student is in the district or school? Write down the assumptions and beliefs associated with these narratives and how they may influence how educators understand the students and families they work with.
- Articulate who is often served well in special education or who tends to receive the most resources and supports. Consider how these narratives relate to the broader demographic and historical context of your work environment. Consider describing what this may look like in an IEP meeting or in a special education classroom (e.g., who receives better services and supports than others).

Theme Generation for the Adapted Critical Cycle Process:

1. Compare and contrast your technical and adaptive responses, either alone or with colleagues.
2. Reflect on how the current context of your work environment explicitly and implicitly impacts educators in your setting and especially in relation to special education service delivery. Also consider how these current contexts relate to historical narratives about your school or district.

3. Reflect on any moral and ethical tensions that arise for you between your technical and adaptive responses.
4. Note the gaps, convergences, and divergences in your reflections.
5. Generate an overarching theme that is responsive to the gaps, convergences, and divergences in your reflections. The theme can start with a statement as simple as "I notice. . ."
6. Consider an object, picture, or artifact that embodies the theme you notice. Consider bringing this "codification" to the adapted critical cycle process.[8]

Enacting the Themes of Chapter 4

Chapter 4 analyzes the second component of the logic of compliance: the status quo. It provides readers with insights into how compliance becomes routinized, fostering institutional inertia that allows for acts of IDEA compliance to continue in ways that may meet organizational needs and priorities but ultimately hinder efforts to achieve equitable outcomes for students. The chapter demonstrated how this inertia can take on a self-sustaining quality, with the organization itself acting as an entity that preserves ineffective educational practices because that is the way it has always been. The chapter encourages readers to consider how taken-for-granted organizational routines reinforce the status quo, even when we understand that established practices may be illogical or ineffective in achieving intended aims. The reflective prompts below are designed to encourage readers to critically examine how organizational systems within schools and districts perpetuate inequitable practices by prioritizing established organizational routines and practices over meaningful reform.

They also encourage readers to assess how educational inequities and inequitable practices persist not necessarily through deliberate bias, but through institutional stagnation and an unquestioned adherence to routine. Finally, they ask readers to reflect on how organizational stability, while offering predictability, serves as a barrier to necessary progress and adaptation.

Technical Compliance

- What are some taken-for-granted, well-established, and well-known policies, practices, and procedures related to special education service delivery that educators readily comply with in your context? Consider what processes and practices do not need to be articulated yet everyone follows, for example, when an IEP meeting will occur, what are the routines people engage in around the meeting?
- What components of the special education process "just happen," where everyone knows what to do without having to look to others for help or guidance? Consider what parts of IDEA these routinized organizational practices relate to.

Adaptive Compliance

- Whose interests and needs are served by well-established special education processes and procedures in your context?
- Whom do you see when you think of a typical IEP meeting, for example? Who is included in routinized and taken-for-granted special education processes and procedures? Consider what might be some underlying assumptions and taken-for-granted narratives about the

way in which students are treated within these routinized practices.

- Who or what group of individuals tends to be able to disrupt organizational inertia? Consider why they can, who they are, and how they relate to the community context and staff in a school or district.

Theme Generation for the Adapted Critical Cycle Process

1. Compare and contrast your technical and adaptive responses either alone or with colleagues.
2. Reflect on organizational routines and practices that persist but may not adequately meet student needs.
3. Reflect on any moral and ethical tensions that arise for you between your technical and adaptive responses.
4. Note the gaps, convergences, and divergences in your reflections.
5. Generate an overarching theme that is responsive to the gaps, convergences, and divergences in your reflections. The theme can start with a statement as simple as "I notice. . ."
6. Consider an object, picture, or artifact that embodies the theme you notice. Consider bringing this "codification" to the adapted critical cycle process.[9]

Enacting the Themes of Chapter 5

Chapter 5 examines the third element of the logic of compliance: good intentions. It provides readers with a framework for understanding how stated good intentions can reinforce rather than disrupt educational inequities, masking the persistence of harmful ideologies embedded within acts of compliance, educational practices, and procedural decision-making. The following reflective prompts are designed to help readers question their assumptions about the neutrality of acts of compliance and to interrogate how racialized and ableist constructions of ability and intelligence can underly bureaucratic structures and the good intentions underlying acts of compliance. The chapter also pushes readers to interrogate how compliance-driven approaches do not inherently require educators to incorporate students' cultural identities and lived experiences into special education policies, practices, and procedures. By engaging with the prompts, readers are urged to recognize how their good intentions, while acting as a bridge between technical compliance and adaptive realities, can conceal and perpetuate exclusionary ideologies and systemic educational inequities.

Technical Compliance

- Conduct an IEP review of a student you know. Examine their specific IEP goals across social, emotional, and academic components. Describe what is prioritized and highlighted in these goals. Consider what you learn about the student from this review.
- Outline and describe the IEP process as it unfolds in your context. Write down a step-by-step list of how IEPs are typically written and what information is gathered and used to fill out IEPs. Consider who is involved in the *writing* of an IEP and whose *voice* is evident in the IEP.

Adaptive Compliance

- After conducting the IEP review for the student you know, reflect on what you know about the student from your interactions with them. Consider how what is written about a student may differ from what is represented in the written document.

- Describe how you integrate a students' cultural identity and lived experience into your educational practice. Consider if these actions are translated to formal special education policies and practices and how they are, or are not, connected.

Theme Generation for the Adapted Critical Cycle Process

1. Compare and contrast your technical and adaptive responses either alone or with colleagues.
2. Reflect on how what you want to do for students—the goodwill you have for your work—may or may not align with the actions you take on a daily basis.
3. Reflect on any moral and ethical tensions that arise for you between your technical and adaptive responses.
4. Note the gaps, convergences, and divergences in your reflections.
5. Generate an overarching theme that is responsive to the gaps, convergences, and divergences in your reflections. The theme can start with a statement as simple as "I notice. . ."
6. Consider an object, picture, or artifact that embodies the theme you notice. Consider bringing this "codification" to the adapted critical cycle process.[10]

Concluding Thoughts

As stated throughout this book, the goal of the text is *praxis*—the ongoing interplay of theory and practice and reflection and action, designed to create critical transformation within the context of political, social, and historical realities. I provide readers with avenues for the bridging of theory and practice, reflection and action, through an exploration of both the technical and adaptive mechanisms of policy implementation dynamics to transform educational systems. At the core of this book is a story about humanization and the need to rehumanize acts of IDEA compliance. The first step in this process is to raise consciousness about the limits of compliance and to critically deconstruct those limitations to challenge and dismantle oppressive systems impacting educators, students, and families. Drawing on Freirean logic, I provided an adapted and transformative process rooted in the notion of critical consciousness—*conscientização*—to rehumanize compliance and to disrupt the status quo to liberate individuals from complying with and recreating oppressive structures.

Freire emphasized that the goal of increasing critical consciousness is not just to move away from oppression but to ensure that liberation does not inadvertently lead to new forms of oppression. Therefore, by making visible the paradox and logic of compliance, readers can begin to identify and name the dehumanizing conditions impacting their work and, ultimately, the students with whom they work. By exposing the limit situations surrounding compliance, the goal is to transform what currently exists and to encourage dialogue that can foster the rehumanization of compliance in service of educational equity.

NOTES

INTRODUCTION

Throughout the book, I move between person-first and identity-first language, drawing from different models of disability and their relationship to disability advocacy, communities, and educational spaces; see Erin E. Andrews et al., "The Evolution of Disability Language: Choosing Terms to Describe Disability," *Disability and health journal* 15, no. 3 (2022): 101328.

1. US Department of Education, *2019 Determination Letters on State Implementation of IDEA*, 2022, www2.ed.gov/fund/data/report/idea/ideafactsheet-determinations-2019.pdf.
2. Martha Minow, *In Brown's Wake: Legacies of America's Educational Landmark*, (Oxford University Press, 2010); Colin Ong-Dean, *Distinguishing Disability: Parents, Privilege, and Special Education* (Chicago: University of Chicago Press, 2009); Perry A. Zirkel, "Does Brown v. Board of Education Play a Prominent Role in Special Education Law," *Journal of Law & Education* 34 (2005): 255.
3. Mitchell L. Yell et al., "The Individualized Education Program: Procedural and Substantive Requirements," *Teaching Exceptional Children* 52, no. 5 (2020): 304–18.
4. Thomas M. Skrtic and K. M. Knackstedt, "Disability, Difference, and Justice: Strong Democratic Leadership for Undemocratic Times," in *Handbook of Leadership and Administration for Special Education*, ed. Jean B. Crockett, Bonnie Billingsley, and Mary Lynn Boscardin (Routledge, 2019).

5. Richard D. Marsico, "The Intersection of Race, Wealth, and Special Education: The Role of Structural Inequities in the IDEA," *New York Law School Law Review* 66 (2021): 207; Beth Harry and Lydia Ocasio-Stoutenburg, "Parent Advocacy for Lives that Matter," *Research and Practice for Persons with Severe Disabilities* 46, no. 3 (2021): 184–98; Yi Li, "Substantively Immaterial? How the IDEA Enables Special Education Labels to be Used as Tools of Inequity," *Disability Law Journal* 4, no. 1 (2023).
6. Perry A. Zirkel, "The Role of Law in Special Education," *Exceptionality* 31, no. 4 (2023): 308–18; Carmen Gomez Mandic et al., "Readability of Special Education Procedural Safeguards," *The Journal of Special Education* 45, no. 4 (2012): 195–203; Russell J. Skiba et al., "Achieving Equity in Special Education: History, Status, and Current Challenges," *Exceptional Children* 74, no. 3 (2008): 264–88; Beth Harry and Janette Klingner, *Why Are So Many Students of Color in Special Education?: Understanding Race and Disability in Schools* (Teachers College Press, 2022).
7. David Pettinicchio, *Politics of Empowerment: Disability Rights and the Cycle of American Policy Reform* (Stanford University Press, 2020).
8. David Pettinicchio, "Strategic Action Fields and the Context of Political Entrepreneurship: How Disability Rights Became Part of the Policy Agenda," in *Research in Social Movements, Conflicts and Change*, ed. Patrick G. Coy (Emerald Group, 2018).
9. In 1975, Congress passed the Education for All Handicapped Children Act (Public Law 94-142), also known as the EHA, to assist states and local agencies in safeguarding the rights of children and youth with disabilities, addressing their individual needs, and improving outcomes for them and their families. This groundbreaking legislation was renamed the Individuals with Disabilities Education Act (IDEA) during its 1990 reauthorization. The most recent reauthorization occurred in 2004, and the Department of Education has since issued updated regulations to guide the law's implementation and interpretation. See https://sites.ed.gov/idea/IDEA-History.

10. Yi Li, "Substantively Immaterial?"; Sarah Triano, "Categorical Eligibility for Special Education: The Enshrinement of the Medical Model in Disability Policy," *Disability Studies Quarterly* 20, no. 4 (2000); Perry A. Zirkel, "Special Education Law: Illustrative Basics and Nuances of Key IDEA Components," *Teacher Education and Special Education* 38, no. 4 (2015): 263–75.
11. Catherine Kramarczuk Voulgarides, Susan Larson Etscheidt, and David I. Hernández-Saca, "Examining Paradoxes of Access in Disability Law: A Critical Analysis of the Least Restrictive Environment," *Journal of Education Policy* (2024): 1–26.
12. Voulgarides et al., "Examining Paradoxes of Access in Disability Law."
13. For example, Beth A. Ferri and David J. Connor, "Tools of Exclusion: Race, Disability, and (re) Segregated Education," *Teachers College Record* 107, no. 3 (2005): 453–74; Alan Gartner and Dorothy Kerzner Lipsky, "Beyond Special Education: Toward a Quality System for All Students," *Harvard Educational Review* 57, no. 4 (1987): 367–96; Jess Gregory, "Not My Responsibility: The Impact of Separate Special Education Systems on Educators' Attitudes toward Inclusion," *Educational Policy Analysis and Strategic Research* 13, no. 1 (2018): 127–48; Elizabeth Kozleski, Alfredo Artiles, and Federico Waitoller, "Equity in Inclusive Education: A Cultural Historical Comparative Perspective," in *The Sage Handbook of Special Education*, ed. Lani Florian, vol. 2 (Sage, 2014); Festus E. Obioker, "Maximizing Access, Equity, and Inclusion in General and Special Education," *Journal of the International Association of Special Education* 12, no. 1 (2011); Justin J. W. Powell, "To Segregate or to Separate? Special Education Expansion and Divergence in the United States and Germany." *Comparative Education Review* 53, no. 2 (2009): 161–87
14. US Department of Education, *43rd Annual Report to Congress on the Implementation of the Individuals with Disabilities Education Act*, Office of Special Education and Rehabilitative Services, Office of Special Education Programs, 2021.
15. C. De Brey at al., *Status and Trends in the Education of Racial and Ethnic Groups 2018 (NCES 2019-038)*, 63, US Department of Education, National Center for Education Statistics, 2019, https://nces.ed.gov/pubsearch.

16. North Cooc, "Disparities in General Education Inclusion for Students of Color with Disabilities: Understanding When and Why," *Journal of School Psychology* 90 (2022): 43–59; Hardy Murphy, Cassandra Cole, and Hannah Bolte, "Race Placed: Special Education Identification and Placement of Black Students," *Educational Policy* (2024); Nicole A. Bannister, "Breaking the Spell of Differentiated Instruction through Equity Pedagogy and Teacher Community," *Cultural Studies of Science Education* 11 (2016): 335–47; Rachel Lambert, "'Indefensible, Illogical, and Unsupported': Countering Deficit Mythologies about the Potential OF Students WITH Learning Disabilities in Mathematics," *Education Sciences* 8, no. 2 (2018): 72; Richard O. Welsh and Shafiqua Little, "The School Discipline Dilemma: A Comprehensive Review of Disparities and Alternative Approaches," *Review of Educational Research* 88, no. 5 (2018): 752–94.
17. Alexandra Aylward Brenda Barrio and Catherine Kramarczuk Voulgarides, "Exclusion from Educational Opportunity in Diversifying Rural Contexts," *Rural Sociology* 86, no. 3 (2021): 559–85; Rachel Elizabeth Fish, "The Racialized Construction of Exceptionality: Experimental Evidence of Race/Ethnicity Effects on Teachers' Interventions," *Social Science Research* 62 (2016): 317–34; Rachel Elizabeth Fish, "Standing out and Sorting in: Exploring the Role of Racial Composition in Racial Disparities in Special Education," *American Educational Research Journal* 56, no. 6 (2019): 2573–2608.
18. Paul L. Morgan and George Farkas, "Are We Helping All the Children that We Are Supposed to be Helping?" *Educational Researcher* 45, no. 3 (2016): 226–28.
19. Jaret Hodges et al., "A Meta-Analysis of Gifted and Talented Identification Practices," *Gifted Child Quarterly* 62, no. 2 (2018): 147–74; Scott J. Peters and Kenneth G. Engerrand, "Equity and Excellence: Proactive Efforts in the Identification of Underrepresented Students for Gifted and talented Services," *Gifted Child Quarterly* 60, no. 3 (2016): 159–71.
20. S. Paul et al., *Annual Disability Statistics Compendium: 2023*, University of New Hampshire, Institute on Disability, 2023.; A. Houtenville and S. Bach, *Annual Report on People with Disabilities*

in America: 2024, Institute on Disability, University of New Hampshire, 2024.

21. Roey Ahram, Catherine Kramarczuk Voulgarides, and Rebecca A. Cruz, "Understanding Disability: High-Quality Evidence in Research on Special Education Disproportionality," *Review of Research in Education* 45, no. 1 (2021): 311–45; Lloyd M. Dunn, "Special Education for the Mildly Retarded—Is Much of It Justifiable?" *Exceptional Children* 35, no. 1 (1968): 5–22; Federico R. Waitoller, Alfredo J. Artiles, and Douglas A. Cheney, "The Miner's Canary: A Review of Overrepresentation Research and Explanations," *Journal of Special Education* 44, no. 1 (2010): 29–49.
22. Marsico, "The Intersection of Race, Wealth, and Special Education"; Keith A. Mayes, *The Unteachables: Disability Rights and the Invention of Black Special Education* (University of Minnesota Press, 2023).
23. Catherine Kramarczuk Voulgarides et al., "Understanding Policy Reverberations Across the Educational Ecosystem to Effectuate Change," *Theory into Practice* 63, no. 4 (2024): 457–68; Edward Fergus, *Solving Disproportionality and Achieving Equity: A Leader's Guide to Using Data to Change Hearts and Minds* (Corwin, 2016); María G. Hernández, David M. Lopez, and Reed Swier, *Dismantling Disproportionality: A Culturally Responsive and sustaining Systems Approach* (Teachers College Press, 2022).
24. Catherine Kramarczuk Voulgarides, Alexandra Aylward, Natasha Strassfeld, et al., "A Critical Examination of Special Education Policy Using a Multi-Layered Systemic Approach for Policy Analysis," *Remedial and Special Education* (2025): 07419325251360336; Voulgarides et al., "Examining Paradoxes of Access in Disability Law." This view is inspired by Urie Bronfenbrenner's ecological systems theory; see *Ecological Systems Theory* (Jessica Kingsley, 1992) and "Toward an Experimental Ecology of Human Development," *American Psychologist* 32, no. 7 (1977): 513–31.
25. Natasha M. Strassfeld, "Education Federalism and Minority Disproportionate Representation Monitoring: Examining IDEA Provisions, Regulations, and Judicial Trends," *Journal of Disability Policy Studies* 30, no. 3 (2019): 138–47; Kimberly Jenkins Robinson, "Disrupting Education Federalism," *Washington University Law Review*, 2015.

26. Harry and Klinger, *Why Are So Many Students of Color in Special Education?*
27. Roey Ahram, Edward Fergus, and Pedro Noguera, "Addressing Racial/Ethnic Disproportionality in Special Education: Case Studies of Suburban School Districts." *Teachers College Record* 113, no. 10 (2011): 2233–66.
28. Ahram et al., "Understanding Disability"; Dunn, "Special Education for the Mildly Retarded"; Waitoller et al., "The Miner's Canary."
29. Meghan M. Burke, "Improving Parental Involvement: Training Special Education Advocates," *Journal of Disability Policy Studies* 23, no. 4 (2013): 225–34; Lydia Ocasio-Stoutenberg, Juanita Davis, and Maria Lewis, "Principals as Co-advocates for Caregivers of Children with Disabilities: Possibilities and Realizations beyond IDEA's Collaborative Ideal," *Journal of Cases in Educational Leadership* 27, no. 4 (2024): 85–104; Zach Rossetti et al., "Parent Perceptions of the Advocacy Expectation in Special Education," *Exceptional Children* 87, no. 4 (2021): 438–57.
30. Janet Decker and Kevin Brady, "Increasing School Employees' Special Education Legal Literacy," *Journal of School Public Relations* 36, no. 3 (2015): 231–59; Elisa Hyman, Dean Hill Rivkin, and Stephen A. Rosenbaum, "How IDEA Fails Families without Means: Causes and Corrections from the Frontlines of Special Education Lawyering," *American Universite Journal of Gender Social Policy and Law* 20 (2011): 107; National Council on Disability, *Federal Monitoring and Enforcement of IDEA Compliance*, 2018. https://www.ncd.gov/sites/default/files/NCD_Monitoring-Enforcement_Accessible.pdf; US Government Accountability Office, *Individuals with Disabilities Education Act: Standards Needed to Improve Identification of Racial and Ethnic Overrepresentation in Special Education*, 2013, https://www.gao.gov/assets/gao-13-137.pdf; Jacqueline M. Nowicki, *Special Education: Varied State Criteria May Contribute to Different in Percentages of Children Served*, GAO-19-348, (US Government Accountability Office, 2019).
31. Catherine Voulgarides, *Does Compliance Matter in Special Education?: IDEA and the Hidden Inequities of Practice* (Teachers College

Press, 2018); Catherine Voulgarides, "The Promises and Pitfalls of Mandating Racial Equity in Special Education," *Phi Delta Kappan* 103, no. 6 (2022): 14–20; Catherine Kramarczuk Voulgarides et al., "Unpacking the Logic of Compliance in Special Education: Contextual Influences on Discipline Racial Disparities in Suburban Schools," *Sociology of Education* 94, no. 3 (2021): 208–26.

32. Patricia Hill Collins and Sirma Bilge, *Intersectionality* (Wiley, 2020); Kimberlé Williams Crenshaw, "Mapping the Margins: Intersectionality, Identity Politics, and Violence against Women of Color," in *The Public Nature of Private Violence*, ed. Martha Albertson (Routledge, 2013).
33. David Isaac Hernández-Saca, Laurie Gutmann Kahn, and Mercedes A. Cannon, "Intersectionality Dis/Ability Research: How Dis/Ability Research in Education Engages Intersectionality to Uncover the Multidimensional Construction of Dis/Abled Experiences," *Review of Research in Education* 42, no. 1 (2018): 286–311.
34. Subini Ancy Annamma, David Connor, and Beth Ferri, "Dis/Ability Critical Race Studies (DisCrit): Theorizing at the Intersections of Race and Dis/Ability," *Race Ethnicity and Education* 16, no. 1 (2013): 1–31.
35. Ronald A. Heifetz, "Mobilizing for Adaptive Work," in *Making Policy Happen*, ed. Leslie Budd, Julie Charlesworth, and Rob Paton (Routledge, 2020); Ronald A. Heifetz, *The Practice of Adaptive Leadership: Tools and Tactics for Changing Your Organization and the World* (Harvard Business Press, 2009); Shane Safir and Jamila Dugan, *Street Data: A Next-Generation Model for Equity, Pedagogy, and School Transformation* (Corwin, 2021); Voulgarides, *Does Compliance Matter in Special Education?*; Voulgarides et al., "Unpacking the Logic of Compliance"; Paulo Freire, *Education: The Practice of Freedom* (Writers and Readers, 1974); Paulo Freire, *Pedagogy of the Oppressed*, 30th anniversary ed (Continuum, 2000); Paulo Freire, "The Banking Concept of Education," in *Thinking About Schools: A Foundation of Education Reader*, ed. Eleanore Blair Hilty (Routledge, 2011).
36. Collins and Bilge, *Intersectionality*.
37. Freire, "The Banking Concept of Education."

38. Freire, "The Banking Concept of Education," 162–63.
39. Freire, *Pedagogy of the Oppressed.*
40. Freire, *Education.*
41. Catherine Voulgarides, "Negotiating Rights in Education: An Examination of US Education Disability Policy," in *Research Handbook on Disability Policy*, ed. Sally Robinson (Edward Elgar, 2023).
42. For sociological organizational theory, see Richard Arum, "Schools and Communities: Ecological and Institutional Dimensions," *Annual Review of Sociology* 26, no. 1 (2000): 395–418; Lauren B. Edelman, *Working Law: Courts, Corporations, and Symbolic Civil Rights* (University of Chicago Press, 2020); John W. Meyer and Brian Rowan, "Institutionalized Organizations: Formal Structure as Myth and Ceremony," *American Journal of Sociology* 83, no. 2 (1977): 340–63; John Richardson and Justin Powell, *Comparing Special Education: Origins to Contemporary Paradoxes* (Stanford University Press, 2011). For disability studies in education, see Ferri and Connor, "Tools of Exclusion"; and Jan W. Valle and David J. Connor, *Rethinking Disability: A Disability Studies Approach to Inclusive Practices* (Routledge, 2019). For DisCrit, see Annamma et al., "Dis/Ability Critical Race Studies." For critical education studies, see Freire, "The Banking Concept of Education"; Freire, *Pedagogy of the Oppressed*; and Mariana Souto-Manning, *Freire, Teaching, and Learning: Culture Circles across Contexts* (Peter Lang, 2010). For special education law, see Kevin Brady et al., *Legal Issues in Special Education: Principles, Policies, and Practices* (Routledge, 2019).
43. For the paradox of compliance, I draw from Alfredo J. Artiles, "Toward an Interdisciplinary Understanding of Educational Equity and Difference: The Case of the Racialization of Ability," *Educational Researcher* 40, no. 9 (2011): 431–45; Richardson and Powell, *Comparing Special Education*; Faye Ginsburg and Rayna Rapp, *Disability Worlds* (Duke University Press, 2024). For the logic of compliance, see Voulgarides, *Does Compliance Matter in Special Education?*
44. See Voulgarides, *Does Compliance Matter in Special Education?*; Voulgarides, "The Promises and Pitfalls"; Voulgarides et al., "Unpacking the Logic of Compliance."

45. Karl E. Weick, "Administering Education in Loosely Coupled Schools," *Phi Delta Kappan* 63, no. 10 (1982): 673–76; Weick, "Educational Organizations as Loosely Coupled Systems," in *The Roots of Logistics*, ed. Peter Klaus and Stefanie Müller (Springer, 2012).
46. Ginsburg and Rapp, *Disability Worlds.*
47. Artiles et al., "Objects of Protection, Enduring Nodes of Difference."
48. Kimberly Jenkins Robinson, "The High Cost of Education Federalism," *Wake Forest Law. Review* 48 (2013): 287.
49. See Joseph P. Bishop and Pedro A. Noguera, "The Ecology of Educational Equity: Implications for Policy," *Peabody Journal of Education* 94, no. 2 (2019): 122–41; Voulgarides et al, "Understanding Policy Reverberations"; Voulgarides, *Does Compliance Matter in Special Education?*; Voulgarides, "The Promises and Pitfalls"; Voulgarides et al., "Unpacking the Logic of Compliance."
50. I draw from educational business literature and the application of these ideas in special education to do so. Safir and Dugan, *Street Data*; Heifetz, "Mobilizing for Adaptive Work"; Heifetz, *The Practice of Adaptive Leadership*; Aydin Bal, Amanda L. Sullivan, and John Harper, "A Situated Analysis of Special Education Disproportionality for Systemic Transformation in an Urban School District," *Remedial and Special Education* 35, no. 1 (2014): 3–14.
51. Bal et al., "A Situated Analysis."
52. Bal et al., "A Situated Analysis."
53. Freire, *Education*; Freire, *Pedagogy of the Oppressed.*
54. Olivia Johnston, *Constructing Composite Narratives: A Step-by-Step Guide for Researchers in the Social Sciences* (Taylor & Francis, 2024).
55. See Caroline Bradbury-Jones Julie Taylor, and O. R. Herber, "Vignette Development and Administration: A Framework for Protecting Research Participants," *International Journal of Social Research Methodology* 17, no. 4 (2014): 427–40; Karen Kaiser, "Protecting Confidentiality," in *The Sage Handbook of Interview Research: The Complexity of the Craft*, ed. Jaber F. Gubrium, James A. Holstein, Amir B. Marvasti, and Karyn D. McKinne (Sage, 2012).

56. Also see John W. Creswell and Cheryl N. Poth, *Qualitative Inquiry and Research Design: Choosing among Five Approaches* (Sage, 2016); Johnston, *Constructing Composite Narratives*; Kyle Pushkarenko et al., "Physical Literacy and the Participant Perspective: Exploring the Value of Physical Literacy According to Individuals Experiencing Disability through Composite Narratives," *Journal of Exercise Science & Fitness* 21, no. 3 (2023): 237–45.
57. Freire, *Education*; Freire, *Pedagogy of the Oppressed.*
58. Freire, *Education*; Freire, *Pedagogy of the Oppressed.*
59. Freire, *Education*; Freire, *Pedagogy of the Oppressed.*
60. Freire, *Education*; Freire, *Pedagogy of the Oppressed.*
61. Henry A. Giroux and Christopher G. Robbins, "Paulo Freire and the Politics of Postcolonialism," in *The Giroux Reader*, ed. Henry Giroux (Routledge, 2015).
62. Mildred Boveda and Subini Ancy Annamma, "Beyond Making a Statement: An Intersectional Framing of the Power and Possibilities of Positioning," *Educational Researcher* 52, no. 5 (2023): 306–14.
63. Freire, *Pedagogy of the Oppressed.*
64. See Boveda and Annamma, "Beyond Making a Statement."

CHAPTER 1

1. John Richardson and Justin Powell, *Comparing Special Education: Origins to Contemporary Paradoxes* (Stanford University Press, 2011).
2. For example, Jennifer L. Erkulwater, "How the Nation's Largest Minority Became White: Race Politics and the Disability Rights Movement, 1970–1980," *Journal of Policy History* 30, no. 3 (2018): 367–99; Sami Schalk, *Black Disability Politics* (Duke University Press, 2022); Margaret C. Wang and Maynard C. Reynolds, "Progressive Inclusion: Meeting New Challenges in Special Education," *Theory into Practice* 35, no. 1 (1996): 20–25.
3. Keith A. Mayes, *The Unteachables: Disability Rights and the Invention of Black Special Education* (University of Minnesota Press, 2023); David Pettinnichio, *Politics of Empowerment: Disability Rights and the Cycle of American Policy Reform* (Stanford University Press, 2020); Richardson and Powell, *Comparing Special Education.*

4. Martha Minow, *In Brown's Wake: Legacies of America's Educational Landmark* (Oxford University Press, 2010).
5. Lindsey Patterson, "The Disability Rights Movement in the United States," *Oxford Handbooks Online*, 2018.
6. Fred Pelka, *What We Have Done: An Oral History of the Disability Rights Movement* (University of Massachusetts Press, 2012).
7. *Brown v. Board of Education of Topeka*, 347 U.S. 483 (1954).
8. Richard Scotch, *From Good Will to Civil Rights: Transforming Federal Disability Policy* (Temple University Press, 2009).
9. Colin Ong-Dean, *Distinguishing Disability: Parents, Privilege, and Special Education* (University of Chicago Press, 2009).
10. Mitchell L. Yell and Denise K. Whitford, "Civil Rights and the Birth of Special Education," in *Disproportionality and Social Justice in Education*, ed. Nicholas Gage et al. (Springer, 2022).
11. Yell and Whitford, "Civil Rights and the Birth of Special Education"; Michael L. Wehmeyer and J. David Smith, "Historical Understandings of Intellectual Disability and the Emergence of Special Education," in *Handbook of Research-Based Practices for Educating Students with Intellectual Disability*, ed. Karrie A. Shogren et al. (Routledge, 2016). And see Natasha M. Strassfeld, "Education Federalism and Minority Disproportionate Representation Monitoring: Examining IDEA Provisions, Regulations, and Judicial Trends," *Journal of Disability Policy Studies* 30, no. 3 (2019): 138–47; Natasha M. Strassfeld, "The Future of IDEA: Monitoring Disproportionate Representation of Minority Students in Special Education and Intentional Discrimination Claims," *Case Western Reserve Law Review*, 67 (2016): 1121.
12. Kevin Brady et al., *Legal Issues in Special Education: Principles, Policies, and Practices* (Routledge, 2019).
13. David F. Bateman and Mitchell L. Yell, *Current Trends and Legal Issues in Special Education* (Corwin, 2019); Brady et al., *Legal Issues in Special Education*; Jacqueline A. Rodriguez and Wendy W. Murawski, *Special Education Law and Policy: From Foundation to Application*, vol. 1 (Plural, 2020).
14. Brady et al., *Legal Issues in Special Education*.

15. Ruth Colker, *Disabled Education: A Critical Analysis of the Individuals with Disabilities Education Act* (New York University Press, 2013).
16. Beth Harry and Janette Klingner, *Why Are So Many Students of Color in Special Education?: Understanding Race and Disability in Schools* (Teachers College Press, 2022).
17. Sally Lindsay et al., "Exploring the Relationships between Race, Ethnicity, and School and Work Outcomes among Youth and Young Adults with Disabilities: A Scoping Review," *Disability and Rehabilitation* 44, no. 25 (2022): 8110–29; Lauren A. Rivera and András Tilsick, "Not in My Schoolyard: Disability Discrimination in Educational Access," *American Sociological Review* 88, no. 2 (2023): 284–321.
18. Claire McKinley Yoder et al., "Disparities in High School Graduation by Identity and Disability Using Intermediate and Long-Term Educational Outcomes," *Journal of School Nursing* 40, no. 3 (2024): 266–74.
19. K. Fuentes et al., "More Than Just Double Discrimination: A Scoping Review of the Experiences and Impact of Ableism and Racism in Employment," *Exceptionality* 28, no. 3 (2020): 176–94.
20. Pettinicchio, *Politics of Empowerment*.
21. Tom Hehir, *New Directions in Special Education: Eliminating Ableism in Policy and Practice* (Harvard Education Press, 2025).
22. Rob Imrie, "Rethinking the Relationships Between Disability, Rehabilitation, and Society," *Disability and Rehabilitation* 19, no. 7 (1997): 263–271.
23. Peter David Blanck and Eilionóir Flynn, *Routledge Handbook of Disability Law and Human Rights* (Routledge, 2017); Tom Shakespeare, "The Social Model of Disability," *The Disability Studies Reader* 2, no. 3 (2006): 197–204.
24. Colin Barnes, "Understanding the Social Model of Disability," Past, Present and Future," in *Routledge Handbook of Disability Studies*, ed. Nick Watson et al. (Routledge, 2019).
25. Michael Oliver, *Understanding Disability: From Theory to Practice* (Bloomsbury, 2018).
26. Michelle R. Nario-Redmond, *Ableism: The Causes and Consequences of Disability Prejudice* (Wiley, 2019).

27. Oliver, *Understanding Disability*; Fiona A. Kumari Campbell, "Exploring Internalized Ableism Using Critical Race Theory," *Disability & Society* 23, no. 2 (2008): 151–62.
28. Lennard J. Davis, *The Disability Studies Reader* (Routledge, 2016); Elizabeth Stringer Keefe, "From Detractive to Democratic: The Duty of Teacher Education to Disrupt Structural Ableism and Reimagine Disability," *Teachers College Record* 124, no. 3 (2022): 115–47; Maria Timberlake, "Recognizing Ableism in Educational Initiatives: Reading Between the Lines," *Research in Educational Policy and Management* 2, no. 1 (2020): 84–100.
29. Angela Frederick and Dara Shifrer, "Race and Disability: From Analogy to Intersectionality," *Sociology of Race and Ethnicity* 5, no. 2 (2019): 200–14; Schalk, *Black Disability Politic*.
30. David Isaac Hernández-Saca, Laurie Gutmann Kahn, and Mercedes A. Cannon, "Intersectionality Dis/Ability Research: How Dis/Ability Research in Education Engages Intersectionality to Uncover the Multidimensional Construction of Dis/Abled Experiences," *Review of Research in Education* 42, no. 1 (2018): 286–311.
31. Chris Bell, "Is disability Studies Actually White Disability Studies?" *The Disability Studies Reader* 5 (2010): 402–10; Phil Smith, "Whiteness, Normal Theory, and Disability Studies," *Disability Studies Quarterly* 24, no. 2 (2004).
32. Jay Dolmage, "Disabled upon Arrival: The Rhetorical Construction of Disability and Race at Ellis Island," *Cultural Critique* 77 (2011): 24–69.
33. Dolmage, "Disabled upon Arrival."
34. Schalk, *Black Disability Politics*.
35. *Willowbrook: The Last Great Disgrace*, directed by Geraldo Rivera, produced by Steve Skinner, Sproutflix, New York, 1972. Also see Susan Flynn, "A History and Sociology of the Willowbrook State School," *International Journal of Disability Development and Education* 64, no. 2 (2017): 1–2.
36. Bronston quoted in Pelka, *What We Have Done*, 175.
37. Rivera quoted in J. M. Valldejuli, "The Racialized History of Disability Activism from the Willowbrooks of this World," *Activist History Review*, November 4, 2019.
38. Kim E. Nielsen, *A Disability History of the United States*, vol. 2 (Beacon Press, 2012).

CHAPTER 2

1. US Department of Education, *2019 Determination Letters on State Implementation of IDEA*, 2022, www2.ed.gov/fund/data/report/idea/ideafactsheet-determinations-2019.pdf.
2. Sarah Hurwitz et al., "Special Education and Individualized Academic Growth: A Longitudinal Assessment of Outcomes for Students with Disabilities," *American Educational Research Journal* 57, no. 2 (2020): 576–611; A. E. Shwartz, B. G. Hopkins, and L. Stiefel, "The Effects of Special Education on the Academic Performance of Students with Learning Disabilities," *Journal of Policy Analysis and Management* 40, no. 2, (2021): 480–520.
3. North Cooc, "National Trends in Special Education and Academic Outcomes for English Learners with Disabilities," *Journal of Special Education* 57, no. 2 (2023): 106–17; Mason G. Haber et al., "What Works, When, for Whom, and with Whom: A Meta-analytic Review of Predictors of Postsecondary Success for Students with Disabilities," *Review of Educational Research* 86, no. 1 (2016): 123–162.
4. Janet Decker and Kevin Brady, "Increasing School Employees' Special Education Legal Literacy," *Journal of School Public Relations* 36, no. 3 (2015): 231–59; Perry A. Zirkel, "Special Education Law: Illustrative Basics and Nuances of Key IDEA Components," *Teacher Education and Special Education* 38, no. 4 (2015): 263–75; Antonis Katsiyannis et al., "Minority Representation in Special Education: 5-Year Trends from 2016–2020," *Advances in Neurodevelopmental Disorders* (2023): 1–14; Roey Ahram, Catherine Kramarczuk Voulgarides, and Rebecca A. Cruz, "Understanding Disability: High-Quality Evidence in Research on Special Education Disproportionality," *Review of Research in Education* 45, no. 1 (2021): 311–45; Federico R. Waitoller, Alfredo J. Artiles, and Douglas A. Cheney, "The Miner's Canary: A Review of Overrepresentation Research and Explanations," *Journal of Special Education* 44, no. 1 (2010): 29–49.
5. US Department of Education, *2019 Determination Letters on State Implementation of IDEA*; National Council on Disability. *Federal Monitoring and Enforcement of IDEA Compliance*, 2018, https://www.ncd.gov/sites/default/files/NCD_Monitoring-Enforcement_Accessible.pdf.

6. Julie Bollmer et al. *A Study of States' Monitoring and Improvement Practices under the Individuals with Disabilities Education Act. NCSER 2011-3001* (National Center for Special Education Research, 2010).
7. National Council on Disability, *Federal Monitoring and Enforcement of IDEA Compliance.*
8. Eileen M. Ahearn, *State Compliance Monitoring Practices: An Update. Final Report*, (National Association of State Directors of Special Education, 1995); Bollmer et al., *A Study of States' Monitoring and Improvement Practices.*
9. Bollmer et al., *A Study of States' Monitoring and Improvement Practices.*
10. National Council on Disability, *Federal Monitoring and Enforcement of IDEA Compliance.*
11. National Council on Disability, *Federal Monitoring and Enforcement of IDEA Compliance.*
12. Benjamin M. Superfine, *Equality in Education Law and Policy, 1954–2010* (Cambridge University Press, 2013).
13. Mitchell L. Yell, James G. Shriner, and Antonis Katsiyannis, "Individuals with Disabilities Education Improvement Act of 2004 and IDEA Regulations of 2006: Implications for Educators, Administrators, and Teacher Trainers," *Focus on Exceptional Children* 39, no. 1 (2006): 1–24.
14. Tom E. C. Smith, "IDEA 2004: Another Round in the Reauthorization Process," *Remedial and Special Education* 26, no. 6 (2005): 314–19.
15. Susan Larson Etscheidt, David Hernandez-Saca, and Catherine Kramarczuk Voulgarides, "Monitoring the Transition Requirements of the Individuals with Disabilities Education Act: A Critique and a Proposal to Expand the Performance Indicators," *Journal of Disability Policy Studies* 35, no. 2 (2024): 128–39; US Government Accountability Office, *Individuals with Disabilities Education Act: Education's Oversight of Racial and Ethnic Groups' Overrepresentation in Special Education Is Hampered by the Flexibility States Have to Define Significant Disproportionality* (GAO-13-137), 2013, https://www.gao.gov/assets/660/652437.pdf.

16. Susan Larson Etscheidt et al., "Monitoring the Transition Requirements."
17. Also see Pierre Gouëdard, "Developing Indicators to Support the Implementation of Education Policies," OECD Education Working Papers, No. 255 (OECD, 2021).
18. The table can be found at the US Department of Education site, https://sites.ed.gov/idea/files/2022_Part-B_SPP-APR_Measurement_Table.pdf.
19. J. Bollmer et al., *Methods for Assessing Racial/Ethnic Disproportionality in Special Education: A Technical Assistance Guide (Revised)* (US Department of Education, Office of Special Programs, 2005), www.ideadata.org. (This is a revised and updated version of the original 2005 publication produced for the US DOE by Westat); Susan Fread Albrecht et al., "Federal Policy on Disproportionality in Special Education: Is It Moving Us Forward?" *Journal of Disability Policy Studies* 23, no. 1 (2012): 14–25.
20. Voulgarides et al., "A Critical Examination of Special Education Policy Using a Multi-Layered Systemic Approach for Policy Analysis," *Remedial and Special Education* (2025): 07419325251360336.
21. US Department of Education, Office of Special Education Programs, *Results-Driven Accountability (RDA) Framework*, 2014, https://sites.ed.gov/idea/rda/.
22. Albrecht et al., "Federal Policy on Disproportionality."
23. John Richardson and Justin Powell, *Comparing Special Education: Origins to Contemporary Paradoxes* (Stanford University Press, 2011).
24. Zach McCall and Thomas Skrtic, "Intersectional Needs Politic: A Policy Frame for the Wicked Problem Of Disproportionality," *Multiple Voices for Ethnically Diverse Exceptional Learners* 11, no. 2 (2009): 14.
25. As highlighted by Perry A. Zirkel in "Does Brown v. Board of Education Play a Prominent Role in Special Education Law," *Journal of Law & Education* 34 (2005): 255
26. Pamela Herd and Donald P. Moynihan, *Administrative Burden: Policymaking by Other Means* (Russell Sage Foundation, 2019); Catherine Voulgarides, *Does Compliance Matter in Special*

Education?: IDEA and the Hidden Inequities of Practice (Teachers College Press, 2018).

27. Robert Merton, "Manifest and Latent Functions," in *Social Theory Re-wired: New Connections to Classical and Contemporary Perspectives*, ed. Wesley Longhofer and Daneil Winchester (Routledge, 2016.)
28. Sam D. Sieber, "Implications for Policy," in *Fatal Remedies: The Ironies of Social Intervention* (Springer, 1981).
29. Karl E. Weick, "Administering Education in Loosely Coupled Schools," *Phi Delta Kappan* 63, no. 10 (1982): 673–76
30. Michael Lipsky, *Street-Level Bureaucracy: Dilemmas of the Individual in Public Service* (Russell Sage Foundation, 2010); Richard Weatherley and Michael Lipsky, "Street-Level Bureaucrats and Institutional Innovation: Implementing Special-Education Reform," *Harvard Educational Review* 47, no. 2 (1977): 171–97
31. Weatherley and Lipsky, "Street-Level Bureaucrats."
32. Voulgarides, *Does Compliance Matter in Special Education?*
33. Lauren B. Edelman, *Working Law: Courts, Corporations, and Symbolic Civil Rights* (University of Chicago Press, 2020).
34. John W. Meyer and Brian Rowan, "Institutionalized Organizations: Formal Structure as Myth and Ceremony," *American Journal of Sociology* 83, no. 2 (1977): 340–63.
35. Edelman, *Working Law.*
36. Laura E. Bray and Jennifer Lin Russel, "Going off Script: Structure and Agency in Individualized Education Program Meetings," *American Journal of Education* 122, no. 3 (2016): 367–98; Argun Saatcioglu and Thomas M. Skrtic, "Categorization by Organizations: Manipulation of Disability Categories in a Racially Desegregated School District," *American Journal of Sociology* 125, no. 1 (2019): 184–260.
37. Voulgarides, *Does Compliance Matter in Special Education?*; Catherine Kramarczuk Voulgarides et al., "Unpacking the Logic of Compliance in Special Education: Contextual Influences on Discipline Racial Disparities in Suburban schools," *Sociology of Education* 94, no. 3 (2021): 208–26.
38. National Council on Disability, *Federal Monitoring and Enforcement of IDEA Compliance.*
39. Voulgarides, *Does Compliance Matter in Special Education?*; Catherine Kramarczuk Voulgarides et al., "Racial and Dis/Ability

Equity-Oriented Educational Leadership Preparation," *Journal of Special Education Preparation* 2, no. 3 (2022): 20–30.

40. Doug Cox, "State Monitoring and Compliance," in *Special Education Leadership*, by Doug Cox and Jennifer Cline (Routledge, 2019); Elisa Hyman, Dean Hill Rivkin, and Stephen A. Rosenbaum, "How IDEA Fails Families without Means: Causes and Corrections from the Frontlines of Special Education Lawyering," *American Universite Journal of Gender Social Policy and Law* 20 (2011): 107
41. Voulgarides et al., "Unpacking the Logic of Compliance"; Kathleen A. King Thorius, *Equity Expansive Technical Assistance for Schools: Education Partnerships to Reverse Racial Disproportionality*, (Teachers College Press, 2023); A. Padilla, Catherine Voulgarides, and R. Bondie, "Disability and Educational Justice: Exploring Intersectional Ways to Disrupt the Logic of Compliance," *Journal of Disability Studies in Education* 1, no. aop (2025): 1–25.
42. Alfredo J. Artiles, "Untangling the Racialization of Disabilities: An Intersectionality Critique across Disability Models," *Du Bois Review* 10, no. 2 (2013): 329–47; Voulgarides et al., "Moving beyond Compliance."
43. Michael Omi and Howard Winant, "Racial Formation," in *The New Social Theory Reader*, ed. Jeffrey C. Alexander and Steven Seidman (Routledge, 2020); Michael Omi and Howard Winant, *Racial Formation in the United States* (Routledge, 2014); Victor Ray, "A Theory of Racialized Organizations," *American Sociological Review* 84, no. 1 (2019): 26–53.
44. Subini Ancy Annamma David Connor, and Beth Ferri, "Dis/Ability Critical Race Studies (DisCrit): Theorizing at the Intersections of Race and Dis/Ability," *Race Ethnicity and Education* 16, no. 1 (2013): 1–31.
45. Edelman, *Working Law*; Meyer and Rowan, "Institutionalized Organizations"; Voulgarides, *Does Compliance Matter in Special Education?*; Voulgarides et al., "Unpacking the Logic of Compliance."
46. Catherine Voulgarides, "Leadership and the Individuals with Disabilities Education Act (IDEA): Is Compliance with IDEA a Path toward Educational Equity?" *Journal of Education Human Resources* 38, no. 2 (2020): 238–57.

CHAPTER 3

1. See Lloyd M. Dunn, "Special Education for the Mildly Retarded—Is Much of It Justifiable?" *Exceptional Children* 35, no. 1 (1968): 5–22.
2. US Department of Education, *2019 Determination Letters on State Implementation of IDEA*, 2022, www2.ed.gov/fund/data/report/idea/ideafactsheet-determinations-2019.pdf; Roey Ahram, Catherine Kramarczuk Voulgarides, and Rebecca A. Cruz, "Understanding Disability: High-Quality Evidence in Research on Special Education Disproportionality," *Review of Research in Education* 45, no. 1 (2021): 311–45; Federico R. Waitoller, Alfredo J. Artiles, and Douglas A. Cheney "The Miner's Canary: A Review of Overrepresentation Research and Explanations," *Journal of Special Education* 44, no. 1 (2010): 29–49.
3. National Center for Educational Statistics, *Students with Disabilities*, US Department of Education, Institute of Education Sciences, 2024, https://nces.ed.gov/programs/coe/indicator/cgg.
4. Melanie Leung-Gagné et al., *Pushed Out: Trends and Disparities in Out-of-School Suspension* (Learning Policy Institute, 2022).
5. Edward Fergus, *Solving Disproportionality and Achieving Equity: A Leader's Guide to Using Data to Change Hearts and Minds* (Corwin, 2016); María Hernández, David M. Lopez, and Reed Swier, *Dismantling Disproportionality: A Culturally Responsive and Sustaining Systems Approach* (Teachers College Press, 2022); Catherine Kramarczuk Voulgarides, Alexandra Aylward, and Pedro A. Noguera, "The Elusive Quest for Equity: An Analysis of How Contextual Factors Contribute to the Likelihood of School Districts Being Legally Cited for Racial Disproportionality in Special Education," *Journal of Law in Society* 15, no. 2 (2013): 241.
6. See Rachel Elizabeth Fish, "The Racialized Construction of Exceptionality. Experimental Evidence of Race/Ethnicity Effects on Teachers' Interventions," *Social Science Research* 62 (2016): 317–34; Amy E. Fisher, Benjamin W. Fisher, and Kirsten S. Raile, "Disciplinary Disparities by Race and Disability: Using DisCrit Theory to Examine the Manifestation Determination Review Process in Special Education in the United States," *Race*

Ethnicity and Education 24, no. 6 (2021): 755–69; Anne Gregory, Russell J. Skiba, and Pedro A. Noguera, "The Achievement Gap and the Discipline Gap: Two Sides of the Same Coin?" *Educational Researcher* 39, no. 1 (2010): 59–68; Beth Harry and Janette Klingner, *Why Are So Many Students of Color in Special Education?: Understanding Race and Disability in Schools* (Teachers College Press, 2022); Daniel J.Losen et al., "Disturbing Inequities: Exploring the Relationship Between Racial Disparities in Special Education Identification and Discipline," *Journal of Applied Research on Children* 5 (2014); Jacqueline M. Nowicki *K–12 Education: Discipline Disparities for Black Students, Boys, and Students with Disabilities. Report to Congressional Requesters*, GAO-18-258 (US Government Accountability Office, 2018) Amanda L. Sullivan, Ethan R. Van Norman, and David A. Klingbeil, "Exclusionary Discipline of Students with Disabilities: Student and School Characteristics Predicting Suspension," *Remedial and Special Education* 35, no. 4 (2014): 199–210; Russell J. Skiba et al., "The Color of Discipline: Sources of Racial and Gender Disproportionality in School Punishment," *Urban Review* 34 (2002): 317–42.

7. See Russell J. Skiba et al., "What Do We Know about Discipline Disparities? New and Emerging Research," *Inequality in School Discipline Research and Practice to Reduce Disparities* (2016): 21–38; Russell J. Skiba et al., "Race Is Not Neutral: A National Investigation of African American and Latino Disproportionality in School Discipline," *School Psychology Review* 40, no. 1 (2011): 85–107.
8. Alexandra Aylward et al., "Deepening the Study of Disproportionality in Special Education: A Contextual Analysis Within Suburban School Districts," *Exceptional Children*, accepted December 1, 2025, forthcoming. See Alexandra Aylward, Brenda Barrio, and Catherine Kramarczuk Voulgarides, "Exclusion from Educational Opportunity in Diversifying Rural Contexts," *Rural Sociology* 86, no. 3 (2021): 559–85; Tamela McNulty Eitle, "Special Education or Racial Segregation: Understanding Variation in the Representation of Black Students in Educable Mentally Handicapped Programs," *Sociological Quarterly* 43, no. 4 (2002): 575–605; Rachel Elizabeth Fish,

"Standing Out and Sorting In: Exploring the Role of Racial Composition in Racial Disparities in Special Education," *American Educational Research Journal* 56, no. 6 (2019): 2573–2608; Aydin Bal, Jennifer Betters-Bubon, and Rachel E. Fish, "A Multilevel Analysis of Statewide Disproportionality in Exclusionary Discipline and the Identification of Emotional Disturbance," *Education and Urban Society* 51, no. 2 (2019): 247–68.

9. Catherine Kramarczuk Voulgarides and Alexandra Aylward, "Enduring Equity Questions: A Sequence Analysis of Citations in Response to Racial Inequity via the Individuals with Disabilities Education Act," *Journal of Disability Policy Studies* 34, no. 1 (2023): 73–85; Voulgarides et al., "The Elusive Quest for Equity."
10. Susan Fread Albrecht et al., "Federal Policy on Disproportionality in Special Education: Is It Moving Us Forward?" *Journal of Disability Policy Studies* 23, no. 1 (2012): 14–25; US Government Accountability Office, *Individuals with Disabilities Education Act: Standards Needed to Improve Identification of Racial and Ethnic Overrepresentation in Special Education*, 2013, https://www.gao.gov/assets/gao-13-137.pdf.
11. Alfredo J. Artiles et al., "Justifying and Explaining Disproportionality, 1968–2008: A Critique of Underlying Views of Culture," *Exceptional Children* 76, no. 3 (2010): 296.
12. Adai A. Tefera et al., "The Aftermath of Disproportionality Citations: Situating Disability-Race Intersections in Historical, Spatial, and Sociocultural Contexts," *American Educational Research Journal* 60, no. 2 (2023): 367–404.
13. Gloria Ladson-Billings, "From the Achievement Gap to the Education Debt: Understanding Achievement in US Schools," *Educational Researcher* 35, no. 7 (2006): 3–12.
14. H. Richard Milner, "Beyond a Test Score: Explaining Opportunity Gaps in Educational Practice," *Journal of Black Studies* 43, no. 6 (2012): 693–718; A. Wade Boykin and Pedro Noguera, *Creating the Opportunity to Learn: Moving from Research to Practice to Close the Achievement Gap* (ASCD, 2011); Prudence L. Carter and Kevin G. Welner, *Closing the Opportunity Gap: What America Must Do to Give Every Child an Even Chance* (Oxford University Press, 2013).

15. Ladson-Billings, "From the Achievement Gap to the Education Debt."
16. Kathleen A. King Thorius and Paulo Tan, "Expanding Analysis of Educational Debt," *Disability Studies and Critical Race Theory in Education* (2016): 87–97; Subini Ancy Annamma et al., "Dis/Ability Critical Race Studies (DisCrit): Theorizing at the Intersections of Race and Dis/Ability," *Race Ethnicity and Education* 16, no. 1 (2013): 1–31; Alfredo J. Artiles, "Untangling the Racialization of Disabilities: An Intersectionality Critique across Disability Models1," *Du Bois Review* 10, no. 2 (2013): 329–47; Amanda L. Sullivan and Alredo J. Artiles, "Theorizing Racial Inequity in Special Education: Applying structural Inequity Theory to Disproportionality," *Urban Education* 46, no. 6 (2011): 1526–52.
17. For example, Michelle Maroto, David Pettinicchio, and Andrew C. Patterson, "Hierarchies of Categorical Disadvantage: Economic Insecurity at the Intersection of Disability, Gender, and Race," *Gender & Society* 33, no. 1 (2019): 64–93; Erin J. McCauley, "The Potential of College Completion: How Disability Shapes Labor Market Activity Differentially by Educational Attainment and disability Type," *Journal of Disability Policy Studies* 30, no. 4 (2020): 213–22.
18. Rebecca A. Cruz et al., "The Effect of School Funding on Opportunity Gaps for Students with Disabilities: Policy and Context in a Diverse Urban District," *Journal of Disability Policy Studies* 33, no. 1 (2022): 3–14; Tammy Kolbe, "Funding Special Education: Charting a Path That Confronts Complexity and Crafts Coherence," National Education Policy Center, 2019; Tammy Kolbe, Elizabeth Dhuey, and Sara Menlove Doutre, "Unequal and Increasingly Unfair: How Federal Policy Creates Disparities in Special Education Funding," *Exceptional Children* 90, no. 1 (2023): 57–75.
19. Nirmala Erevelles and Andrea Minear, "Unspeakable Offenses: Untangling Race and Disability in Discourses of Intersectionality," *Journal of Literary and Cultural Disability Studies* 4, no. 2 (2010): 127–45; Clyde Chitty, *Eugenics, Race and Intelligence in Education* (A & C Black, 2009); Ann Gibson Winfield, "The Burden Our Children Bear: The Legacy of Eugenic Ideology,"

in *Contemporary Issues in Equity, Democracy, and Public Education*, ed. Felicity Crawford et al. (Routledge, 2024), 17–29.
20. Colin Ong-Dean, *Distinguishing Disability: Parents, Privilege, and Special Education* (University of Chicago Press, 2009), 3.
21. Harry and Klingner, *Why Are So Many Students of Color in Special Education?*
22. Beth Harry and Lydia Occasio-Stoutenberg, *Meeting Families Where They Are: Building Equity Through Advocacy with Diverse Schools and Communities* (Teachers College Press, 2020); Beth Harry and Lydia Occasio-Stoutenberg "Parent Advocacy for Lives that Matter," *Research and Practice for Persons with Severe Disabilities* 46, no. 3 (2021): 184–98.; Jamie N. Pearson et al., "Experiences of Family Peer Advocates Supporting Black Families Raising Autistic Children," *Exceptional Children* 91, no. 1 (2024): 57–73; Catherine Voulgarides, "Equity, Parental/Caregiver 'Power,' and Disability Policy in the US Context," *International Journal of Inclusive Education* 28, no. 4 (2024): 326–43.
23. Zach McCall and Thomas Skrtic, "Intersectional Needs Politics: A Policy Frame for the Wicked Problem of Disproportionality," *Multiple Voices for Ethnically Diverse Exceptional Learners* 11, no. 2 (2009): 14.
24. Geoffrey C. Bowker and Susan Leigh Star, *Sorting Things Out: Classification and Its Consequences* (MIT Press, 1999).
25. See Dunn, "Special Education for the Mildly Retarded."
26. Zeus Leonardo and Alicia A. Broderick, "Smartness as Property: A Critical Exploration of Intersections between Whiteness and Disability Studies," *Teachers College Record* 113, no. 10 (2011): 2214.
27. Voulgarides, "Equity, Parental/Caregiver 'Power,' and Disability Policy."
28. McCall and Skrtic, "Intersectional Needs Politics," 16; Thomas M. Skrtic, *Behind Special Education* (Love Publishing Company, 1991) Thomas Skrtic, "An Organizational Analysis of the Overrepresentation of Poor and Minority Students in Special Education," *Multiple Voices for Ethnically Diverse Exceptional Learners* 6, no. 1 (2003): 41–57.
29. Leonardo and Broderick, "Smartness as Property," 2214.
30. Ladson-Billings, "From the Achievement Gap to the Education Debt."

CHAPTER 4

1. Peter David Blanck and Eilionóir Flynn, eds., *Routledge Handbook of Disability Law and Human Rights* (Routledge, 2017); Keith A. Mayes, *The Unteachables: Disability Rights and the Invention of Black Special Education* (University of Minnesota Press, 2023); Fred Pelka, *What We Have Done: An Oral History of the Disability Rights Movement* (University of Massachusetts Press, 2012); Gelila Selassie and Denny Chan, "The Power and Limits of Law to Fight Structural Ageism, Ableism, and Racism," *Generations* 47, no. 1 (2023): 1–10.
2. Frank Dobbin and Alexandra Kalev, "The Civil Rights Revolution at Work: What Went Wrong," *Annual Review of Sociology* 47, no. 1 (2021): 281–303; Samuel Lucas, *Theorizing Discrimination in an Era of Contested Prejudice: Discrimination in the United States* (Temple University Press, 2009).
3. Lauren B. Edelman, *Working Law: Courts, Corporations, and Symbolic Civil Rights* (University of Chicago Press, 2020).
4. For a discussion of fragmented harm, see Charles M. Payne, *Getting What We Ask For: The Ambiguity of Success and Failure in Urban Education* (Praeger, 1984); and Mica Pollock, *Because of Race: How Americans Debate Harm and Opportunity in Our Schools* (Princeton University Press, 2010). For neoinstitutional framework, see Richard Arum, "Schools and Communities: Ecological and Institutional Dimensions," *Annual Review of Sociology* 26, no. 1 (2000): 395–418; John W. Meyer and Brian Rowan, "Institutionalized Organizations: Formal Structure as Myth and Ceremony," *American Journal of Sociology* 83, no. 2 (1977): 340–63; and Walter W. Powell and Paul J. DiMaggio, *The New Institutionalism in Organizational Analysis* (University of Chicago Press, 2012).
5. Powell and DiMaggio, *The New Institutionalism in Organizational Analysis*; Paul J. DiMaggio and Walter W. Powell. "The Iron Cage Revisited: Institutional Isomorphism and Collective Rationality in Organizational Fields," *American Sociological Review* 48, no. 2 (1983): 147–60
6. Payne, *Getting What We Ask For*; Payne, *So Much Reform, So Little Change: The Persistence of Failure in Urban Schools*, vol. 8 (Harvard Education Press, 2008).

7. Valencia, *Achieving Equal Educational Opportunity for Students of Color: Disrupting Structural Racism–An American Imperative* (Teachers College Press, 2024); Valencia, *Dismantling Contemporary Deficit Thinking: Educational Thought and Practice* (Routledge, 2010); Payne, *Getting What We Ask For*; Payne, *So Much Reform*.
8. See Catherine Voulgarides, *Does Compliance Matter in Special Education?: IDEA and the Hidden Inequities of Practice* (Teachers College Press, 2018); Catherine Voulgarides, "The Promises and Pitfalls of Mandating Racial Equity in Special Education," *Phi Delta Kappan* 103, no. 6 (2022): 14–20.
9. Arum, "Schools and Communities."
10. David Baker, *The Schooled Society: The Educational Transformation of Global Culture* (Stanford University Press, 2020); Alexander W. Wiseman and David P. Baker, "The Symbiotic Relationship Between Empirical Comparative Research on Education and Neo-institutional Theory," in *The Impact of Comparative Education Research on Institutional Theory*, eds. David P. Baker and Alexander W. Wiseman (Emerald, 2006); Alexander W. Wiseman, M. Fernanda Astiz, and David P. Baker, "Comparative Education Research Framed by Neo-institutional Theory: A Review of Diverse Approaches and Conflicting Assumptions," *Compare* 44, no. 5 (2014): 688–709.
11. Meyer and Rowan, "Institutionalized Organizations."
12. Voulgarides, *Does Compliance Matter in Special Education*?
13. Karl E. Weick, "Administering Education in Loosely Coupled Schools," *Phi Delta Kappan* 63, no. 10 (1982): 673–76.
14. Meyer and Rowan, "Institutionalized Organizations."
15. Lauren B. Edelman and Shauhin A. Talesh, "To Comply or Not to Comply—That Isn't the Question: How Organizations Construct the Meaning of Compliance," in *Explaining Compliance: Business Responses to Regulation*, ed. Christine Parker and Vibek Leimann (Edward Elgar, 2011).
16. These ideas have been applied to civil rights law, equal opportunity employment, and antidiscrimination policies to analyze how these measures have also not achieved their intended aims. See Lauren B. Edelman, "Legal Environments and Organizational Governance: The Expansion of due Process in the American Workplace," *American Journal of Sociology* 95, no.

6 (1990): 1401–40; Lauren B. Edelman, Christopher Uggen, and Howard S. Erlanger, "The Endogeneity of Legal Regulation: Grievance Procedures as Rational Myth," *American Journal of Sociology* 105, no. 2 (1999): 406–54.

17. Edelman, "Legal Environments and Organizational Governance"; W. Richard Scott, *Institutions and Organizations: Ideas and Interests* (Sage, 2008).
18. James Q. Wilson, *Bureaucracy: What Government Agencies Do and Why They Do It* (Hachette, 2019).
19. Perry A. Zirkel, "The Role of Law in Special Education," *Exceptionality* 31, no. 4 (2023): 308–18.
20. See John W. Meyer, Georg Krücken, and Gili S. Drori, *World Society: The Writings of John W. Meyer* (Oxford University Press, 2009).
21. John W. Meyer, *Organizational Factors Affecting Legalization in Education* (Institute for Research on Educational Finance and Governance, School of Education, Stanford University, 1981); Brian Rowan, H. Meyer, and B. Rowan, "The New Institutionalism the Study of Educational Organizations: Changing Ideas for Changing Times," *The New Institutionalism in Education* (2006): 15–32
22. Randall Collins, *The Credential Society: An Historical Sociology of Education and Stratification* (Columbia University Press, 2019); Hans Heinrich Gerth, Max Weber, and Wright Mills, *From Max Weber: Essays in Sociology* (Routledge, 2013); Max Weber, "The Rationalization of Education and Training," in *Social Stratification, Class, Race, and Gender in Sociological Perspective*, 2nd ed. (Routledge, 2019); Weber, "Rational-Legal Authority and Bureaucracy," in *Policy Process: A Reader*, ed. Michael Hill (Routledge, 1997).
23. Bo Dong, "A Systematic Review of the Organizational Inertia Literature and Future Outlook," *International Journal of Education and Humanities* 8, no. 2 (2023): 119–23; Powell and DiMaggio, *The New Institutionalism in Organizational Analysis*; Michael T. Hannan and John Freeman, "Structural Inertia and Organizational Change," *American Sociological Review* (1984): 149–64.
24. John Richardson and Justin Powell, *Comparing Special Education: Origins to Contemporary Paradoxes* (Stanford University Press, 2011).

25. John Richardson and Justin Powell, *Comparing Special Education.*
26. Laura E. Bray and Jennifer Lin Russell, "Going off Script: Structure and Agency in Individualized Education Program Meetings," *American Journal of Education* 122, no. 3 (2016): 367–98; Hugh Mehan, "Language and Power in Organizational Process," *Discourse Processes* 10, no. 4 (1987): 291–301; Thomas M. Skrtic, Wayne Sailor, and Kathleen Gee, "Voice, Collaboration, and Inclusion: Democratic Themes in Educational and Social Reform Initiatives," *Remedial and Special Education* 17, no. 3 (1996): 142–57; Sally Tomlinson, *A Sociology of Special and Inclusive Education* (Routledge, 2017).
27. Harry, "Restructuring the Participation of African-American Parents in Special Education," *Exceptional Children* 59, no. 2 (1992): 123–31; Sally Tomlinson, *The Politics of Race, Class and Special Education: The Selected Works of Sally Tomlinson* (Routledge, 2014).
28. Beth Harry, Norma Allen, and Margaret McLaughlin, "Communication versus Compliance: African-American Parents' Involvement in Special Education," *Exceptional Children* 61, no. 4 (1995): 364–77.
29. Catherine Kramarczuk Voulgarides et al., "Understanding Policy Reverberations Across the Educational Ecosystem to Effectuate Change," *Theory into Practice* 63, no. 4 (2024): 457–68; Meghan M. Burke and Samantha E. Goldman, "Documenting the Experiences of Special Education Advocates," *Journal of Special Education* 51, no. 1 (2017): 3–13; Meghan M. Burke, Kristina Rios, and Chung eun Lee, "Exploring the Special Education Advocacy Process According to Families and Advocates," *Journal of Special Education* 53, no. 3 (2019): 131–41; Erin Phillips, "When Parents Aren't Enough: External Advocacy in Special Education," *Yale Law Journal* 117 (2007): 1802.
30. Edelman, "Legal Environments and Organizational Governance."
31. Ian F. Haney López, "Institutional Racism: Judicial Conduct and a New Theory of Racial Discrimination," *Yale Law Journal* 109 (1999): 1717; Ian F. Haney López,"White by Law 10th Anniversary Edition: The Legal Construction of Race," in *White by Law 10th Anniversary Edition: The Legal Construction of Race* (New York University Press, 2006).

CHAPTER 5

1. Richard R. Valencia and Daniel G. Solórzano, "Contemporary Deficit Thinking," in *The Evolution of Deficit Thinking*, ed. Richard R. Valencia (Routledge, 2012).
2. Subini Ancy Annamma, David Connor, and Beth Ferri, "Dis/Ability Critical Race Studies (DisCrit): Theorizing at the Intersections of Race and Dis/Ability," *Race Ethnicity and Education* 16, no. 1 (2013): 1–31
3. Drrick A. Bell, "Who's Afraid of Critical Race Theory?" *University of Illinois Law Review* 4, no. 3 (1995): 823–46; Richard Delgado and Jean Stefanic, "Critical Race Theory: Past, Present, and Future," *Current Legal Problems* 51, no. 1 (1998): 467; Daniel G. Solórzano, "Critical Race Theory's Intellectual Roots: My Email Epistolary with Derrick Bell," in *Handbook of Critical Race Theory in Education*, eds. Marvin Lynn and Adrienne D. Dixson (Routledge, 2021).
4. Cheryl I. Harris, "Reflections on Whiteness as Property," *Harvard Law Review* 134 (2020): 1; Cheryl I. Harris, "Whiteness as Property," *Harvard Law Review* 106 (1993): 1707–91
5. Delgado and Stefanic, "Critical Race Theory"; Harris, "Reflections on Whiteness as Property"; Harris, "Whiteness as Property."
6. Natasha M Strassfeld, "The Future of IDEA: Monitoring Disproportionate Representation of Minority Students in Special Education and Intentional Discrimination Claims," *Case Western Reserve Law Review* 67 (2016): 1121.
7. Fiona A. Kumari Campbell, "Exploring Internalized Ableism Using Critical Race Theory," *Disability & Society* 23, no. 2 (2008): 151–62; Sarah Diem and Anjalé D. Welton, *Anti-Racist Educational Leadership and Policy: Addressing Racism in Public Education* (Routledge, 2020); Elizabeth Stringer Keefe, "From Detractive to Democratic: The Duty of Teacher Education to Disrupt Structural Ableism and Reimagine Disability," *Teachers College Record* 124, no. 3 (2022): 115–47; Anjalé D. Welton, Devean R. Owens, and Eboni M. Zamani-Gallaher, "Anti-Racist Change: A Conceptual Framework for Educational Institutions to Take Systemic Action," *Teachers College Record* 120, no. 14 (2018): 1–22.

8. Keith A. Mayes, *The Unteachables: Disability Rights and the Invention of Black Special Education* (University of Minnesota Press, 2023); Kim E. Nielsen, *A Disability History of the United States*, vol. 2 (Beacon Press, 2012.)
9. Robert A. Wilson and Joshua St. Pierre. "Eugenics and Disability," *Rethinking Disability: World Perspectives in Culture and Society* 93 (2016); Robyn M. Powell, "Confronting Eugenics Means Finally Confronting Its Ableist Roots," *William and Mary Journal of Race, Gender, and Social Justice* 27 (2020): 607; Michael Rembis, "Disability and the History of Eugenics," in *The Oxford Handbook of Disability History*, ed. Michael Remis, Catherine Kudlick, and Kim E. Nielsen (Oxford University Press, 2018); Jay Dolmage, "Disabled upon Arrival: The Rhetorical Construction of Disability and Race at Ellis Island," *Cultural Critique* 77 (2011): 24–69.
10. Nirmala Erevelles, Anne Kanga, and Renee Middleton,"How Does It Feel to Be a Problem? Race, Disability, and Exclusion in Educational Policy," in *Who Benefits from Special Education?: Remediating (Fixing) Other People's Children* (Routledge, 2006); Nirmala Erevelles, *Disability and Difference in Global Contexts: Enabling a Transformative Body Politic* (Palgrave Macmillan, 2011).
11. Martha Minow, *In Brown's Wake: Legacies of America's Educational Landmark* (Oxford University Press, 2010).
12. Thomas P. Dirth and Glenn A. Adams, "Decolonial Theory and Disability Studies: On the Modernity/Coloniality of Ability," *Journal of Social and Political Psychology* 7, no. 1 (2019): 260–89; Catherine Kramarczuk Voulgarides et al., "Educational Inequality and the Paradox of Dis/Ability Rights in a Schooled Society: Moving Towards an Intersectional Discursive, Material, and Emotive Approach," *Educational Review* 76, no. 1 (2024): 181–198.
13. David Isaac Hernández-Saca, Catherine Kramarczuk Voulgarides, and Susan Larson Etscheidt, "A Critical Systematic Literature Review of Global Inclusive Education Using an Affective, Intersectional, Discursive, Emotive and Material Lens," *Education Sciences* 13, no. 12 (2023): 1212.
14. Voulgarides et al., "Educational Inequality." See also David Isaac Hernández-Saca and Mercedes Adell Cannon, "Interrogating Disability Epistemologies: Towards Collective

Dis/Ability Intersectional Emotional, Affective and Spiritual Autoethnographies for Healing," *International Journal of Qualitative Studies in Education* 32, no. 3 (2019): 243–62.

15. Alfredo J. Artiles, "Untangling the Racialization of Disabilities: An Intersectionality Critique across Disability Models," *Du Bois Review* 10, no. 2 (2013): 331.
16. To this point, Frederick and Shifrer stated, "Because legal rights tend to operate around singular-identity statuses, people who experience multiple forms of inequality, and for whom racism and ableism are powerful, inter-locking forces in their lives, cannot as easily benefit from the legal rights model, which demands proof of blatant and intentional discrimination directed at an individual on the basis of a singular aspect of the victim's identity"; Angela Frederick and Dara Shifrer, "Race and Disability: From Analogy to Intersectionality," *Sociology of Race and Ethnicity* 5, no. 2 (2019): 200–14. See also Samuel R. Bagenstos, "From Integrationism to Equal Protection: TenBroek and the Next 25 Years of Disability Rights," *University of St. Thomas Law Journal* 13 (2016): 13; Linda R. Shaw, Fong Chan, and Brian T. McMahon, "Intersectionality and Disability Harassment: The Interactive Effects of Disability, Race, Age, and Gender," *Rehabilitation Counseling Bulletin* 55, no. 2 (2012): 82–91; Dean Spade, "Intersectional Resistance and Law Reform," *Signs: Journal of Women in Culture and Society* 38, no. 4 (2013): 1031–55. See also Adai A. Tefera and Gustavo E. Fischman, "Beyond Good Intentions in Special Education Policy: Engaging with Critical Disability Intersectional Research," *Qualitative Inquiry* 30, no. 1 (2024): 48–58; Adai A. Tefera, Jeanne M. Powers, and Gustavo E. Fischman, "Intersectionality in Education: A Conceptual Aspiration and Research Imperative," *Review of Research in Education* 42, no. 1 (2018): vii–xvii.
17. Kathleen A. King Thorius, *Equity Expansive Technical Assistance for Schools: Education Partnerships to Reverse Racial Disproportionality* (Teachers College Press, 2023); María G. Hernández, David M. Lopez, and Reed Swier, *Dismantling Disproportionality: A Culturally Responsive and Sustaining Systems Approach* (Teachers College Press, 2022).

18. Tarun Kumar Vashisth, Sushil Nifadkar, and Rajesh Chandwani, "Organizational Socialization of Employees with Blindness: Navigating Ableism in Diverse Spaces," *Academy of Management Proceedings* 2024, no. 1 (2024): 12933; Koen Van Lear, Eline Jammaers, and Wendy Hoeven, "Disabling Organizational Spaces: Exploring the Processes through Which Spatial Environments Disable Employees with Impairments," *Organization* 29, no. 6 (2022): 1018–35; Alexis Padilla, Catherine Voulgarides, and Rhonda Bondie, "Disability and Educational Justice: Exploring Intersectional Ways to Disrupt the Logic of Compliance," *Journal of Disability Studies in Education* 1, no. aop (2025): 1–25.
19. Victor Ray, "A Theory of Racialized Organizations," *American Sociological Review* 84, no. 1 (2019): 26–53.
20. Frederick and Shifrer, "Race and Disability."
21. Subini Ancy Annamma, Darrell D. Jackson, and Deb Morrison, "Conceptualizing Color-Evasiveness: Using Dis/Ability Critical Race Theory to Expand a Color-Blind Racial Ideology in Education and Society," *Race Ethnicity and Education* 20, no. 2 (2017): 147–62; Lissa Stapleton and Liam James, "Not Another All White Study: Challenging Color-Evasiveness Ideology in Disability Scholarship (Practice Brief)," *Journal of Postsecondary Education and Disability* 33, no. 3 (2020): 215–22; Kathleen A. King Thorius, "Facilitating En/Counters with Special Education's Cloak of Benevolence in Professional Learning to Eliminate Racial Disproportionality in Special Education," *International Journal of Qualitative Studies in Education* 32, no. 3 (2019): 323–40; Sally Tomlinson, *The Politics of Race, Class and Special Education: The Selected Works of Sally Tomlinson* (Routledge, 2014).
22. Thorius; "Facilitating En/Counters."
23. Angelina E. Castagno, ed., *The Price of Nice: How Good Intentions Maintain Educational Inequity* (University of Minnesota Press, 2019), xix.
24. Angelina E. Castagno, *Educated in Whiteness: Good Intentions and Diversity in Schools* (University of Minnesota Press, 2014); Sylvia Mac, "Niceness in Special Education: An Ethnographic Case Study of Benevolence, Goodness, and Paternalism at Colina Cedro Charter High School," in *The Price of Nice: How Good*

Intentions Maintain Educational Inequity, ed. Angelina E. Castagno (University of Minnesota Press, 2019).

25. On this point, Saito had this to say: "People working to enact and support race-neutral public policies may ignore the ways in which race is already present in the ideologies and practices of the larger society that shape the formation and implementation of policies. As a result, policies that appear race neutral may in fact be structured in ways that have racialized outcomes. This occurs because the policies do nothing to counter the ways in which race is already present, and thus the policies serve to reinforce racialized practices." Leland T. Saito, *The Politics of Exclusion* (Stanford University Press, 2009), 4. See also H. Richard Milner and E. Self, "Getting Real about Race: Colorblindness as Complicit Instructional Ineffectiveness," *National Journal of Urban Education & Practice* 6, no. 1 (2012): 1–19; Thorius, "Facilitating En/Counters."
26. Russell J. Skiba et al., "The Color of Discipline: Sources of Racial and Gender Disproportionality in School Punishment," *Urban Review* 34 (2002): 317–42.
27. Russell J. Skiba et al., "The Color of Discipline," 332.
28. Daniel J. Losen et al., "Disturbing Inequities: Exploring the Relationship between Racial Disparities in Special Education Identification and Discipline," *Journal of Applied Research on Children* 5 (2014); Rebecca A. Cruz, Saili S. Kulkarni, and Allison R. Firestone, "A QuantCrit Analysis of Context, Discipline, Special Education, and Disproportionality," *AERA Open* 7 (2021): 23328584211041354; Sarah Hurwitz et al., "Special Education and Individualized Academic Growth: A Longitudinal Assessment of Outcomes for Students with Disabilities," *American Educational Research Journal* 57, no. 2 (2020): 576–611.
29. Castagno, ed., *The Price of Nice*; Susan Baglieri and Priya Lalvani, *Undoing Ableism: Teaching about Disability in K–12 Classrooms* (Routledge, 2019).
30. Lisa Delpit, *Other People's Children: Cultural Conflict in the Classroom* (New Press, 2006).
31. Mike Cole, "Critical Race Theory in Education, Marxism and Abstract Racial Domination," *British Journal of Sociology of Education* 33, no. 2 (2012): 167–83; Cheryl E. Matias, *Feeling White:*

Whiteness, Emotionality, and Education (Springer, 2016); Cheryl E. Matias and Michalinos Zemblyas, "'When Saying You Care Is Not Really Caring': Emotions of Disgust, Whiteness Ideology, and Teacher Education," *Critical Studies in Education* 55, no. 3 (2014): 319–37

32. Alicia Broderick and Priya Lalvani, "Dysconscious Ableism: Toward a Liberatory Praxis in Teacher Education." *International Journal of Inclusive Education* 21, no. 9 (2017): 894–905; Gloria Ladson-Billings and William F. Tate, "Toward a Critical Race Theory of Education," *Teachers College Record* 97, no. 1 (1995): 47–68.
33. Thorius, "Facilitating En/Counters."
34. Annamma et al., "Dis/Ability Critical Race Studies."
35. See Tyrone C. Howard, "Culturally Responsive Pedagogy," in *Transforming Multicultural Education Policy and Practice: Expanding Educational Opportunity*, ed. James A. Banks (Teachers College Press, 2021); Gloria Ladson-Billings, "Toward a Theory of Culturally Relevant Pedagogy," *American Educational Research Journal* 32, no. 3 (1995): 465–91; Django Paris and H. Sammy Alim, *Culturally Sustaining Pedagogies: Teaching and Learning for Justice in a Changing World* (Teachers College Press, 2017).
36. Geneva Gay, *Culturally Responsive Teaching: Theory, Research, and Practice* (Teachers College Press, 2018).
37. Django Paris, "Culturally Sustaining Pedagogy: A Needed Change in Stance, Terminology, and Practice," *Educational Researcher* 41, no. 3 (2012): 93–97.
38. Howard, "Culturally Responsive Pedagogy."
39. Shernaz García and Alba Ortiz, "A Framework for Culturally and Linguistically Responsive Design of Response-to-Intervention Models," *Multiple Voices for Ethnically Diverse Exceptional Learners* 11, no. 1 (2008): 24–41; Federico R. Waitoller and Kathleen A. King Thorius, "Cross Pollinating Culturally Sustaining Pedagogy and Universal Design for Learning: Toward an Inclusive Pedagogy that Accounts for Dis/Ability," *Harvard Educational Review* 86, no. 3 (2016): 366–89.
40. Thorius, "Facilitating En/Counters."
41. Annamma et al., "Dis/ability Critical Race Studies."
42. Brenda L. Barrio et al., "Designing Culturally Responsive and Relevant Individualized Educational Programs," *Intervention in School and Clinic* 53, no. 2 (2017): 114–19.

43. Connor and Ferri, "Historicizing Dis/ability: Creating Normalcy, Containing Difference," in *Foundations of Disability Studies*, eds. Matthew Wappett and Katrina Arndt (Palgrave Macmillan, 2013); Thorius, "Facilitating En/Counters."

CHAPTER 6

1. Paulo Freire, *Education: The Practice of Freedom* (Writers and Readers, 1974); Paulo Freire, *Pedagogy of the Oppressed*, 30th anniversary ed. (Continuum, 2000).
2. Aaliyah El-Amin et al., "Critical Consciousness: A Key to Student Achievement," *Phi Delta Kappan* 98, no. 5 (2017): 18–23.
3. Catherine Voulgarides, *Does Compliance Matter in Special Education?: IDEA and the Hidden Inequities of Practice* (Teachers College Press, 2018); Catherine Voulgarides, "The Promises and Pitfalls of Mandating Racial Equity in Special Education," *Phi Delta Kappan* 103, no. 6 (2022): 14–20; Catherine Kramarczuk Voulgarides et al., "Unpacking the Logic of Compliance in Special Education: Contextual Influences on Discipline Racial Disparities in Suburban schools," *Sociology of Education* 94, no. 3 (2021): 208–26.
4. Rayna Rapp and Faye Ginsburg, "The Paradox of Recognition: Success or Stigma for Children with Learning Disabilities," in *Contesting Recognition: Culture, Identity and Citizenship*, ed. Janice McLaughlin, Peter Phillmore, and Diane Richards (Palgrave Macmillan, 2011).
5. Alfredo J. Artiles, Sherman Dorn, and Aydin Bal, "Objects of Protection, Enduring Nodes of Difference: Disability Intersections with 'Other' Differences, 1916 to 2016," *Review of Research in Education* 40, no. 1 (2016): 777–820.
6. Lloyd M. Dunn, "Special Education for the Mildly Retarded—Is Much of It Justifiable?" *Exceptional Children* 35, no. 1 (1968): 5–22; Federico R. Waitoller, Alfredo J. Artiles, and Douglas A. Cheney, "The Miner's Canary: A Review of Overrepresentation Research and Explanations," *Journal of Special Education* 44, no. 1 (2010): 29–49; Roey Ahram, Catherine Kramarczuk Voulgarides, and Rebecca A. Cruz, "Understanding Disability: High-Quality Evidence in Research on Special Education Disproportionality," *Review of Research in Education* 45, no. 1 (2021): 311–45.

7. Gloria Ladson-Billings, "From the Achievement Gap to the Education Debt: Understanding Achievement in US Schools," *Educational Researcher* 35, no. 7 (2006): 3–12.
8. Freire, *Education: The Practice of Freedom*; Freire, *Pedagogy of the Oppressed*.
9. Patricia Hill Collins and Sima Bilge, *Intersectionality* (Wiley, 2020).
10. Paulo Freire, "The Banking Concept of Education," in *Thinking about Schools: A Foundation of Education Reader*, ed. Eleanore Blair Hilty (Routledge, 2011).
11. Freire, *Pedagogy of the Oppressed*.
12. Artiles, "Objects of Protection"; Rapp and Ginsberg, "The Paradox of Recognition."
13. Freire, *Education: The Practice of Freedom*.
14. Henry A. Giroux, "Rethinking Education as the Practice of Freedom: Paulo Freire and the Promise of Critical Pedagogy," *Policy Futures in Education* 8, no. 6 (2010): 715–21; Peter McInerney, "Toward a Critical Pedagogy of Engagement for Alienated Youth: Insights from Freire and school-Based Research," *Critical Studies in Education* 50, no. 1 (2009): 23–35.
15. Giroux, "Rethinking Education as the Practice of Freedom," 716.
16. Collins and Bilge, *Intersectionality*.
17. Collins and Bilge, *Intersectionality*, 162–63.
18. Maria Ceci Misoczky, "Paulo Freire and the Praxis of Liberation: Education, Organization and Ethics," *Management Learning* 55, no. 1 (2024): 124–40.
19. Mariana Souto-Manning, *Freire, Teaching, and Learning: Culture Circles across Contexts* (Peter Lang, 2010), 33.
20. Souto-Manning, *Freire, Teaching, and Learning*; Mariana Souto-Manning, "Transforming University-Based Teacher Education: Preparing Asset-, Equity-, and Justice-Oriented Teachers within the Contemporary Political Context," *Teachers College Record* 121, no. 6 (2019): 1–26
21. Souto-Manning, *Freire, Teaching, and Learning*, 36.
22. Souto-Manning, *Freire, Teaching, and Learning*, 36.
23. Souto-Manning, *Freire, Teaching, and Learning*, 19.
24. Souto-Manning, *Freire, Teaching, and Learning*, 37–38.

25. Souto-Manning, *Freire, Teaching, and Learning*, 35.
26. Freire, *Education: The Practice of Freedom.*
27. Souto-Manning, *Freire, Teaching, and Learning*, 42.

CHAPTER 7

1. Paulo Freire, *Education: The Practice of Freedom* (Writers and Readers, 1974); Paulo Freire, *Pedagogy of the Oppressed*, 30th anniversary ed. (Continuum, 2000).
2. Mildred Boveda and Subini Ancy Annamma, "Beyond Making a Statement: An Intersectional Framing of the Power and Possibilities of Positioning," *Educational Researcher* 52, no. 5 (2023): 306–14.
3. Patricia Hill Collins, *On Intellectual Activism* (Temple University Press, 2012).
4. Boveda and Annamma, "Beyond Making a Statement."
5. Patricia Hill Collins, *Black Feminist Thought: Knowledge, Consciousness, and the Politics of Empowerment*, 2nd ed. (Routledge, 2009).
6. Collins, *Black Feminist Thought.*
7. Orla Higgins Averill, Claudia Rinaldi, and U. S. E. L. Collaborative, "Multi-tier System of Supports (MTSS)," *District Administration* 48, no. 8 (2011): 91–95.
8. Kent McIntosh and Steve Goodman, *Integrated Multi-tiered Systems of Support: Blending RTI and PBIS* (Guilford, 2016); George Sugai and Robert H. Horner, "Responsiveness-to-Intervention and School-Wide Positive Behavior Supports: Integration of Multi-tiered System Approaches," *Exceptionality* 17, no. 4 (2009): 223–37.
9. Sheri Berkeley et al., "A Snapshot of RTI Implementation Implementation a Decade Later: New Picture, Same Story," *Journal of Learning Disabilities* 53, no. 5 (2020): 332–42; Wendy M. Reinke et al., "Problem Solving within an RTI Framework: Roles and Functions of Effective Teams," in *Handbook of Response to Intervention and Multi-tiered Systems of Support*, ed. Shane R. Jimerdson, Matthew K. Burns, and Amanda VanDerHeyden (Routledge, 2018); Jingyuan Zhang et al., "Response to Intervention(RTI)/Multi-tiered Systems of Support (MTSS): A Nationwide Analysis," *Journal of Educational Leadership and Policy Studies* 7, no. 1 (2023): n1.

10. Katherine Clemens et al., "Proactively Pivot: Guidance on Adapting the PBIS Framework in Response to Crises to Support Students with Disabilities," *Teaching Exceptional Children* 55, no. 1 (2022): 40–47; Brooke C. Shuster et al., "Including Students with Disabilities in Positive Behavioral Interventions and Supports: Experiences and Perspectives of Special Educators," *Journal of Positive Behavior Interventions* 19, no. 3 (2017): 143–57.
11. See Sugai and Horner, "Responsiveness-to-Intervention."
12. Sugai and Horner, "Responsiveness-to-Intervention."
13. McIntosh and Goodman, *Integrated Multi-tiered Systems of Support.*
14. Sarah V. Arden et al., "Toward More Effective Tiered Systems: Lessons from National Implementation Efforts," *Exceptional Children* 83, no. 3 (2017): 269–80; Kaitlin M. Leonard et al., "Implementing MTSS in Beginning Reading: Tools and Systems to Support Schools and Teachers," *Learning Disabilities Research and Practice* 34, no. 2 (2019): 110–17.
15. Joseph Calvin Gagnon, Brian R. Barber, and Ilker Soyturk, "Policies and Practices Supporting Positive Behavioral Interventions and Supports (PBIS) Implementation in High-Poverty Florida Middle Schools," *Exceptionality* 28, no. 3 (2020): 176–94; Amanda L. Sullivan et al., "No 'Top of the Triangle Kids': Toward Conceptual Clarity of Students, Behavior, and Tiers in MTSS to Advance Social Justice," *Journal of School Psychology* 106 (2024): 101325.
16. Yolanda Anyon et al., "An Exploration Between Student Racial Background and the School Sub-contexts of Office Discipline Referrals: A Critical Race Theory Analysis," *Race Ethnicity and Education* 21, no. 3 (2018): 390–406
17. Michael John Orosco and Janette Klingner, "One School's Implementation of RTI with English Language Learners: 'Referring into RTI,'" *Journal of Learning Disabilities* 43, no. 3 (2010): 269–88; Kathleen A. King Thorius et al., "A Critical Practice Analysis of Response to Intervention Appropriation in an Urban School," *Remedial and Special Education* 35, no. 5 (2014): 287–99.
18. McIntosh and Goodman, *Integrated Multi-tiered Systems of Support*; Brandi Simenson et al., "Supporting Students' Social, Emotional, and Behavior (SEB) Growth Through Tier 2 and

3 Intervention Within a Multi-tiered System of Supports (MTSS) Framework," in *Handbook of Classroom Management*, ed. Edward J. Sabornie and Dorothy L. Esplelage (Routledge, 2022).

19. McIntosh and Goodman, *Integrated Multi-tiered Systems of Support.*
20. Lindsay M. Fallon, Margarida Veiga, and George Sugai, "Strengthening MTSS for Behavior (MTSS-B) to Promote Racial Equity," *School Psychology Review* 52, no. 5 (2023): 518–33; Kent McIntosh, Ambra L. Green, and Nikole Hollins-Sims, "Improving School Climate Within Multi-tiered Systems of Support," in *Creating an Inclusive School Climate: A School Psychology Model for Supporting Marginalized Students* (Routledge, 2023).

APPENDIX

1. Edward Fergus, *Solving Disproportionality and Achieving Equity: A Leader's Guide to Using Data to Change Hearts and Minds* (Corwin, 2016); Kathleen A. King Thorius, *Equity Expansive Technical Assistance for Schools: Education Partnerships to Reverse Racial Disproportionality* (Teachers College Press, 2023); María G. Hernández, David M. Lopez, and Reed Swier, "Dismantling Disproportionality*: A Culturally Responsive and sustaining Systems Approach* (Teachers College Press, 2022); Catherine Voulgarides et al., "Moving beyond Compliance and Toward Equity to Address Racial Disproportionality," *Intervention in School and Clinic* 60, no. 2 (2024): 108–18.
2. Paulo Freire, *Pedagogy of the Oppressed*, 30th anniversary ed. (Continuum, 2000).
3. Freire, *Pedagogy of the Oppressed.*
4. Mariana Souto-Manning, *Freire, Teaching, and Learning: Culture Circles Across Contexts* (Peter Lang, 2010).
5. Mariana Souto-Manning, *Freire, Teaching, and Learning.*
6. Gloria Ladson-Billings, "From the Achievement Gap to the Education Debt: Understanding Achievement in US Schools," *Educational Researcher* 35, no. 7 (2006): 3–12.
7. See Fergus, *Solving Disproportionality and Achieving Equity.*
8. Souto-Manning, *Freire, Teaching, and Learning.*
9. Souto-Manning, *Freire, Teaching, and Learning.*
10. Souto-Manning, *Freire, Teaching, and Learning.*

BIBLIOGRAPHY

Ahearn, Eileen M. *State Compliance Monitoring Practices: An Update. Final Report*. National Association of State Directors of Special Education, 1995.

Ahram, Roey, Edward Fergus, and Pedro Noguera. "Addressing Racial/Ethnic Disproportionality in Special Education: Case Studies of Suburban School Districts." *Teachers College Record* 113, no. 10 (2011): 2233–66.

Ahram, Roey, Catherine Kramarczuk Voulgarides, and Rebecca A. Cruz. "Understanding Disability: High-Quality Evidence in Research on Special Education Disproportionality." *Review of Research in Education* 45, no. 1 (2021): 311–45.

Albrecht, Susan Fread, Russell J. Skiba, Daniel J. Losen, Choong-Geun Chung, and Laura Middelberg. "Federal Policy on Disproportionality in Special Education: Is It Moving Us Forward?" *Journal of Disability Policy Studies* 23, no. 1 (2012): 14–25.

Andrews, Erin E., Robyn M. Powell, and Kara Ayers. "The Evolution of Disability Language: Choosing Terms to Describe Disability." *Disability and health journal* 15, no. 3 (2022): 101328.

Annamma, Subini Ancy, David Connor, and Beth Ferri. "Dis/Ability Critical Race Studies (DisCrit): Theorizing at the Intersections of Race and Dis/Ability." *Race Ethnicity and Education* 16, no. 1 (2013): 1–31.

Annamma, Subini Ancy, Darrell D. Jackson, and Deb Morrison. "Conceptualizing Color-Evasiveness: Using Dis/Ability Critical Race Theory to Expand a Color-Blind Racial Ideology in Education and Society." *Race Ethnicity and Education* 20, no. 2 (2017): 147–62.

Anyon, Yolanda, Chalane Lechuga, Debora Ortega, Barbara Downing, Eldridge Greer, and John Simmons. "An Exploration of the Relationships Between Student Racial Background and the School Sub-contexts of Office Discipline Referrals: A Critical Race Theory Analysis." *Race Ethnicity and Education* 21, no. 3 (2018): 390–406.

Arden, Sarah V., Allison Gruner Gandhi, Rebecca Zumeta Edmonds, and Louis Danielson. "Toward More Effective Tiered Systems: Lessons from National Implementation Efforts." *Exceptional Children* 83, no. 3 (2017): 269–80.

Artiles, Alfredo J. "Toward an Interdisciplinary Understanding of Educational Equity and Difference: The Case of the Racialization of Ability." *Educational Researcher* 40, no. 9 (2011): 431–45.

Artiles, Alfredo J. "Untangling the Racialization of Disabilities: An Intersectionality Critique Across Disability Models." *Du Bois Review* 10, no. 2 (2013): 329–47.

Artiles, Alfredo J., Sherman Dorn, and Aydin Bal. "Objects of Protection, Enduring Nodes of Difference: Disability Intersections with 'Other' Differences, 1916 to 2016." *Review of Research in Education* 40, no. 1 (2016): 777–820.

Artiles, Alfredo J., Elizabeth B. Kozleski, Stanley C. Trent, David Osher, and Alba Ortiz. "Justifying and Explaining Disproportionality, 1968–2008: A Critique of Underlying Views of Culture." *Exceptional Children* 76, no. 3 (2010): 279–99.

Arum, Richard. "Schools and Communities: Ecological and Institutional Dimensions." *Annual Review of Sociology* 26, no. 1 (2000): 395–418.

Averill, Orla Higgins, Claudia Rinaldi, and U. S. E. L. Collaborative. "Multi-tier System of Supports (MTSS)." *District Administration* 48, no. 8 (2011): 91–95.

Aylward, Alexandra, Brenda Barrio, and Catherine Kramarczuk Voulgarides. "Exclusion from Educational Opportunity in Diversifying Rural Contexts." *Rural Sociology* 86, no. 3 (2021): 559–85.

Bagenstos, Samuel R. "From Integrationism to Equal Protection: TenBroek and the Next 25 Years of Disability Rights." *University of St. Thomas Law Journal* 13 (2016): 13.

Baglieri, Susan, and Priya Lalvani. *Undoing Ableism: Teaching about Disability in K–12 Classrooms*. Routledge, 2019.

Baker, David. *The Schooled Society: The Educational Transformation of Global Culture*. Stanford University Press, 2020.

Bal, Aydin, Jennifer Betters-Bubon, and Rachel E. Fish. "A Multilevel Analysis of Statewide Disproportionality in Exclusionary Discipline and the Identification of Emotional Disturbance." *Education and Urban Society* 51, no. 2 (2019): 247–68.

Bal, Aydin, Amanda L. Sullivan, and John Harper. "A Situated Analysis of Special Education Disproportionality for Systemic Transformation in an Urban School District." *Remedial and Special Education* 35, no. 1 (2014): 3–14.

Bannister, Nicole A. "Breaking the Spell of Differentiated Instruction through Equity Pedagogy and Teacher Community." *Cultural Studies of Science Education* 11 (2016): 335–47.

Barnes, Colin. "Understanding the Social Model of Disability: Past, Present and Future." In *Routledge Handbook of Disability Studies*, edited by Nick Watson, Alan Roulstone, and Carol Thomas. Routledge, 2019.

Barrio, Brenda L., Darcy Miller, Yun-Ju Hsiao, Michael Dunn, Sara Petersen, Aleksandra Hollingshead, and Susan Banks. "Designing Culturally Responsive and Relevant Individualized Educational Programs." *Intervention in School and Clinic* 53, no. 2 (2017): 114–19.

Bateman, David F., and Mitchell L. Yell, eds. *Current Trends and Legal Issues in Special Education*. Corwin, 2019.

Bell, Chris. "Is disability Studies Actually White Disability Studies." *The Disability Studies Reader* 5 (2010): 402–10.

Bell, Derrick A. "Who's Afraid of Critical Race Theory?" *University of Illinois Law Review* 4, no. 3 (1995): 823–46.

Berkeley, Sheri, David Scanlon, Tessie R. Bailey, Jason C. Sutton, and Donna M. Sacco. "A Snapshot of RTI Implementation a Decade Later: New Picture, Same Story." *Journal of Learning Disabilities* 53, no. 5 (2020): 332–42.

Bishop, Joseph P., and Pedro A. Noguera. "The Ecology of Educational Equity: Implications for Policy." *Peabody Journal of Education* 94, no. 2 (2019): 122–41.

Blanck, Peter David, and Eilionóir Flynn, eds. *Routledge Handbook of Disability Law and Human Rights*. Routledge, 2017.

Bollmer, Julia M., James W. Bethel, Tom E. Munk, and Amy R. Bitterman, eds. *Methods for Assessing Racial/Ethnic Disproportionality in Special Education: A Technical Assistance Guide (Revised)*. US Department of Education, Office of Special Programs, Washington, DC, 2005. www.ideadata.org.

Bollmer, J., R. Cronin, M. Brauen, B. Howell, P. Fletcher, R. Gonin, and F. Jenkins. *A Study of States' Monitoring and Improvement Practices Under the Individuals with Disabilities Education Act. NCSER 2011-3001*. National Center for Special Education Research. 2010.

Bonilla-Silva, Eduardo. *Racism without Racists: Color-Blind Racism and the Persistence of Racial Inequality in America*. Rowman & Littlefield, 2021.

Boveda, Mildred, and Subini Ancy Annamma. "Beyond Making a Statement: An Intersectional Framing of the Power and Possibilities of Positioning." *Educational Researcher* 52, no. 5 (2023): 306–14.

Boykin, A. Wade, and Pedro Noguera. *Creating the Opportunity to Learn: Moving from Research to Practice to Close the Achievement Gap*. ASCD, 2011.

Bradbury-Jones, Caroline, Julie Taylor, and O. R. Herber. "Vignette Development and Administration: A Framework for Protecting Research Participants." *International Journal of Social Research Methodology* 17, no. 4 (2014): 427–40.

Braddock, David L., and Susan L. Parish. "An Institutional History of Disability." In *Handbook of Disability Studies*. Sage, 2001.

Brady, Kevin, Charles Russo, Cynthia Dieterich, and Allan Osborne Jr. *Legal Issues in Special Education: Principles, Policies, and Practices*. Routledge, 2019.

Bray, Laura E., and Jennifer Lin Russell. "Going off Script: Structure and Agency in Individualized Education Program Meetings." *American Journal of Education* 122, no. 3 (2016): 367–98.

Broderick, Alicia, and Priya Lalvani. "Dysconscious Ableism: Toward a Liberatory Praxis in Teacher Education." *International Journal of Inclusive Education* 21, no. 9 (2017): 894–905.

Bronfenbrenner, Urie. *Ecological Systems Theory*. Jessica Kingsley, 1992.

Bronfenbrenner, Urie. "Toward an Experimental Ecology of Human Development." *American Psychologist* 32, no. 7 (1977): 513–31.

Brown v. Board of Education of Topeka (1952).

Brusnahan, Lynn Stansberry, Erin Maguire, Elizabeth A. Harkins Monaco, Adam Leckie, Sheila Bailey, and Marcus Fuller. "Leading with an Equity Lens: Addressing the Intersection of Racism and Ableism in Public Schools." *Teaching Exceptional Children* 55, no. 5 (2023): 302–13.

Burke, Meghan M. "Improving Parental Involvement: Training Special Education Advocates." *Journal of Disability Policy Studies* 23, no. 4 (2013): 225–34.

Burke, Meghan M., and Samantha E. Goldman. "Documenting the Experiences of Special Education Advocates." *Journal of Special Education* 51, no. 1 (2017): 3–13.

Burke, Meghan M., Kristina Rios, and Chung eun Lee. "Exploring the Special Education Advocacy Process According to Families and Advocates." *Journal of Special Education* 53, no. 3 (2019): 131–41.

Byron, Reginald A., and Vincent J. Roscigno. "Bureaucracy, Discrimination, and the Racialized Character of Organizational Life." In *Race, Organizations, and the Organizing Process*. Emerald, 2019.

Campbell, Fiona A. Kumari. "Exploring Internalized Ableism Using Critical Race Theory." *Disability & Society* 23, no. 2 (2008): 151–62.

Carter, Prudence L., and Kevin G. Welner, eds. *Closing the Opportunity Gap: What America Must Do to Give Every Child an Even Chance*. Oxford University Press, 2013.

Castagno, Angelina E. *Educated in Whiteness: Good Intentions and Diversity in Schools*. University of Minnesota Press, 2014.

Castagno, Angelina E., ed. *The Price of Nice: How Good Intentions Maintain Educational Inequity*. University of Minnesota Press, 2019.

Chitty, Clyde. *Eugenics, Race and Intelligence in Education*. A & C Black, 2009.

Chordiya, Rashmi, and Adana Protonentis. "Healing from Intersectional White Supremacy Culture and Ableism: Disability Justice as an Antidote." *Journal of Social Equity and Public Administration* 2, no. 1 (2024): 127–52.

Clemens, Katharine, Luke Borowski, Mary Donovan, Katherine Meyer, Kathryn Dooley, and Brandi Simonsen. "Proactively Pivot: Guidance on Adapting the PBIS Framework in Response to Crises to Support Students with Disabilities." *Teaching Exceptional Children* 55, no. 1 (2022): 40–47.

Cole, Mike. "Critical Race Theory in Education, Marxism and Abstract Racial Domination." *British Journal of Sociology of Education* 33, no. 2 (2012): 167–83.

Colker, Ruth. *Disabled Education: A Critical Analysis of the Individuals with Disabilities Education Act*. New York University Press, 2013.

Collins, Patricia Hill. *Black Feminist Thought: Knowledge, Consciousness, and the Politics of Empowerment*. 2nd ed. Routledge, 2009.

Collins, Patricia Hill. *On Intellectual Activism*. Temple University Press, 2012.

Collins, Patricia Hill, and Sirma Bilge. *Intersectionality*. Wiley, 2020.

Collins, Randall. *The Credential Society: An Historical Sociology of Education and Stratification*. Columbia University Press, 2019.

Connor, David J., and Beth A. Ferri. "Historicizing Dis/ability: Creating Normalcy, Containing Difference." In *Foundations of Disability Studies*, ed. Matthew Wappett and Katrina Arndt. Palgrave Macmillan, 2013.

Connor, David J., and Beth A. Ferri. "Integration and Inclusion—A Troubling Nexus: Race, Disability, and Special Education." *Journal of African American History* 90, no. 1–2 (2005): 107–27.

Cooc, North. "Disparities in General Education Inclusion for Students of Color with Disabilities: Understanding When and Why." *Journal of School Psychology* 90 (2022): 43–59.

Cooc, North. "National Trends in Special Education and Academic Outcomes for English Learners with Disabilities." *Journal of Special Education* 57, no. 2 (2023): 106–17.

Cox, Doug. "State Monitoring and Compliance." In *Special Education Leadership*, by Doug Cox and Jennifer Cline. Routledge, 2019.

Crenshaw, Kimberlé Williams. "Mapping the Margins: Intersectionality, Identity Politics, and Violence against Women of Color." In *The Public Nature of Private Violence*, ed. Martha Albertson. Routledge, 2013.

Crenshaw, Kimberlé Williams, Luke Charles Harris, Daniel Martinez HoSang, and George Lipsitz, eds. *Seeing Race Again: Countering Colorblindness across the Disciplines*. University of California Press, 2019.

Creswell, John W., and Cheryl N. Poth. *Qualitative Inquiry and Research Design: Choosing among Five Approaches*. Sage, 2016.

Cruz, Rebecca A., Saili S. Kulkarni, and Allison R. Firestone. "A QuantCrit Analysis of Context, Discipline, Special Education, and Disproportionality." *AERA Open* 7 (2021): 23328584211041354.

Cruz, Rebecca A., Joon-Ho Lee, Alexandra G. Aylward, and Catherine Kramarczuk Voulgarides. "The Effect of School Funding on Opportunity Gaps for Students with Disabilities: Policy and Context in a Diverse Urban District." *Journal of Disability Policy Studies* 33, no. 1 (2022): 3–14.

Davis, Lennard J. *The Disability Studies Reader*. Routledge, 2016.

de Brey, C., L. Musu, J. McFarland, S. Wilkinson-Flicker, M. Diliberti, A. Zhang, C. Branstetter, and X. Wang X. *Status and Trends in the Education of Racial and Ethnic Groups 2018 (NCES 2019-038)*. US Department of Education. National Center for Education Statistics, 2019. https://nces.ed.gov/pubsearch.

Decker, Janet, and Kevin Brady. "Increasing School Employees' Special Education Legal Literacy." *Journal of School Public Relations* 36, no. 3 (2015): 231–59.

Delgado, Richard, and Jean Stefancic. "Critical Race Theory: Past, Present, and Future." *Current Legal Problems* 51, no. 1 (1998): 467.

Delpit, Lisa. *Other People's Children: Cultural Conflict in the Classroom*. New Press, 2006.

Diem, Sarah, and Anjalé D. Welton. *Anti-Racist Educational Leadership and Policy: Addressing Racism in Public Education*. Routledge, 2020.

DiMaggio, Paul J., and Walter W. Powell. "The Iron Cage Revisited: Institutional Isomorphism and Collective Rationality in Organizational Fields." *American Sociological Review* 48, no. 2 (1983): 147–60.

Dirth, Thomas P., and Glenn A. Adams. "Decolonial Theory and Disability Studies: On the Modernity/Coloniality of Ability." *Journal of Social and Political Psychology* 7, no. 1 (2019): 260–89.

Dobbin, Frank, and Alexandra Kalev. "The Civil Rights Revolution at Work: What Went Wrong." *Annual Review of Sociology* 47, no. 1 (2021): 281–303.

Dolmage, Jay. "Disabled upon Arrival: The Rhetorical Construction of Disability and Race at Ellis Island." *Cultural Critique* 77 (2011): 24–69.

Dong, Bo. "A Systematic Review of the Organizational Inertia Literature and Future Outlook." *International Journal of Education and Humanities* 8, no. 2 (2023): 119–23.

Dunn, Lloyd M. "Special Education for the Mildly Retarded—Is Much of It Justifiable?" *Exceptional Children* 35, no. 1 (1968): 5–22.

Edelman, Lauren B. "Legal Ambiguity and Symbolic Structures: Organizational Mediation of Civil Rights Law." *American journal of Sociology* 97, no. 6 (1992): 1531–1576.

Edelman, Lauren B. "Legal Environments and Organizational Governance: The Expansion of due Process in the American Workplace." *American Journal of Sociology* 95, no. 6 (1990): 1401–40.

Edelman, Lauren B. *Working Law: Courts, Corporations, and Symbolic Civil Rights*. University of Chicago Press, 2020.

Edelman, Lauren B., and Shauhin A. Talesh. "To Comply or Not to Comply—That Isn't the Question: How Organizations Construct the Meaning of Compliance." In *Explaining Compliance: Business Responses to Regulation*, ed. Christine Parker and Vibek Leimann. Edward Elgar, 2011.

Edelman, Lauren B., Christopher Uggen, and Howard S. Erlanger. "The Endogeneity of Legal Regulation: Grievance Procedures as Rational Myth." *American Journal of Sociology* 105, no. 2 (1999): 406–54.

Eitle, Tamela McNulty. "Special Education or Racial Segregation: Understanding Variation in the Representation of Black Students in Educable Mentally Handicapped Programs." *Sociological Quarterly* 43, no. 4 (2002): 575–605.

El-Amin, Aaliyah, Scott Seider, Daren Graves, Jalene Tamerat, Shelby Clark, Madora Soutter, Jamie Johannsen, and Saira Malhotra. "Critical Consciousness: A Key to Student Achievement." *Phi Delta Kappan* 98, no. 5 (2017): 18–23.

Erkulwater, Jennifer L. "How the Nation's Largest Minority Became White: Race Politics and the Disability Rights Movement, 1970–1980." *Journal of Policy History* 30, no. 3 (2018): 367–99.

Erevelles, Nirmala. *Disability and Difference in Global Contexts: Enabling a Transformative Body Politic*. Palgrave Macmillan, 2011.

Erevelles, Nirmala, Anne Kanga, and Renee Middleton. "How Does It Feel to Be a Problem? Race, Disability, and Exclusion in Educational Policy." In *Who Benefits from Special Education?: Remediating (Fixing) Other People's Children*. Routledge, 2006.

Erevelles, Nirmala, and Andrea Minear. "Unspeakable Offenses: Untangling Race and Disability in Discourses of Intersectionality." *Journal of Literary and Cultural Disability Studies* 4, no. 2 (2010): 127–45.

Etscheidt, Susan Larson, David Hernandez-Saca, and Catherine Kramarczuk Voulgarides. "Monitoring the Transition Requirements of the Individuals with Disabilities Education Act: A Critique and a Proposal to Expand the Performance Indicators." *Journal of Disability Policy Studies* 35, no. 2 (2024): 128–39.

Fallon, Lindsay M., Margarida Veiga, and George Sugai. "Strengthening MTSS for Behavior (MTSS-B) to Promote Racial Equity." *School Psychology Review* 52, no. 5 (2023): 518–33.

Fenwick, Tara, and Richard Edwards. "Considering Materiality in Educational Policy: Messy Objects and Multiple Reals." *Educational Theory* 61, no. 6 (2011): 709–26.

Fergus, Edward. *Solving Disproportionality and Achieving Equity: A Leader's Guide to Using Data to Change Hearts and Minds*. Corwin, 2016.

Ferri, Beth A., and David J. Connor. "Tools of Exclusion: Race, Disability, and (re) Segregated Education." *Teachers College Record* 107, no. 3 (2005): 453–74.

Fish, Rachel Elizabeth. "The Racialized Construction of Exceptionality: Experimental Evidence of Race/Ethnicity Effects on Teachers' Interventions." *Social Science Research* 62 (2016): 317–34.

Fish, Rachel Elizabeth. "Standing out and Sorting in: Exploring the Role of Racial Composition in Racial Disparities in Special Education." *American Educational Research Journal* 56, no. 6 (2019): 2573–2608.

Fisher, Amy E., Benjamin W. Fisher, and Kirsten S. Railey. "Disciplinary Disparities by Race and Disability: Using DisCrit Theory to Examine the Manifestation Determination Review Process in Special Education in the United States." *Race Ethnicity and Education* 24, no. 6 (2021): 755–69.

Fleischer, Doris, and Fleischer Doris Zames. *The Disability Rights Movement: From Charity to Confrontation*. Temple University Press, 2012.

Flynn, Susan. "A History and Sociology of the Willowbrook State School." *International Journal of Disability Development and Education* 64, no. 2 (2017): 1–2.

Frederick, Angela, and Dara Shifrer. "Race and Disability: From Analogy to Intersectionality." *Sociology of Race and Ethnicity* 5, no. 2 (2019): 200–14.

Freire, Paulo. "The Banking Concept of Education." In *Thinking about Schools: A Foundations of Education Reader*, ed. Elanor Blair Hilty. Routledge, 2018.

Freire, Paulo. "The Banking Concept of Education." In *Thinking about Schools: A Foundation of Education Reader*, ed. Eleanore Blair Hilty. Routledge, 2011.

Freire, Paulo. *Education: The Practice of Freedom*. Writers and Readers, 1974.

Freire, Paulo. *Pedagogy of the Oppressed*. 30th anniversary ed. Continuum, 2000.

Fuentes, K., S. Hsu, S. Patel, and S. Lindsay, S. "More Than Just Double Discrimination: A Scoping Review of the Experiences and Impact of Ableism and Racism in Employment." *Disability and Rehabilitation* 46, no. 4 (2024): 650–71.

Gagnon, Joseph Calvin, Brian R. Barber, and Ilker Soyturk. "Policies and Practices Supporting Positive Behavioral Interventions and Supports (PBIS) Implementation in High-Poverty Florida Middle Schools." *Exceptionality* 28, no. 3 (2020): 176–94.

García, Shernaz, and Alba Ortiz. "A Framework for Culturally and Linguistically Responsive Design of Response-to-Intervention Models." *Multiple Voices for Ethnically Diverse Exceptional Learners* 11, no. 1 (2008): 24–41.

Gartner, Alan, and Dorothy Kerzner Lipsky. "Beyond Special Education: Toward a Quality System for All Students." *Harvard Educational Review* 57, no. 4 (1987): 367–96.

Gay, Geneva. *Culturally Responsive Teaching: Theory, Research, and Practice*. Teachers College Press, 2018.

Gerth, Hans Heinrich, Max Weber, and Wright Mills. *From Max Weber: Essays in Sociology*. Routledge, 2013.

Gillborn, David. "Ability, Selection and Institutional Racism in Schools." *Culture and Learning: Access and Opportunity in the Classroom* (2004): 279–97.

Gillborn, David. "Education Policy as an Act of White Supremacy: Whiteness, Critical Race Theory and Education Reform." *Journal of Education Policy* 20, no. 4 (2005): 485–505.

Ginsburg, Faye, and Rayna Rapp. *Disability Worlds*. Duke University Press, 2024.

Giroux, Henry A. "Rethinking Education as the Practice of Freedom: Paulo Freire and the Promise of Critical Pedagogy." *Policy Futures in Education* 8, no. 6 (2010): 715–21.

Giroux, Henry A., and Christopher G. Robbins. "Paulo Freire and the Politics of Postcolonialism." In *The Giroux Reader*, ed. Henry Giroux. Routledge, 2015.

Gouëdard, Pierre. "Developing Indicators to Support the Implementation of Education Policies." OECD Education Working Papers, No. 255. OECD, 2021.

Gregory, Anne, Russell J. Skiba, and Pedro A. Noguera. "The Achievement Gap and the Discipline Gap: Two Sides of the Same Coin?" *Educational Researcher* 39, no. 1 (2010): 59–68.

Gregory, Jess. "Not My Responsibility: The Impact of Separate Special Education Systems on Educators' Attitudes toward Inclusion." *Educational Policy Analysis and Strategic Research* 13, no. 1 (2018): 127–48.

Haber, Mason G., Valerie L. Mazzotti, April L. Mustian, Dawn A. Rowe, Audrey L. Bartholomew, David W. Test, and Catherine H. Fowler. "What Works, When, for Whom, and with Whom: A Meta-analytic Review of Predictors of Postsecondary Success for Students with Disabilities." *Review of Educational Research* 86, no. 1 (2016): 123–162.

Hannan, Michael T., and John Freeman. "Structural Inertia and Organizational Change." *American Sociological Review* (1984): 149–64.

Harris, Cheryl I. "Reflections on Whiteness as Property." *Harvard Law Review* 134 (2020): 1.

Harris, Cheryl I. "Whiteness as Property." *Harvard Law Review* 106 (1993): 1707–91.

Harry, Beth. "Collaboration with Culturally and Linguistically Diverse Families: Ideal versus Reality. *Exceptional Children* 74, no. 3 (2008): 372–88.

Harry, Beth. "Restructuring the Participation of African-American Parents in Special Education." *Exceptional Children* 59, no. 2 (1992): 123–31.

Harry, Beth, Norma Allen, and Margaret McLaughlin. "Communication versus Compliance: African-American Parents' Involvement in Special Education." *Exceptional Children* 61, no. 4 (1995): 364–77.

Harry, Beth, and Janette Klingner. *Why Are So Many Students of Color in Special Education?: Understanding Race and Disability in Schools*. Teachers College Press, 2022.

Harry, Beth, and Lydia Ocasio-Stoutenburg. *Meeting Families Where They Are: Building Equity Through Advocacy with Diverse Schools and Communities*. Teachers College Press, 2020.

Harry, Beth, and Lydia Ocasio-Stoutenburg. "Parent Advocacy for Lives that Matter." *Research and Practice for Persons with Severe Disabilities* 46, no. 3 (2021): 184–98.

Hehir, Tom. *New Directions in Special Education: Eliminating Ableism in Policy and Practice*. Harvard Education Press, 2025.

Heifetz, Ronald A. "Mobilizing for Adaptive Work." In *Making Policy Happen*, ed. Leslie Budd, Julie Charlesworth, and Rob Paton. Routledge, 2020.

Heifetz, Ronald A. *The Practice of Adaptive Leadership: Tools and Tactics for Changing Your Organization and the World*. Harvard Business Press, 2009.

Herd, Pamela, and Donald P. Moynihan. *Administrative Burden: Policymaking by Other Means*. Russell Sage Foundation, 2019.

Hernández, María G., David M. Lopez, and Reed Swier. *Dismantling Disproportionality: A Culturally Responsive and Sustaining Systems Approach*. Teachers College Press, 2022.

Hernández-Saca, David Isaac, and Mercedes Adell Cannon. "Interrogating Disability Epistemologies: Towards Collective Dis/Ability Intersectional Emotional, Affective and Spiritual Autoethnographies for Healing." *International Journal of Qualitative Studies in Education* 32, no. 3 (2019): 243–62.

Hernández-Saca, David Isaac, Laurie Gutmann Kahn, and Mercedes A. Cannon. "Intersectionality Dis/Ability Research: How Dis/Ability Research in Education Engages Intersectionality to Uncover the Multidimensional Construction of Dis/Abled Experiences." *Review of Research in Education* 42, no. 1 (2018): 286–311.

Hernández-Saca, David Isaac, Catherine Kramarczuk Voulgarides, and Susan Larson Etscheidt. "A Critical Systematic Literature Review of Global Inclusive Education Using an Affective, Intersectional, Discursive, Emotive and Material Lens." *Education Sciences* 13, no. 12 (2023): 1212.

Hodges, Jaret, Juliana Tay, Yukiko Maeda, and Marcia Gentry. "A Meta-Analysis of Gifted and Talented Identification Practices." *Gifted Child Quarterly* 62, no. 2 (2018): 147–74.

Houtenville, A., and S. Bach. *Annual Report on People with Disabilities in America: 2024. Institute on Disability*, University of New Hampshire, 2024.

Howard, Tyrone C. "Culturally Responsive Pedagogy." In *Transforming Multicultural Education Policy and Practice: Expanding Educational Opportunity*, ed. James A. Banks. Teachers College Press, 2021.

Hurwitz, Sarah, Brea Perry, Emma D. Cohen, and Russell Skiba. "Special Education and Individualized Academic Growth: A Longitudinal Assessment of Outcomes for Students with

Disabilities." *American Educational Research Journal* 57, no. 2 (2020): 576–611.

Hyman, Elisa, Dean Hill Rivkin, and Stephen A. Rosenbaum. "How IDEA Fails Families without Means: Causes and Corrections from the Frontlines of Special Education Lawyering." *American Universite Journal of Gender Social Policy and Law* 20 (2011): 107.

Imrie, Rob. "Rethinking the Relationships Between Disability, Rehabilitation, and Society." *Disability and rehabilitation* 19, no. 7 (1997): 263–271.

Individuals with Disabilities Education Act, 20 U.S.C. § 1400 (2004).

Johnston, Olivia. *Constructing Composite Narratives: A Step-by-Step Guide for Researchers in the Social Sciences*. Taylor & Francis, 2024.

Katsiyannis, Antonis, Dalun Zhang, Idean Ettekal, Wen-Hsuan Chang, Peizhen Li, Bronwyn Bigger, and Melissa Hullett. "Minority Representation in Special Education: 5-Year Trends from 2016–2020." *Advances in Neurodevelopmental Disorders* (2023): 1–14.

Keefe, Elizabeth Stringer. "From Detractive to Democratic: The Duty of Teacher Education to Disrupt Structural Ableism and Reimagine Disability." *Teachers College Record* 124, no. 3 (2022): 115–47.

Ladson-Billings, Gloria. "From the Achievement Gap to the Education Debt: Understanding Achievement in US Schools." *Educational Researcher* 35, no. 7 (2006): 3–12.

Ladson-Billings, Gloria. "Toward a Theory of Culturally Relevant Pedagogy." *American Educational Research Journal* 32, no. 3 (1995): 465–91.

Ladson-Billings, Gloria, and William F. Tate. "Toward a Critical Race Theory of Education." *Teachers College Record* 97, no. 1 (1995): 47–68.

Lalvani, Priya, and Alicia A. Broderick. "Institutionalized Ableism and the Misguided 'Disability Awareness Day': Transformative Pedagogies for Teacher Education." *Equity and Excellence in Education* 46, no. 4 (2013): 468–83.

Lambert, Rachel. "'Indefensible, Illogical, and Unsupported': Countering Deficit Mythologies about the Potential OF Students WITH Learning Disabilities in Mathematics." *Education Sciences* 8, no. 2 (2018): 72.

Leonard, Kaitlin M., Michael D. Coyne, Ashley C. Oldham, Darci Burns, and Margie B. Gillis. "Implementing MTSS in Beginning Reading: Tools and Systems to Support Schools and Teachers." *Learning Disabilities Research and Practice* 34, no. 2 (2019): 110–17.

Leonardo, Zeus, and Alicia A. Broderick. "Smartness as Property: A Critical Exploration of Intersections between Whiteness and Disability Studies." *Teachers College Record* 113, no. 10 (2011): 2206–32.

Leung-Gagné, Melanie, Jennifer McCombs, Caitlin Scott, and Daniel J. Losen. *Pushed out: Trends and Disparities in Out-of-School Suspension*. Learning Policy Institute, 2022.

Li, Yi. "Substantively Immaterial? How the IDEA Enables Special Education Labels to be Used as Tools of Inequity." *Disability Law Journal* 4, no. 1 (2023).

Lindsay, Sally, Azar Varahra, Hiba Ahmed, Sara Abrahamson, Sierra Pulver, Mara Primucci, and Karen Wong. "Exploring the Relationships between Race, Ethnicity, and School and Work Outcomes among Youth and Young Adults with Disabilities: A Scoping Review." *Disability and Rehabilitation* 44, no. 25 (2022): 8110–29.

Lipsky, Michael. *Street-Level Bureaucracy: Dilemmas of the Individual in Public Service*. Russell Sage Foundation, 2010.

López, Ian F. Haney. "Institutional Racism: Judicial Conduct and a New Theory of Racial Discrimination." *Yale Law Journal* 109 (1999): 1717.

López, Ian F. Haney. "White by Law 10th Anniversary Edition: The Legal Construction of Race." In *White by Law 10th Anniversary Edition: The Legal Construction of Race*. New York University Press, 2006.

Losen, Daniel J., Cheri Hodson, Jongyeon Ee, and Tia E. Martinez. "Disturbing Inequities: Exploring the Relationship between Racial Disparities in Special Education Identification and Discipline." *Journal of Applied Research on Children* 5, no. 2 (2014).

Lucas, Samuel. *Theorizing Discrimination in an Era of Contested Prejudice: Discrimination in the United States*. Temple University Press, 2009.

Mac, Sylvia. "Niceness in Special Education: An Ethnographic Case Study of Benevolence, Goodness, and Paternalism at Colina Cedro Charter High School." In *The Price of Nice: How Good Intentions Maintain Educational Inequity*, ed. Angelina E. Castagno. University of Minnesota Press, 2019.

Mandic, Carmen Gomez, Rima Rudd, Thomas Hehir, and Dolores Acevedo-Garcia. "Readability of special education procedural safeguards." *The Journal of Special Education* 45, no. 4 (2012): 195–203.

Maroto, Michelle, David Pettinicchio, and Andrew C. Patterson. "Hierarchies of Categorical Disadvantage: Economic Insecurity at the Intersection of Disability, Gender, and Race." *Gender & Society* 33, no. 1 (2019): 64–93.

Marsico, Richard. D. "The Intersection of Race, Wealth, and Special Education: The Role of Structural Inequities in the IDEA." *New York Law School Law Review 66* (2021): 207.

Matias, Cheryl E. *Feeling White: Whiteness, Emotionality, and Education*. Springer, 2016.

Matias, Cheryl E., and Michalinos Zembylas. "'When Saying You Care Is Not Really Caring': Emotions of Disgust, Whiteness Ideology, and Teacher Education." *Critical Studies in Education* 55, no. 3 (2014): 319–37.

Mayes, Keith A. *The Unteachables: Disability Rights and the Invention of Black Special Education*. University of Minnesota Press, 2023.

Mayorga-Gallo, Sarah. *Behind the White Picket Fence: Power and Privilege in a Multiethnic Neighborhood*. University of North Carolina Press, 2014.

Mayorga-Gallo, Sarah. "The White-Centering Logic of Diversity Ideology." *American Behavioral Scientist* 63, no. 13 (2019): 1789–1809.

McInerney, Peter. "Toward a Critical Pedagogy of Engagement for Alienated Youth: Insights from Freire and school-Based Research." *Critical Studies in Education* 50, no. 1 (2009): 23–35.

McIntosh, Kent, and Steve Goodman. *Integrated Multi-tiered Systems of Support: Blending RTI and PBIS*. Guilford, 2016.

McIntosh, Kent, Ambra L. Green, and Nikole Hollins-Sims. "Improving School Climate Within Multi-tiered Systems of

Support." In *Creating an Inclusive School Climate: A School Psychology Model for Supporting Marginalized Students*. Routledge, 2023.

McCall, Zach, and Thomas Skrtic. "Intersectional Needs Politics: A Policy Frame for the Wicked Problem of Disproportionality." *Multiple Voices for Ethnically Diverse Exceptional Learners* 11, no. 2 (2009): 3–23.

McCauley, Erin J. "The Potential of College Completion: How Disability Shapes Labor Market Activity Differentially by Educational Attainment and disability Type." *Journal of Disability Policy Studies* 30, no. 4 (2020): 213–22.

Mehan, Hugh. "Language and Power in Organizational Process." *Discourse Processes* 10, no. 4 (1987): 291–301.

Merton, Robert. "Manifest and Latent Functions." In *Social Theory Re-wired: New Connections to Classical and Contemporary Perspectives*, eds. Wesley Longhofer and Daneil Winchester. Routledge, 2016.

Meyer, John W. *Organizational Factors Affecting Legalization in Education*. Institute for Research on Educational Finance and Governance, School of Education, Stanford University, 1981.

Meyer, John W., Georg Krücken, and Gili S. Drori. *World Society: The Writings of John W. Meyer*. Oxford University Press, 2009.

Meyer, John W., and Brian Rowan. "Institutionalized Organizations: Formal Structure as Myth and Ceremony." *American Journal of Sociology* 83, no. 2 (1977): 340–63.

Mills v. Board of Education of the District of Columbia, 348 F. Supp. 866 (D.D.C. 1972).

Milner, H. Richard. "Beyond a Test Score: Explaining Opportunity Gaps in Educational Practice." *Journal of Black Studies* 43, no. 6 (2012): 693–718.

Milner, H. Richard, and E. Self. "Getting Real about Race: Colorblindness as Complicit Instructional Ineffectiveness." *National Journal of Urban Education & Practice* 6, no. 1 (2012): 1–19.

Minow, Martha. *In Brown's Wake: Legacies of America's Educational Landmark*. Oxford University Press, 2010.

Misoczky, Maria Ceci. "Paulo Freire and the Praxis of Liberation: Education, Organization and Ethics." *Management Learning* 55, no. 1 (2024): 124–40.

Morgan, Paul L., and George Farkas. "Are We Helping All the Children that We Are Supposed to be Helping?" *Educational Researcher* 45, no. 3 (2016): 226–28.

Murphy, Hardy, Cassandra Cole, and Hannah Bolte. "Race Placed: Special Education Identification and Placement of Black Students." *Educational Policy* (2024).

Nario-Redmond, Michelle R. *Ableism: The Causes and Consequences of Disability Prejudice*. Wiley, 2019.

National Center for Education Statistics. *Students with Disabilities*. US Department of Education, Institute of Education Sciences, 2024. https://nces.ed.gov/programs/coe/indicator/cgg.

National Council on Disability. *Federal Monitoring and Enforcement of IDEA Compliance*. 2018. https://www.ncd.gov/sites/default/files/NCD_Monitoring-Enforcement_Accessible.pdf.

Nielsen, Kim E. *A Disability History of the United States*. Vol. 2. Beacon Press, 2012.

Nowicki, Jacqueline M. "K–12 Education: Discipline Disparities for Black Students, Boys, and Students with Disabilities. Report to Congressional Requesters. GAO-18-258." US Government Accountability Office, 2018.

Nowicki, Jacqueline M. "Special Education: Varied State Criteria May Contribute to Differences in Percentages of Children Served. Report to Congressional Requesters. GAO-19-348." US Government Accountability Office, 2019.

Obiakor, Festus E. "Maximizing Access, Equity, and Inclusion in General and Special Education." *Journal of the International Association of Special Education* 12, no. 1 (2011).

Ocasio-Stoutenburg, Lydia, Juanita Davis, and Maria Lewis. "Principals as Co-advocates for Caregivers of Children with Disabilities: Possibilities and Realizations beyond IDEA's Collaborative Ideal." *Journal of Cases in Educational Leadership* 27, no. 4 (2024): 85–104.

Oliver, Michael. *Understanding Disability: From Theory to Practice*. Bloomsbury, 2018.

Omi, Michael, and Howard Winant. "Racial Formation." In *The New Social Theory Reader*, ed. Jeffrey C. Alexander and Steven Seidman. Routledge, 2020.

Omi, Michael, and Howard Winant. *Racial Formation in the United States*. Routledge, 2014.

Ong-Dean, Colin. *Distinguishing Disability: Parents, Privilege, and Special Education*. University of Chicago Press, 2009.

Orosco, Michael John, and Janette Klingner. "One School's Implementation of RTI with English Language Learners: 'Referring into RTI.'" *Journal of Learning Disabilities* 43, no. 3 (2010): 269–88.

Padilla, Alexis, Catherine Voulgarides, and Rhonda Bondie. "Disability and Educational Justice: Exploring Intersectional Ways to Disrupt the Logic of Compliance." *Journal of Disability Studies in Education* 1, no. aop (2025): 1–25.

Paris, Django. "Culturally Sustaining Pedagogy: A Needed Change in Stance, Terminology, and Practice." *Educational Researcher* 41, no. 3 (2012): 93–97.

Paris, Django, and H. Samy Alim, eds. *Culturally Sustaining Pedagogies: Teaching and Learning for Justice in a Changing World*. Teachers College Press, 2017.

Patterson, Lindsey. "The Disability Rights Movement in the United States." *Oxford Handbooks Online*, 2018.

Paul, S., S. Rogers, S. Bach, and A. J. Houtenville. *Annual Disability Statistics Compendium: 2023*. University of New Hampshire, Institute on Disability, 2023.

Payne, Charles M. *Getting What We Ask For: The Ambiguity of Success and Failure in Urban Education*. Praeger, 1984.

Payne, Charles M. *So Much Reform, So Little Change: The Persistence of Failure in Urban Schools*. Vol. 8. Harvard Education Press, 2008.

Pearson, Jamie N., Lonnie DC Manns, Jared H. Stewart-Ginsburg, DeVoshia L. Mason Martin, and Janelle A. Johnson. "Experiences of Family Peer Advocates Supporting Black Families Raising Autistic Children." *Exceptional Children* 91, no. 1 (2024): 57–73.

Pelka, Fred. *What We Have Done: An Oral History of the Disability Rights Movement*. University of Massachusetts Press, 2012.

Pennsylvania Association for Retarded Citizens (PARC) v. Commonwealth of Pennsylvania, 343 F. Supp. 279 (E.D. Pa. 1972).

Peters, Scott J., and Kenneth G. Engerrand. "Equity and Excellence: Proactive Efforts in the Identification of Underrepresented Students for Gifted and talented Services." *Gifted Child Quarterly* 60, no. 3 (2016): 159–71.

Pettinicchio, David. *Politics of Empowerment: Disability Rights and the Cycle of American Policy Reform*. Stanford. University Press, 2020.

Pettinicchio, David. "Strategic Action Fields and the Context of Political Entrepreneurship: How Disability Rights Became Part of the Policy Agenda." In *Research in Social Movements, Conflicts and Change*, ed. Patrick G. Coy. Emerald Group, 2018.

Phillips, Erin. "When Parents Aren't Enough: External Advocacy in Special Education." *Yale Law Journal* 117 (2007): 1802.

Pollock, Mica. *Because of Race: How Americans Debate Harm and Opportunity in Our Schools*. Princeton University Press, 2010.

Powell, Justin J. W. "To Segregate or to Separate? Special Education Expansion and Divergence in the United States and Germany." *Comparative Education Review* 53, no. 2 (2009): 161–87.

Powell, Robyn M. "Confronting Eugenics Means Finally Confronting Its Ableist Roots." *William and Mary Journal of Race, Gender, and Social Justice* 27 (2020): 607.

Powell, Walter W., and Paul J. DiMaggio, eds. *The New Institutionalism in Organizational Analysis*. University of Chicago Press, 2012.

Pushkarenko, Kyle, Mikaeli Cavell, Nicholas Gosse, and Emilie Michalovic. "Physical Literacy and the Participant Perspective: Exploring the Value of Physical Literacy According to Individuals Experiencing Disability through Composite Narratives." *Journal of Exercise Science & Fitness* 21, no. 3 (2023): 237–45.

Rapp, Rayna, and Faye Ginsburg. "The Paradox of Recognition: Success or Stigma for Children with Learning Disabilities." In *Contesting Recognition: Culture, Identity and Citizenship*, eds. Janice McLaughlin, Peter Phillmore, and Diane Richards. Palgrave Macmillan, 2011.

Ray, Victor. "A Theory of Racialized Organizations." *American Sociological Review* 84, no. 1 (2019): 26–53.

Ray, Victor, Pamela Herd, and Donald Moynihan. "Racialized Burdens: Applying Racialized Organization Theory to the

Administrative State." *Journal of Public Administration Research and Theory* 33, no. 1 (2023): 139–52.

Reinke, Wendy M., Wesley Sims, Daniel Cohen, and Keith C. Herman. "Problem Solving within an RTI Framework: Roles and Functions of Effective Teams." In *Handbook of Response to Intervention and Multi-tiered Systems of Support*, eds. Shane R. Jimerdson, Matthew K. Burns, and Amanda VanDerHeyden. Routledge, 2018.

Rembis, Michael. "Disability and the History of Eugenics." In *The Oxford Handbook of Disability History*, eds. Michael Remis, Catherine Kudlick, and Kim E. Nielsen. Oxford University Press, 2018.

Richardson, John, and Justin Powell. *Comparing Special Education: Origins to Contemporary Paradoxes*. Stanford University Press, 2011.

Rivera, Lauren A., and András Tilcsik. "Not in My Schoolyard: Disability Discrimination in Educational Access." *American Sociological Review* 88, no. 2 (2023): 284–321.

Robinson, Kimberly Jenkins. "Disrupting Education Federalism." *Washington University Law Review* 92, no. 4 (2015): 959–1018.

Robinson, Kimberly Jenkins. "The High Cost of Education Federalism." *Wake Forest Law. Review* 48 (2013): 287.

Rodriguez, Jacqueline A., and Wendy W. Murawski. *Special Education Law and Policy: From Foundation to Application*. Vol. 1. Plural, 2020.

Rossetti, Zach, Meghan M. Burke, Oscar Hughes, Kristen Schraml-Block, Javier I. Rivera, Kristina Rios, Janeth Aleman Tovar, and James D. Lee. "Parent Perceptions of the Advocacy Expectation in Special Education." *Exceptional Children* 87, no. 4 (2021): 438–57.

Rowan, Brian, H. Meyer, and B. Rowan. "The New Institutionalism and the Study of Educational Organizations: Changing Ideas for Changing Times." *The New Institutionalism in Education* (2006): 15–32.

Saatcioglu, Argun, and Thomas M. Skrtic. "Categorization by Organizations: Manipulation of Disability Categories in a Racially Desegregated School District." *American Journal of Sociology* 125, no. 1 (2019): 184–260.

Safir, Shane, and Jamila Dugan. *Street Data: A Next-Generation Model for Equity, Pedagogy, and School Transformation*. Corwin, 2021.

Saito, Leland T. *The Politics of Exclusion: The Failure of Race-Neutral Policies in Urban America*. Stanford University Press, 2009.

Schwartz, A. E., B. G. Hopkins, and L. Stiefel. "The Effects of Special Education on the Academic Performance of Students with Learning Disabilities." *Journal of Policy Analysis and Management* 40, no. 2, (2021): 480–520.

Schalk, Sami. *Black Disability Politics*. Duke University Press, 2022.

Scott, W. Richard. *Institutions and Organizations: Ideas and Interests*. Sage, 2008.

Scotch, Richard. *From Good Will to Civil Rights: Transforming Federal Disability Policy*. Temple University Press, 2009.

Selassie, Gelila, and Denny Chan. "The Power and Limits of Law to Fight Structural Ageism, Ableism, and Racism." *Generations* 47, no. 1 (2023): 1–10.

Shakespeare, Tom. "The Social Model of Disability." *The Disability Studies Reader* 2, no. 3 (2006): 197–204.

Shaw, Linda R., Fong Chan, and Brian T. McMahon. "Intersectionality and Disability Harassment: The Interactive Effects of Disability, Race, Age, and Gender." *Rehabilitation Counseling Bulletin* 55, no. 2 (2012): 82–91.

Shuster, Brooke C., Jenny R. Gustafson, Abbie B. Jenkins, Blair P. Lloyd, Erik W. Carter, and Caitlin F. Bernstein. "Including Students with Disabilities in Positive Behavioral Interventions and Supports: Experiences and Perspectives of Special Educators." *Journal of Positive Behavior Interventions* 19, no. 3 (2017): 143–57.

Sieber, Sam D. "Implications for Policy." In *Fatal Remedies: The Ironies of Social Intervention*. Springer, 1981.

Simonsen, Brandi, Jennifer Freeman, Anthony J. Gambino, Sandra Sears, Katherine Meyer, and Robert Hoselton. "An Exploration of the Relationship between PBIS and Discipline Outcomes for Students with Disabilities." *Remedial and Special Education* 43, no. 5 (2022): 287–300.

Simonsen, Brandi, Karen Robbie, Katherine Meyer, Jennifer Freeman, Susannah Everett, and Adam B. Feinberg. "Supporting Students' Social, Emotional, and Behavior (SEB) Growth

Through Tier 2 and 3 Intervention Within a Multi-tiered System of Supports (MTSS) Framework." In *Handbook of Classroom Management*, eds. Edward J. Sabornie and Dorothy L. Esplelage. Routledge, 2022.

Skiba, Russell J., Mariella I. Arredondo, Chrystal Gray, and M. Karega Rausch. "What Do We Know about Discipline Disparities? New and Emerging Research." *Inequality in School Discipline: Research and Practice to Reduce Disparities* (2016): 21–38.

Skiba, Russell J., Robert H. Horner, Choong-Geun Chung, M. Karega Rausch, Seth L. May, and Tary Tobin. "Race Is Not Neutral: A National Investigation of African American and Latino Disproportionality in School Discipline." *School Psychology Review* 40, no. 1 (2011): 85–107.

Skiba, Russell J., Robert S. Michael, Abra Carroll Nardo, and Reece L. Peterson. "The Color of Discipline: Sources of Racial and Gender Disproportionality in School Punishment." *Urban Review* 34 (2002): 317–42.

Skiba, Russell J., A. B. Simmons, S. Ritter, A. C. Gibb, M. K. Rausch, J. Cuadrado, and C. G. Chung. "Achieving Equity in Special Education: History, Status, and Current Challenges." *Exceptional Children* 74, no. 3 (2008): 264–88.

Skrtic, Thomas M. *Behind Special Education*. Love Publishing Company, 1991.

Skrtic, Thomas M. "The Special Education Paradox: Equity as the Way to Excellence." *Harvard Educational Review* 61, no. 2 (1991): 148–207.

Skrtic, Thomas M., and K. M. Knackstedt. "Disability, Difference, and Justice: Strong Democratic Leadership for Undemocratic Times." In *Handbook of Leadership and Administration for Special Education*, eds. Jean B. Crockett, Bonnie Billingsley, and Mary Lynn Boscardin. Routledge, 2019.

Skrtic, Thomas M., Wayne Sailor, and Kathleen Gee. "Voice, Collaboration, and Inclusion: Democratic Themes in Educational and Social Reform Initiatives." *Remedial and Special Education* 17, no. 3 (1996): 142–57.

Smith, Anne, and Elizabeth B. Kozleski. "Witnessing Brown: Pursuit of an Equity Agenda in American Education." *Remedial and Special Education* 26, no. 5 (2005): 270–80.

Smith, Phil. "Whiteness, Normal Theory, and Disability Studies." *Disability Studies Quarterly* 24, no. 2 (2004).

Smith, Tom E. C. "IDEA 2004: Another Round in the Reauthorization Process." *Remedial and Special Education* 26, no. 6 (2005): 314–19.

Solórzano, Daniel G. "Critical Race Theory's Intellectual Roots: My Email Epistolary with Derrick Bell." In *Handbook of Critical Race Theory in Education*, eds. Marvin Lynn and Adrienne D. Dixson. Routledge, 2021.

Souto-Manning, Mariana. *Freire, Teaching, and Learning: Culture Circles across Contexts*. Peter Lang, 2010.

Souto-Manning, Mariana. "Transforming University-Based Teacher Education: Preparing Asset-, Equity-, and Justice-Oriented Teachers within the Contemporary Political Context." *Teachers College Record* 121, no. 6 (2019): 1–26.

Spade, Dean. "Intersectional Resistance and Law Reform." *Signs: Journal of Women in Culture and Society* 38, no. 4 (2013): 1031–55.

Stapleton, Lissa, and Liam James. "Not Another All White Study: Challenging Color-Evasiveness Ideology in Disability Scholarship (Practice Brief)." *Journal of Postsecondary Education and Disability* 33, no. 3 (2020): 215–22.

Star, Susan Leigh, and Geoffrey Bowker. "Sorting Things Out." *Classification and Its Consequences*. MIT Press, 1999.

Strassfeld, Natasha M. "Education Federalism and Minority Disproportionate Representation Monitoring: Examining IDEA Provisions, Regulations, and Judicial Trends." *Journal of Disability Policy Studies* 30, no. 3 (2019): 138–47.

Strassfeld, Natasha M. "The Future of IDEA: Monitoring Disproportionate Representation of Minority Students in Special Education and Intentional Discrimination Claims." *Case Western Reserve Law Review*. 67 (2016): 1121.

Sugai, George, and Robert H. Horner. "Responsiveness-to-Intervention and School-Wide Positive Behavior Supports: Integration of Multi-tiered System Approaches." *Exceptionality* 17, no. 4 (2009): 223–37.

Sugai, George, and Robert H. Horner. "Sustaining and Scaling Positive Behavioral Interventions and Supports: Implementation

Drivers, Outcomes, and Considerations." *Exceptional Children* 86, no. 2 (2020): 120–36.

Sullivan, Amanda L., and Alfredo J. Artiles. "Theorizing Racial Inequity in Special Education: Applying structural Inequity Theory to Disproportionality." *Urban Education* 46, no. 6 (2011): 1526–52.

Sullivan, Amanda L., Ethan R. Van Norman, and David A. Klingbeil. "Exclusionary Discipline of Students with Disabilities: Student and School Characteristics Predicting Suspension." *Remedial and Special Education* 35, no. 4 (2014): 199–210.

Sullivan, Amanda L., Mollie Weeks, Faith G. Miller, Thuy Nguyen, Tara Kulkarni, Shay Williams, and Jiwon Kim. "No 'Top of the Triangle Kids': Toward Conceptual Clarity of Students, Behavior, and Tiers in MTSS to Advance Social Justice." *Journal of School Psychology* 106 (2024): 101325.

Superfine, Benjamin M. *Equality in Education Law and Policy, 1954–2010*. Cambridge University Press, 2013.

Tefera, Adai A., and Gustavo E. Fischman. "Beyond Good Intentions in Special Education Policy: Engaging with Critical Disability Intersectional Research." *Qualitative Inquiry* 30, no. 1 (2024): 48–58.

Tefera, Adai A., Jeanne M. Powers, and Gustavo E. Fischman. "Intersectionality in Education: A Conceptual Aspiration and Research Imperative." *Review of Research in Education* 42, no. 1 (2018): vii–xvii.

Thorius, Kathleen A. King. *Equity Expansive Technical Assistance for Schools: Education Partnerships to Reverse Racial Disproportionality*. Teachers College Press, 2023.

Thorius, Kathleen A. King. "Facilitating En/Counters with Special Education's Cloak of Benevolence in Professional Learning to Eliminate Racial Disproportionality in Special Education." *International Journal of Qualitative Studies in Education* 32, no. 3 (2019): 323–40.

Thorius, Kathleen A. King, Brendan D. Maxcy, Erin Macey, and Adrienne Cox. "A Critical Practice Analysis of Response to Intervention Appropriation in an Urban School." *Remedial and Special Education* 35, no. 5 (2014): 287–99.

Thorius, Kathleen A. King, and Paulo Tan. "Expanding Analysis of Educational Debt." *Disability Studies and Critical Race Theory in Education* (2016): 87–97.

Timberlake, Maria. "Recognizing Ableism in Educational Initiatives: Reading Between the Lines." *Research in Educational Policy and Management* 2, no. 1 (2020): 84–100.

Tomlinson, Sally. *The Politics of Race, Class and Special Education: The Selected Works of Sally Tomlinson*. Routledge, 2014.

Tomlinson, Sally. *A Sociology of Special and Inclusive Education*. Routledge, 2017.

Triano, Sarah. "Categorical Eligibility for Special Education: The Enshrinement of the Medical Model in Disability Policy." *Disability Studies Quarterly* 20, no. 4 (2000).

US Department of Education. *2019 Determination Letters on State Implementation of IDEA*. 2022. www2.ed.gov/fund/data/report/idea/ideafactsheet-determinations-2019.pdf.

US Department of Education. *43rd Annual Report to Congress on the Implementation of the Individuals with Disabilities Education Act*. Office of Special Education and Rehabilitative Services, Office of Special Education Programs, 2021.

US Government Accountability Office. *Individuals with Disabilities Education Act: Standards Needed to Improve Identification of Racial and Ethnic Overrepresentation in Special Education*. 2013. https://www.gao.gov/assets/gao-13-137.pdf.

Valencia, Richard R. *Achieving Equal Educational Opportunity for Students of Color: Disrupting Structural Racism–An American Imperative*. Teachers College Press, 2024.

Valencia, Richard R. *Dismantling Contemporary Deficit Thinking: Educational Thought and Practice*. Routledge, 2010.

Valencia, Richard R., and Daniel G. Solórzano. "Contemporary Deficit Thinking." In *The Evolution of Deficit Thinking*, ed. Richard R. Valencia. Routledge, 2012.

Valldejuli, J. M. "The Racialized History of Disability Activism from the Willowbrooks of this World." *Activist History Review*, November 4, 2019.

Valle, Jan W., and David J. Connor. *Rethinking Disability: A Disability Studies Approach to Inclusive Practices*. Routledge, 2019.

Van Laer, Koen, Eline Jammaers, and Wendy Hoeven. "Disabling Organizational Spaces: Exploring the Processes through Which Spatial Environments Disable Employees with Impairments." *Organization* 29, no. 6 (2022): 1018–35.

Vashisth, Tarun Kumar, Sushil Nifadkar, and Rajesh Chandwani. "Organizational Socialization of Employees with Blindness: Navigating Ableism in Diverse Spaces." *Academy of Management Proceedings* 2024, no. 1 (2024): 12933.

Voulgarides, Catherine. *Does Compliance Matter in Special Education?: IDEA and the Hidden Inequities of Practice*. Teachers College Press, 2018.

Voulgarides, Catherine. "Equity, Parental/Caregiver 'Power,' and Disability Policy in the US Context." *International Journal of Inclusive Education* 28, no. 4 (2024): 326–43.

Voulgarides, Catherine. "Leadership and the Individuals with Disabilities Education Act (IDEA): Is Compliance with IDEA a Path toward Educational Equity?" *Journal of Education Human Resources* 38, no. 2 (2020): 238–57.

Voulgarides, Catherine. "Negotiating Rights in Education: An Examination of US Education Disability Policy." In *Research Handbook on Disability Policy*, ed. Sally Robinson. Edward Elgar, 2023.

Voulgarides, Catherine. "The Promises and Pitfalls of Mandating Racial Equity in Special Education." *Phi Delta Kappan* 103, no. 6 (2022): 14–20.

Voulgarides, Catherine. "Special Education Racial Inequity and the Educational Debt." *Urban Education* (2023): 00420859231153407.

Voulgarides, Catherine Kramarczuk, and Alexandra Aylward. "Enduring Equity Questions: A Sequence Analysis of Citations in Response to Racial Inequity via the Individuals with Disabilities Education Act." *Journal of Disability Policy Studies* 34, no. 1 (2023): 73–85.

Voulgarides, Catherine Kramarczuk, Alexandra Aylward, and Pedro A. Noguera. "The Elusive Quest for Equity: An Analysis of How Contextual Factors Contribute to the Likelihood of School Districts Being Legally Cited for Racial Disproportionality in Special Education." *Journal of Law in Society* 15, no. 2 (2013): 241.

Voulgarides, Catherine Kramarczuk, Alexandra Aylward, Natasha Strassfeld, et al. "A Critical Examination of Special Education Policy Using a Multi-Layered Systemic Approach for Policy Analysis." *Remedial and Special Education* (2025): 07419325251360336.

Voulgarides, Catherine Kramarczuk, Alexandra Aylward, Adai Tefera, Alfredo J. Artiles, Sarah L. Alvarado, and Pedro Noguera. "Unpacking the Logic of Compliance in Special Education: Contextual Influences on Discipline Racial Disparities in Suburban schools." *Sociology of Education* 94, no. 3 (2021): 208–26.

Voulgarides, Catherine Kramarczuk, Rebecca Cruz, Natasha Strassfeld, Alexandra Aylward, Roey Ahram, and Allison Firestone. "Understanding Policy Reverberations Across the Educational Ecosystem to Effectuate Change." *Theory into Practice* 63, no. 4 (2024): 457–68.

Voulgarides, Catherine Kramarczuk, Susan Larson Etscheidt, and David I. Hernández-Saca. "Educational Inequality and the Paradox of Dis/Ability Rights in a Schooled Society: Moving towards an Intersectional Discursive, Material, and Emotive Approach." *Educational Review* 76, no. 1 (2024): 181–98.

Voulgarides, Catherine Kramarczuk, Susan Larson Etscheidt, and David I. Hernández-Saca. "Examining Paradoxes of Access in Disability Law: A Critical Analysis of the Least Restrictive Environment." *Journal of Education Policy* (2024): 1–26.

Voulgarides, Catherine Kramarczuk, Susan Larson Etscheidt, and David I. Hernández-Saca. "Racial and Dis/Ability Equity-Oriented Educational Leadership Preparation." *Journal of Special Education Preparation* 2, no. 3 (2022): 20–30.

Voulgarides, Catherine, John Jacobs, David Lopez, and Brenda L. Barrio. "Moving beyond Compliance and Toward Equity to Address Racial Disproportionality." *Intervention in School and Clinic* 60, no. 2 (2024): 108–18.

Voulgarides, Catherine, Patrick Jean-Pierre, and Natalie Zwerger "The Case of Racial Disproportionality in Special Education." In *The Complex Web of Inequality in North American Schools: Investigating Educational Policies for Social Justice*, ed. Gilberto

Q. Conchas, Briana M. Hinga, Miguel N. Abad, and Kris D. Gutiérrez. Routledge 2019.

Voulgarides, Catherine Kramarczuk, and Adai Tefera. "Reframing the Racialization of Disabilities in Policy." *Theory into Practice* 56, no. 3 (2017): 161–68.

Voulgarides, Catherine Kramarczuk, Sarah L. Woulfin, Natasha Strassfeld, and Isabel Meltzer. "Consequential Intersections: Examining Equity Expressions and Experiences within Special Education Ecosystems." *AERA Open* 10 (2024): 23328584241230056.

Voulgarides, Catherine Kramarczuk, Natalie Zwerger, and Pedro Noguera. *Identifying the Root Causes of Disproportionality*. New York University Technical Assistance Center on Disproportionality, 2013.

Waitoller, Federico R., and Alfredo J. Artiles. "A Decade of Professional Development Research for Inclusive Education: A Critical Review and Notes for a Research Program." *Review of Educational Research* 83, no. 3 (2013): 319–56.

Waitoller, Federico R., Alfredo J. Artiles, and Douglas A. Cheney. "The Miner's Canary: A Review of Overrepresentation Research and Explanations." *Journal of Special Education* 44, no. 1 (2010): 29–49.

Waitoller, Federico R., and Kathleen A. King Thorius. "Cross-Pollinating Culturally Sustaining Pedagogy and Universal Design for Learning: Toward an Inclusive Pedagogy that Accounts for Dis/ability." *Harvard Educational Review* 86, no. 3 (2016): 366–89.

Wang, Margaret C., and Maynard C. Reynolds. "Progressive Inclusion: Meeting New Challenges in Special Education." *Theory into Practice* 35, no. 1 (1996): 20–25.

Weatherley, Richard, and Michael Lipsky. "Street-Level Bureaucrats and Institutional Innovation: Implementing Special-Education Reform." *Harvard Educational Review* 47, no. 2 (1977): 171–97.

Weber, Max. "The Rationalization of Education and Training." In *Social Stratification, Class, Race, and Gender in Sociological Perspective*, 2nd ed. Routledge, 2019.

Weber, Max. "Rational-Legal Authority and Bureaucracy." In *Policy Process: A Reader*, ed. Michael Hill. Routledge, 1997.

Wehmeyer, Michael L., and J. David Smith. "Historical Understandings of Intellectual Disability and the Emergence of Special Education." In *Handbook of Research-Based Practices for Educating Students with Intellectual Disability*, eds. Karrie A. Shogren, LaRon A. Scott, Evan E. Dean, and Brad Linnenkamo. Routledge, 2016.

Weick, Karl E. "Administering Education in Loosely Coupled Schools." *Phi Delta Kappan* 63, no. 10 (1982): 673–76.

Weick, Karl E. "Educational Organizations as Loosely Coupled Systems." In *The Roots of Logistics*, eds. Peter Klaus and Stefanie Müller. Springer, 2012.

Welsh, Richard O., and Shafiqua Little. "The School Discipline Dilemma: A Comprehensive Review of Disparities and Alternative Approaches." *Review of Educational Research* 88, no. 5 (2018): 752–94.

Welton, Anjalé D., Devean R. Owens, and Eboni M. Zamani-Gallaher. "Anti-racist Change: A Conceptual Framework for Educational Institutions to Take Systemic Action." *Teachers College Record* 120, no. 14 (2018): 1–22.

Wilson, James Q. *Bureaucracy: What Government Agencies Do and Why They Do It.* Hachette, 2019.

Wilson, Robert A., and Joshua St. Pierre. "Eugenics and Disability." *Rethinking Disability: World Perspectives in Culture and Society* 93 (2016).

Winfield, Ann Gibson. "The Burden Our Children Bear: The Legacy of Eugenics Ideology." In *Contemporary Issues in Equity, Democracy, and Public Education*, pp. 17–29. Routledge, 2024.

Wiseman, Alexander W., and David P. Baker. "The Symbiotic Relationship Between Empirical Comparative Research on Education and Neo-institutional Theory." In *The Impact of Comparative Education Research on Institutional Theory*, eds. David P. Baker and Alexander W. Wiseman. Emerald, 2006.

Wiseman, Alexander W., M. Fernanda Astiz, and David P. Baker. "Comparative Education Research Framed by Neo-institutional Theory: A Review of Diverse Approaches and Conflicting Assumptions." *Compare* 44, no. 5 (2014): 688–709.

Winfield, Ann Gibson. *Eugenics and Education in America: Institutionalized Racism and the Implications of History, Ideology, and Memory*. Vol. 18. Peter Lang, 2007.

Yell, Mitchell L., James Collins, Gerda Kumpiene, and David Bateman. "The individualized education program: Procedural and substantive requirements." *Teaching Exceptional Children* 52, no. 5 (2020): 304–318.

Yell, Mitchell L., James G. Shriner, and Antonis Katsiyannis. "Individuals with Disabilities Education Improvement Act of 2004 and IDEA Regulations of 2006: Implications for Educators, Administrators, and Teacher Trainers." *Focus on Exceptional Children* 39, no. 1 (2006): 1–24.

Yell, Mitchell L., and Denise K. Whitford. "Civil Rights and the Birth of Special Education." In *Disproportionality and Social Justice in Education*, eds. Nicholas Gage, Luke J. Rapa, Denise K. Whitford, and Antonis Katsiyannos. Springer, 2022.

Yoder, Claire McKinley, M. A. Cantrell, and J. L. Hinkle. "Disparities in High School Graduation by Identity and Disability Using Intermediate and Long-Term Educational Outcomes." *Journal of School Nursing* 40, no. 3 (2024): 266–74.

Zhang, Jingyuan, Ronald C. Martella, Sungwoo Kang, and Busra Yilmaz Yenioglu. "Response to Intervention (RTI)/ Multi-tiered Systems of Support (MTSS): A Nationwide Analysis." *Journal of Educational Leadership and Policy Studies* 7, no. 1 (2023): n1.

Zirkel, Perry A. "Does Brown v. Board of Education Play a Prominent Role in Special Education Law." *Journal of Law & Education* 34 (2005): 255.

Zirkel, Perry A. "The Role of Law in Special Education." *Exceptionality* 31, no. 4 (2023): 308–18.

Zirkel, Perry A. "Special Education Law: Illustrative Basics and Nuances of Key IDEA Components." *Teacher Education and Special Education* 38, no. 4 (2015): 263–75.

ACKNOWLEDGMENTS

I wrote this book for those of us working as educators in K–12 school systems. The book's central purpose is to show how our professional decisions and personal biographies influence how we provide or hinder educational opportunities for students, in particular disabled students across K–12 school settings. My hope is that this book will be a vital resource for practitioners and a tool that promotes criticality about a seemingly benign act shrouded in good intentions and a civil rights legacy—that of compliance with the Individuals with Disabilities Education Act.

In the pages of this book, I try to make the concept of compliance visible, accessible, and actionable as an equity lever. I reflect on more than a decade of classroom and research experiences to highlight how we can foster community among professionals, students, caregivers, and the broader communities we serve. By challenging the status quo and reframing routine policy compliance as a lever for equity, we can create more inclusive and just educational spaces. I wrote this with the greater hope of giving the professionals in complex educational systems the chance to pause and reconnect with our purpose: who we are, why we do this work, and how our belief in and love for our children and students can continue to guide us.

I would also like to acknowledge support for portions of this research provided by the PSC-CUNY Research Award from The City University of New York.

ABOUT THE AUTHOR

Dr. Catherine Kramarczuk Voulgarides is an associate professor at the City University of New York (CUNY) Hunter College, a faculty affiliate at the Roosevelt House Public Policy Institute at Hunter College, and a faculty affiliate of the Urban Education Program at the CUNY Graduate Center. With expertise in qualitative and mixed-methods approaches, she investigates the complex factors contributing to racial disparities in special education through a systems-level lens focused on policy compliance. She critically examines the limitations of legal protections in promoting equity for students with disabilities, exploring the historical, political, structural, and procedural barriers that perpetuate educational inequality. She also works in collaboration with state and local partners to inform and improve policies and practices in dynamic research to practice partnerships. Prior to her academic career, Dr. Voulgarides was a special education teacher in the New York City public school system, where she gained first-hand experience with the challenges and complexities that she continues to study to date in her career.

INDEX